The Complete Air Fryer Cookbook for Beginners

800 Affordable, Quick & Easy Air Fryer Recipes | Fry, Bake, Grill & Roast Most Wanted Family Meals | 21-Day Meal Plan

Dr Camilla Moore

Chapter 6: Seafood & Fish Recipes 148

Chapter 7: Meatless Meals Recipes 167

Introduction

In this book, we have to see a healthy diet popularly known as a ketogenic diet. It will change the eating habits of many people and gives them a healthy lifestyle. When you consume lower carbohydrates and increase fat and protein consumption. It will help you to decrease the blood sugar level and cholesterol levels and also decrease your overall body weight. Keto diet is very effective on rapid weight loss.

Here in this book, we have chosen a healthy keto diet and the air fryer for the healthy way of cooking your keto foods. An air fryer is a versatile cooking appliance cooks your foods by circulating very hot air from the food basket. You can cook chicken, fry French fries, bake cakes and biscuits, grill meat, roast vegetables in a single appliance. It fries your French fries into very less oil, it just requires a tablespoon of oil to fry your French fries. An air fryer is the best option for those people who are disappointed due to the lack of crispiness into their French fries. It makes your French fries tender from inside and crisp from outside. In this book, we have to see different types of 450 healthy and delicious recipes. Here we have made different and fabulous ketogenic recipes into the air fryer. In this book, we also see the benefits of the ketogenic diet and air frying foods.

My goal is here that you should understand the health benefits of a ketogenic diet and also enjoy delicious quick and easy air fryer recipes. I hope the information found in this book helps you to make healthy and affordable recipes at home.

Chapter1: Air Fryer Basics

What is an Air Fryer?

An air fryer is one of the magical cooking appliances which help to cook various delicious and tasty dishes at home. The air fryer works like a convection oven. It cooks food by circulating very hot air into an air fryer chamber. You can fry French fries with very less oil required. It saves more than 80percent of oil while frying or cooking food. Most of the people are disappointed due to the lack of crispiness in their food. The air fryer makes your food crispy and tasty.

Air fryer circulates hot air into food basket with the help of a fan. These fans are located on the top of the food basket. Using this fan air fryer circulates quick and even air around the food basket. Due to this, your food is cook evenly on all sides. It is one of the best choices for those people who love fried food most but also hate about the extra calories.

The Benefits of Air Fryer

The air fryer comes with various benefits some of them are described as follows:

1. Requires less oil and fats

Compare to other traditional fryer Air fryer requires very less oil to fry. It saves more than 80 percent of oil during cooking. Just a tablespoon of oil fries your French fries make it tender from inside and crispy from outside.

2. Saves nutritional values

Traditional deep-frying method destroys essential vitamin and minerals from your food. Air fryer fries your food by blowing the very hot air into a food basket. Air frying your food helps to maintain essential vitamins and nutrients into your food.

3. Versatile cooking options

Air fryer is not only used for frying purpose but also cooks, roasts, grill and bake delicious food for you. It works like a multi-cooker do all the operations into a single pot.

4. Reduce the risk of heart-related disease

Eating deep-fried food is not a healthy choice for your body. Air fryer requires very less oil to fry your food. It also maintains essential vitamins and nutrients into your food. This will help to reduce heart-related disease.

5. Automatic cooking programs

Most of the air fryer comes with pre-programmed auto cook buttons. These auto cooking functions are nothing but commonly used programs like French fries, chicken fries, chips, etc.

You just need to press auto cook function button your air fryer automatically adjusts the time and temperature of your air fryer.

Chapter 2: Snack & Appetizers Recipes

Buffalo Cauliflower Wings

Preparation Time: 10 minutes; Cooking Time: 14 minutes; Serve:4
Ingredients:

- 1 cauliflower head, cut into florets
- 1 tbsp butter, melted
- 1/2 cup buffalo sauce
- Pepper
- Salt

Directions:

1. Spray air fryer basket with cooking spray.
2. In a bowl, mix together buffalo sauce, butter, pepper, and salt.
3. Add cauliflower florets into the air fryer basket and cook at 400 F for 7 minutes.
4. Transfer cauliflower florets into the buffalo sauce mixture and toss well.
5. Again, add cauliflower florets into the air fryer basket and cook for 7 minutes more at 400 F.
6. Serve and enjoy.

Nutritional Value (Amount per Serving):

- Calories 44
- Fat 3 g
- Carbohydrates 3.8 g
- Sugar 1.6 g
- Protein 1.3 g
- Cholesterol 8 mg

Air Fry Bacon

Preparation Time: 5 minutes; Cooking Time: 10 minutes; Serve:11
Ingredients:

- 11 bacon slices

Directions:

1. Place half bacon slices in air fryer basket.
2. Cook at 400 F for 10 minutes.
3. Cook remaining half bacon slices using same steps.
4. Serve and enjoy.

Nutritional Value (Amount per Serving):

- Calories 103
- Fat 7.9 g
- Carbohydrates 0.3 g
- Sugar 0 g
- Protein 7 g
- Cholesterol 21 mg

Crunchy Bacon Bites

Preparation Time: 5 minutes; Cooking Time: 10 minutes; Serve:4
Ingredients:

- 4 bacon strips, cut into small pieces
- 1/2 cup pork rinds, crushed
- 1/4 cup hot sauce

Directions:

1. Add bacon pieces in a bowl.
2. Add hot sauce and toss well.
3. Add crushed pork rinds and toss until bacon pieces are well coated.
4. Transfer bacon pieces in air fryer basket and cook at 350 F for 10 minutes.
5. Serve and enjoy.

Nutritional Value (Amount per Serving):
- Calories 112
- Fat 9.7 g
- Carbohydrates 0.3 g
- Sugar 0.2 g
- Protein 5.2 g
- Cholesterol 3 mg

Easy Jalapeno Poppers

Preparation Time: 10 minutes; Cooking Time: 13 minutes; Serve:5

Ingredients:
- 5 jalapeno peppers, slice in half and deseeded
- 2 tbsp salsa
- 4 oz goat cheese, crumbled
- 1/4 tsp chili powder
- 1/2 tsp garlic, minced
- Pepper
- Salt

Directions:
1. In a small bowl, mix together cheese, salsa, chili powder, garlic, pepper, and salt.
2. Spoon cheese mixture into each jalapeno halves and place in air fryer basket.
3. Cook jalapeno poppers at 350 F for 13 minutes.
4. Serve and enjoy.

Nutritional Value (Amount per Serving):
- Calories 111
- Fat 8.3 g
- Carbohydrates 2.1 g
- Sugar 1.2 g
- Protein 7.3 g
- Cholesterol 24 mg

Perfect Crab Dip

Preparation Time: 5 minutes; Cooking Time: 7 minutes; Serve:4

Ingredients:
- 1 cup crabmeat
- 2 tbsp parsley, chopped
- 2 tbsp fresh lemon juice
- 2 tbsp hot sauce
- 1/2 cup green onion, sliced
- 2 cups cheese, grated
- 1/4 cup mayonnaise
- 1/4 tsp pepper
- 1/2 tsp salt

Directions:
1. In a 6-inch dish, mix together crabmeat, hot sauce, cheese, mayo, pepper, and salt.
2. Place dish in air fryer basket and cook dip at 400 F for 7 minutes.
3. Remove dish from air fryer.
4. Drizzle dip with lemon juice and garnish with parsley.
5. Serve and enjoy.

Nutritional Value (Amount per Serving):

- Calories 313
- Fat 23.9 g
- Carbohydrates 8.8 g

- Sugar 3.1 g
- Protein 16.2 g
- Cholesterol 67 mg

Spinach Dip

Preparation Time: 10 minutes; Cooking Time: 40 minutes; Serve:8

Ingredients:

- 8 oz cream cheese, softened
- 1/4 tsp garlic powder
- 1/2 cup onion, minced
- 1/3 cup water chestnuts, drained and chopped
- 1 cup mayonnaise
- 1 cup parmesan cheese, grated
- 1 cup frozen spinach, thawed and squeeze out all liquid
- 1/2 tsp pepper

Directions:

1. Spray air fryer baking dish with cooking spray.
2. Add all ingredients into the bowl and mix until well combined.
3. Transfer bowl mixture into the prepared baking dish and place dish in air fryer basket.
4. Cook at 300 F for 35-40 minutes. After 20 minutes of cooking stir dip.
5. Serve and enjoy.

Nutritional Value (Amount per Serving):

- Calories 220
- Fat 20.5 g
- Carbohydrates 9.3 g

- Sugar 2.3 g
- Protein 3.8 g
- Cholesterol 41 mg

Italian Dip

Preparation Time: 10 minutes; Cooking Time: 12 minutes; Serve:8

Ingredients:

- 8 oz cream cheese, softened
- 1 cup mozzarella cheese, shredded
- 1/2 cup roasted red peppers
- 1/3 cup basil pesto
- 1/4 cup parmesan cheese, grated

Directions:

1. Add parmesan cheese and cream cheese into the food processor and process until smooth.
2. Transfer cheese mixture into the air fryer pan and spread evenly.
3. Pour basil pesto on top of cheese layer.
4. Sprinkle roasted pepper on top of basil pesto layer.
5. Sprinkle mozzarella cheese on top of pepper layer and place dish in air fryer basket.
6. Cook dip at 250 F for 12 minutes.
7. Serve and enjoy.

Nutritional Value (Amount per Serving):

- Calories 115
- Fat 10.7 g
- Carbohydrates 1.6 g

- Sugar 0.6 g
- Protein 3.6 g
- Cholesterol 34 mg

Sweet Potato Tots

Preparation Time: 10 minutes; Cooking Time: 31 minutes; Serve: 24

Ingredients:
- 2 sweet potatoes, peeled
- 1/2 tsp cajun seasoning
- Salt

Directions:
1. Add water in large pot and bring to boil. Add sweet potatoes in pot and boil for 15 minutes. Drain well.
2. Grated boil sweet potatoes into a large bowl using a grated.
3. Add cajun seasoning and salt in grated sweet potatoes and mix until well combined.
4. Spray air fryer basket with cooking spray.
5. Make small tot of sweet potato mixture and place in air fryer basket.
6. Cook at 400 F for 8 minutes. Turn tots to another side and cook for 8 minutes more.
7. Serve and enjoy.

Nutritional Value (Amount per Serving):
- Calories 15
- Fat 0 g
- Carbohydrates 3.5 g
- Sugar 0.1 g
- Protein 0.2 g
- Cholesterol 0 mg

Stuffed Mushrooms

Preparation Time: 10 minutes; Cooking Time: 15 minutes; Serve: 24

Ingredients:
- 24 mushrooms, caps and stems diced
- 1 1/2 tbsp mozzarella cheese, shredded
- 1/2 cup sour cream
- 1 cup cheddar cheese, shredded
- 2 bacon slices, diced
- 1 small onion, diced
- 1/2 onion, diced
- 1/2 bell pepper, diced

Directions:
1. Add diced mushrooms stems, bacon, carrot, onion, and bell pepper in pan and heat over medium heat.
2. Cook vegetable mixture until softened, about 5 minutes.
3. Stir in sour cream and cheddar cheese and cook until cheese is melted, about 2 minutes.
4. Preheat the air fryer 350 F.
5. Stuff vegetable cheese mixture into the mushroom cap and place in air fryer basket. Sprinkle mozzarella cheese on top.
6. Cook mushrooms for 8 minutes or until cheese is melted.
7. Serve and enjoy.

Nutritional Value (Amount per Serving):
- Calories 97
- Fat 7.4 g
- Carbohydrates 1.5 g
- Sugar 0.6 g
- Protein 6.4 g
- Cholesterol 20 mg

Herb Zucchini Slices

Preparation Time: 10 minutes; Cooking Time: 15 minutes; Serve: 4

Ingredients:

- 2 zucchinis, slice in half lengthwise and cut each half through middle
- 1 tbsp olive oil
- 4 tbsp parmesan cheese, grated
- 2 tbsp almond flour
- 1 tbsp parsley, chopped
- Pepper
- Salt

Directions:

1. Preheat the air fryer to 350 F.
2. In a bowl, mix together cheese, parsley, oil, almond flour, pepper, and salt.
3. Top zucchini pieces with cheese mixture and place in the air fryer basket.
4. Cook zucchini for 15 minutes at 350 F.
5. Serve and enjoy.

Nutritional Value (Amount per Serving):

- Calories 157
- Fat 11.4 g
- Carbohydrates 5.1 g
- Sugar 1.7 g
- Protein 11 g
- Cholesterol 20 mg

Ranch Kale Chips

Preparation Time: 5 minutes; Cooking Time: 5 minutes; Serve: 4

Ingredients:

- 4 cups kale, stemmed
- 1 tbsp nutritional yeast flakes
- 2 tsp ranch seasoning
- 2 tbsp olive oil
- 1/4 tsp salt

Directions:

1. Add all ingredients into the large mixing bowl and toss well.
2. Spray air fryer basket with cooking spray.
3. Add kale in air fryer basket and cook for 4-5 minutes at 370 F. Shake halfway through.
4. Serve and enjoy.

Nutritional Value (Amount per Serving):

- Calories 102
- Fat 7 g
- Carbohydrates 8 g
- Sugar 0 g
- Protein 3 g
- Cholesterol 0 mg

Curried Sweet Potato Fries

Preparation Time: 10 minutes; Cooking Time: 20 minutes; Serve: 3

Ingredients:

- 2 small sweet potatoes, peel and cut into fries shape
- 1/4 tsp coriander
- 1/2 tsp curry powder
- 2 tbsp olive oil
- 1/4 tsp sea salt

Directions:

1. Add all ingredients into the large mixing bowl and toss well.
2. Spray air fryer basket with cooking spray.
3. Transfer sweet potato fries in the air fryer basket.
4. Cook for 20 minutes at 370 F. Shake halfway through.
5. Serve and enjoy.

Nutritional Value (Amount per Serving):
- Calories 118
- Fat 9 g
- Carbohydrates 9 g
- Sugar 2 g
- Protein 1 g
- Cholesterol 0 mg

Roasted Almonds

Preparation Time: 5 minutes; Cooking Time: 8 minutes; Serve: 8
Ingredients:
- 2 cups almonds
- 1/4 tsp pepper
- 1 tsp paprika
- 1 tbsp garlic powder
- 1 tbsp soy sauce

Directions:
1. Add pepper, paprika, garlic powder, and soy sauce in a bowl and stir well.
2. Add almonds and stir to coat.
3. Spray air fryer basket with cooking spray.
4. Add almonds in air fryer basket and cook for 6-8 minutes at 320 F. Shake basket after every 2 minutes.
5. Serve and enjoy.

Nutritional Value (Amount per Serving):
- Calories 143
- Fat 11.9 g
- Carbohydrates 6.2 g
- Sugar 1.3 g
- Protein 5.4 g
- Cholesterol 0 mg

Crispy Zucchini Fries

Preparation Time: 10 minutes; Cooking Time: 10 minutes; Serve: 4
Ingredients:
- 2 medium zucchinis, cut into fries shape
- 1/2 tsp garlic powder
- 1 tsp Italian seasoning
- 1/2 cup parmesan cheese, grated
- 1/2 cup almond flour
- 1 egg, lightly beaten
- Pepper
- Salt

Directions:
1. Add egg in a bowl and whisk well.
2. In a shallow bowl, mix together almond flour, spices, parmesan cheese, pepper, and salt.
3. Spray air fryer basket with cooking spray.
4. Dip zucchini fries in egg then coat with almond flour mixture and place in the air fryer basket.

5. Cook zucchini fries for 10 minutes at 400 F.
6. Serve and enjoy.

Nutritional Value (Amount per Serving):
- Calories 147
- Fat 10 g
- Carbohydrates 6 g
- Sugar 3 g
- Protein 9 g
- Cholesterol 49 mg

Cauliflower Dip

Preparation Time: 10 minutes; Cooking Time: 40 minutes; Serve: 10
Ingredients:
- 1 cauliflower head, cut into florets
- 1 1/2 cups parmesan cheese, shredded
- 2 tbsp green onions, chopped
- 2 garlic clove
- 1 tsp Worcestershire sauce
- 1/2 cup sour cream
- 3/4 cup mayonnaise
- 8 oz cream cheese, softened
- 2 tbsp olive oil

Directions:
1. Toss cauliflower florets with olive oil.
2. Add cauliflower florets into the air fryer basket and cook at 390 F for 20-25 minutes. Shake basket halfway through.
3. Add cooked cauliflower, 1 cup parmesan cheese, green onion, garlic, Worcestershire sauce, sour cream, mayonnaise, and cream cheese into the food processor and process until smooth.
4. Transfer cauliflower mixture into the 7-inch dish and top with remaining parmesan cheese.
5. Place dish in air fryer basket and cook at 360 F for 10-15 minutes.
6. Serve and enjoy.

Nutritional Value (Amount per Serving):
- Calories 308
- Fat 29 g
- Carbohydrates 3 g
- Sugar 1 g
- Protein 7 g
- Cholesterol 51 mg

Pepperoni Chips

Preparation Time: 2 minutes; Cooking Time: 8 minutes; Serve: 6
Ingredients:
- 6 oz pepperoni slices

Directions:
1. Place one batch of pepperoni slices in the air fryer basket.
2. Cook for 8 minutes at 360 F.
3. Cook remaining pepperoni slices using same steps.
4. Serve and enjoy.

Nutritional Value (Amount per Serving):
- Calories 51
- Fat 1 g

- Carbohydrates 2 g
- Sugar 1.3 g
- Protein 0 g
- Cholesterol 0 mg

Crispy Eggplant

Preparation Time: 5 minutes; Cooking Time: 20 minutes; Serve: 4
Ingredients:
- 1 eggplant, cut into 1-inch pieces
- 1/2 tsp Italian seasoning
- 1 tsp paprika
- 1/2 tsp red pepper
- 1 tsp garlic powder
- 2 tbsp olive oil

Directions:
1. Add all ingredients into the large mixing bowl and toss well.
2. Transfer eggplant mixture into the air fryer basket.
3. Cook at 375 F for 20 minutes. Shake basket halfway through.
4. Serve and enjoy.

Nutritional Value (Amount per Serving):
- Calories 99
- Fat 7.5 g
- Carbohydrates 8.7 g
- Sugar 4.5 g
- Protein 1.5 g
- Cholesterol 0 mg

Steak Nuggets

Preparation Time: 10 minutes; Cooking Time: 15 minutes; Serve: 4
Ingredients:
- 1 lb beef steak, cut into chunks
- 1 large egg, lightly beaten
- 1/2 cup pork rind, crushed
- 1/2 cup parmesan cheese, grated
- 1/2 tsp salt

Directions:
1. Add egg in a small bowl.
2. In a shallow bowl, mix together pork rind, cheese, and salt.
3. Dip each steak chunk in egg then coat with pork rind mixture and place on a plate. Place in refrigerator for 30 minutes.
4. Spray air fryer basket with cooking spray.
5. Preheat the air fryer to 400 F.
6. Place steak nuggets in air fryer basket and cook for 15-18 minutes or until cooked. Shake after every 4 minutes.
7. Serve and enjoy.

Nutritional Value (Amount per Serving):
- Calories 609
- Fat 38 g
- Carbohydrates 2 g
- Sugar 0.4 g
- Protein 63 g
- Cholesterol 195 mg

Cheese Bacon Jalapeno Poppers

Preparation Time: 10 minutes; Cooking Time: 5 minutes; Serve: 5

Ingredients:
- 10 fresh jalapeno peppers, cut in half and remove seeds
- 2 bacon slices, cooked and crumbled
- 1/4 cup cheddar cheese, shredded
- 6 oz cream cheese, softened

Directions:
1. In a bowl, combine together bacon, cream cheese, and cheddar cheese.
2. Stuff each jalapeno half with bacon cheese mixture.
3. Spray air fryer basket with cooking spray.
4. Place stuffed jalapeno halved in air fryer basket and cook at 370 F for 5 minutes.
5. Serve and enjoy.

Nutritional Value (Amount per Serving):
- Calories 195
- Fat 17.3 g
- Carbohydrates 3.2 g
- Sugar 1 g
- Protein 7.2 g
- Cholesterol 52 mg

Cabbage Chips

Preparation Time: 10 minutes; Cooking Time: 30 minutes; Serve: 6
Ingredients:
- 1 large cabbage head, tear cabbage leaves into pieces
- 2 tbsp olive oil
- 1/4 cup parmesan cheese, grated
- Pepper
- Salt

Directions:
1. Preheat the air fryer to 250 F.
2. Add all ingredients into the large mixing bowl and toss well.
3. Spray air fryer basket with cooking spray.
4. Divide cabbage in batches.
5. Add one cabbage chips batch in air fryer basket and cook for 25-30 minutes at 250 F or until chips are crispy and lightly golden brown.
6. Serve and enjoy.

Nutritional Value (Amount per Serving):
- Calories 96
- Fat 5.1 g
- Carbohydrates 12.1 g
- Sugar 6.7 g
- Protein 3 g
- Cholesterol 1 mg

Healthy Broccoli Tots

Preparation Time: 10 minutes; Cooking Time: 25 minutes; Serve: 4
Ingredients:
- 1 lb broccoli, chopped
- 1/2 cup almond flour
- 1/4 cup ground flaxseed
- 1/2 tsp garlic powder
- 1 tsp salt

Directions:
1. Add broccoli into the microwave-safe bowl and microwave for 3 minutes.

2. Transfer steamed broccoli into the food processor and process until it looks like rice.
3. Transfer broccoli to a large mixing bowl.
4. Add remaining ingredients into the bowl and mix until well combined.
5. Spray air fryer basket with cooking spray.
6. Make small tots from broccoli mixture and place into the air fryer basket.
7. Cook broccoli tots for 12 minutes at 375 F.
8. Serve and enjoy.

Nutritional Value (Amount per Serving):
- Calories 161
- Fat 9.2 g
- Carbohydrates 12.8 g
- Sugar 2.1 g
- Protein 7.5 g
- Cholesterol 0 mg

Crispy & Healthy Kale Chips

Preparation Time: 5 minutes; Cooking Time: 5 minutes; Serve: 2
Ingredients:
- 1 bunch of kale, remove stem and cut into pieces
- 1/2 tsp garlic powder
- 1 tsp olive oil
- 1/2 tsp salt

Directions:
1. Preheat the air fryer to 370 F.
2. Add all ingredients into the large bowl and toss well.
3. Transfer kale mixture into the air fryer basket and cook for 3 minutes.
4. Shake basket well and cook for 2 minutes more.
5. Serve and enjoy.

Nutritional Value (Amount per Serving):
- Calories 37
- Fat 1 g
- Carbohydrates 6 g
- Sugar 1 g
- Protein 3 g
- Cholesterol 0 mg

Juicy Meatballs

Preparation Time: 10 minutes; Cooking Time: 14 minutes; Serve: 5
Ingredients:
- 1 lb ground beef
- 1 tsp garlic powder
- 1 egg, lightly beaten
- 1/2 onion, diced
- 1/4 tsp pepper
- 1 tsp salt

Directions:
1. Spray air fryer basket with cooking spray.
2. Preheat the air fryer to 390 F.
3. Add all ingredients into the bowl and mix until well combined.
4. Make balls from meat mixture and place into the air fryer basket.
5. Cook meatballs for 14 minutes. Shake basket 3-4 times while cooking.
6. Serve and enjoy.

Nutritional Value (Amount per Serving):
- Calories 259
- Fat 18 g
- Carbohydrates 3 g
- Sugar 0.5 g
- Protein 17 g
- Cholesterol 95 mg

Bacon Jalapeno Poppers

Preparation Time: 10 minutes; Cooking Time: 8 minutes; Serve: 10
Ingredients:
- 10 jalapeno peppers, cut in half and remove seeds
- 1/3 cup cream cheese, softened
- 5 bacon strips, cut in half

Directions:
1. Preheat the air fryer to 370 F.
2. Stuff cream cheese into each jalapeno half.
3. Wrap each jalapeno half with half bacon strip and place in the air fryer basket.
4. Cook for 6-8 minutes.
5. Serve and enjoy.

Nutritional Value (Amount per Serving):
- Calories 83
- Fat 7.4 g
- Carbohydrates 1.3 g
- Sugar 0.5 g
- Protein 2.8 g
- Cholesterol 9 mg

BBQ Chicken Wings

Preparation Time: 10 minutes; Cooking Time: 15 minutes; Serve: 4
Ingredients:
- 1 lb chicken wings
- 1/2 cup BBQ sauce, sugar-free
- 1/4 tsp garlic powder
- Pepper

Directions:
1. Preheat the air fryer to 400 F.
2. Season chicken wings with garlic powder and pepper and place into the air fryer basket.
3. Cook chicken wings for 15 minutes. Shake basket 3-4 times while cooking.
4. Transfer cooked chicken wings in a large mixing bowl. Pour BBQ sauce over chicken wings and toss to coat.
5. Serve and enjoy.

Nutritional Value (Amount per Serving):
- Calories 263
- Fat 8.5 g
- Carbohydrates 11.5 g
- Sugar 8 g
- Protein 32 g
- Cholesterol 100 mg

Healthy Vegetable Kabobs

Preparation Time: 10 minutes; Cooking Time: 10 minutes; Serve: 4
Ingredients:
- 1/2 onion
- 1 zucchini

- 1 eggplant
- 2 bell peppers
- Pepper
- Salt

Directions:
1. Cut all vegetables into 1-inch pieces.
2. Thread vegetables onto the soaked wooden skewers and season with pepper and salt.
3. Place skewers into the air fryer basket and cook for 10 minutes at 390 F. Turn halfway through.
4. Serve and enjoy.

Nutritional Value (Amount per Serving):
- Calories 61
- Fat 0.5 g
- Carbohydrates 14 g
- Sugar 8 g
- Protein 2 g
- Cholesterol 0 mg

Shrimp Kabobs

Preparation Time: 10 minutes; Cooking Time: 8 minutes; Serve: 2
Ingredients:
- 1 cup shrimp
- 1 lime juice
- 1 garlic clove, minced
- 1/4 tsp pepper
- 1/8 tsp salt

Directions:
1. Preheat the air fryer to 350 F.
2. Add shrimp, lime juice, garlic, pepper, and salt into the bowl and toss well.
3. Thread shrimp onto the soaked wooden skewers and place into the air fryer basket.
4. Cook for 8 minutes. Turn halfway through.
5. Serve and enjoy.

Nutritional Value (Amount per Serving):
- Calories 75
- Fat 1 g
- Carbohydrates 4 g
- Sugar 0.5 g
- Protein 13 g
- Cholesterol 160 mg

Mild & Sweet Shishito Peppers

Preparation Time: 5 minutes; Cooking Time: 5 minutes; Serve: 2
Ingredients:
- 20 shishito Peppers
- 1 tbsp olive oil
- Salt

Directions:
1. Add shishito peppers into the bowl and toss with olive oil.
2. Add shishito peppers into the air fryer basket and cook at 390 F for 5 minutes. Shake halfway through.
3. Season shishito peppers with salt.
4. Serve and enjoy.

Nutritional Value (Amount per Serving):

- Calories 20
- Fat 1 g
- Carbohydrates 5 g

- Sugar 2 g
- Protein 1 g
- Cholesterol 0 mg

Healthy Tofu Steaks

Preparation Time: 10 minutes; Cooking Time: 35 minutes; Serve: 4
Ingredients:

- 1 package tofu, press and remove excess liquid
- 1/4 tsp dried thyme
- 1/4 cup lemon juice
- 2 tbsp lemon zest

- 3 garlic cloves, minced
- 1/4 cup olive oil
- Pepper
- Salt

Directions:
1. Cut tofu into eight pieces.
2. In a bowl, mix together olive oil, thyme, lemon juice, lemon zest, garlic, pepper, and salt.
3. Add tofu into the bowl and coat well and place in the refrigerator for overnight.
4. Spray air fryer basket with cooking spray.
5. Place marinated tofu into the air fryer basket and cook at 350 F for 30-35 minutes. Turn halfway through.
6. Serve and enjoy.

Nutritional Value (Amount per Serving):
- Calories 195
- Fat 16 g
- Carbohydrates 5 g

- Sugar 1 g
- Protein 7 g
- Cholesterol 0 mg

Lemon Tofu

Preparation Time: 10 minutes; Cooking Time: 15 minutes; Serve: 4
Ingredients:

- 1 lb tofu, drained and pressed
- 1 tbsp arrowroot powder
- 1 tbsp tamari
- For sauce:
- 2 tsp arrowroot powder

- 2 tbsp erythritol
- 1/2 cup water
- 1/3 cup lemon juice
- 1 tsp lemon zest

Directions:
1. Cut tofu into cubes. Add tofu and tamari into the zip-lock bag and shake well.
2. Add 1 tbsp arrowroot into the bag and shake well to coat the tofu. Set aside for 15 minutes.
3. Meanwhile, in a bowl, mix together all sauce ingredients and set aside.
4. Spray air fryer basket with cooking spray.
5. Add tofu into the air fryer basket and cook at 390 F for 10 minutes. Shake halfway through.

6. Add cooked tofu and sauce mixture into the pan and cook over medium-high heat for 3-5 minutes.
7. Serve and enjoy.

Nutritional Value (Amount per Serving):

- Calories 112
- Fat 3 g
- Carbohydrates 13 g
- Sugar 8 g
- Protein 8 g
- Cholesterol 0 mg

Air Fried Cheese Sticks

Preparation Time: 10 minutes; Cooking Time: 8 minutes; Serve: 4 minutes

Ingredients:

- 6 mozzarella cheese sticks
- 1/4 tsp garlic powder
- 1 tsp Italian seasoning
- 1/3 cup almond flour
- 1/2 cup parmesan cheese, grated
- 1 large egg, lightly beaten
- 1/4 tsp sea salt

Directions:

1. In a small bowl, whisk the egg.
2. In a shallow bowl, mix together almond flour, parmesan cheese, Italian seasoning, garlic powder, and salt.
3. Dip mozzarella cheese stick in egg then coat with almond flour mixture and place on a plate. Place in refrigerator for1 hour.
4. Spray air fryer basket with cooking spray.
5. Place prepared mozzarella cheese sticks into the air fryer basket and cook at 375 F for 8 minutes.
6. Serve and enjoy.

Nutritional Value (Amount per Serving):

- Calories 245
- Fat 18 g
- Carbohydrates 3 g
- Sugar 2 g
- Protein 19 g
- Cholesterol 0 mg

Broccoli Cheese Nuggets

Preparation Time: 10 minutes; Cooking Time: 15 minutes; Serve: 4

Ingredients:

- 1/4 cup almond flour
- 2 cups broccoli florets, cooked until soft
- 1 cup cheddar cheese, shredded
- 2 egg whites
- 1/8 tsp salt

Directions:

1. Preheat the air fryer to 325 F.
2. Spray air fryer basket with cooking spray.
3. Add cooked broccoli into the bowl and using masher mash broccoli into the small pieces.
4. Add remaining ingredients to the bowl and mix well to combine.
5. Make small nuggets from broccoli mixture and place into the air fryer basket.

6. Cook broccoli nuggets for 15 minutes. Turn halfway through.
7. Serve and enjoy.

Nutritional Value (Amount per Serving):
- Calories 175
- Fat 13 g
- Carbohydrates 5 g
- Sugar 1 g
- Protein 12 g
- Cholesterol 30 mg

Chicken Jalapeno Poppers

Preparation Time: 10 minutes; Cooking Time: 20 minutes; Serve: 12
Ingredients:
- 1/2 cup chicken, cooked and shredded
- 6 jalapenos, halved and seed removed
- 1/4 cup green onion, sliced
- 1/4 cup Monterey jack cheese, shredded
- 1/4 tsp garlic powder
- 4 oz cream cheese
- 1/4 tsp dried oregano
- 1/4 tsp dried basil
- 1/4 tsp salt

Directions:
1. Preheat the air fryer to 370 F.
2. Spray air fryer basket with cooking spray.
3. Mix all ingredients in a bowl except jalapenos.
4. Spoon 1 tablespoon mixture into each jalapeno halved and place into the air fryer basket.
5. Cook jalapeno for 20 minutes.
6. Serve and enjoy.

Nutritional Value (Amount per Serving):
- Calories 105
- Fat 8.5 g
- Carbohydrates 1.5 g
- Sugar 0.7 g
- Protein 6.3 g
- Cholesterol 35 mg

Artichoke Dip

Preparation Time: 10 minutes; Cooking Time: 24 minutes; Serve: 6
Ingredients:
- 15 oz artichoke hearts, drained
- 1 tsp Worcestershire sauce
- 3 cups arugula, chopped
- 1 cup cheddar cheese, shredded
- 1 tbsp onion, minced
- 1/2 cup mayonnaise

Directions:
1. Preheat the air fryer to 325 F.
2. Add all ingredients into the blender and blend until smooth.
3. Pour artichoke mixture into air fryer baking dish and place into the air fryer basket.
4. Cook dip for 24 minutes.
5. Serve with vegetables and enjoy.

Nutritional Value (Amount per Serving):
- Calories 190
- Fat 13 g

- Carbohydrates 13 g
- Sugar 2.5 g
- Protein 7.5 g
- Cholesterol 25 mg

Crab Mushrooms

Preparation Time: 10 minutes; Cooking Time: 8 minutes; Serve: 16

Ingredients:
- 16 mushrooms, clean and chop stems
- 1/4 tsp chili powder
- 1/4 tsp onion powder
- 1/4 cup mozzarella cheese, shredded
- 2 oz crab meat, chopped
- 8 oz cream cheese, softened
- 2 tsp garlic, minced
- 1/4 tsp pepper

Directions:
1. In a mixing bowl, mix together stems, chili powder, onion powder, pepper, cheese, crabmeat, cream cheese, and garlic until well combined.
2. Stuff mushrooms with bowl mixture and place into the air fryer basket.
3. Cook mushrooms at 370 F for 8 minutes.
4. Serve and enjoy.

Nutritional Value (Amount per Serving):
- Calories 59
- Fat 5.1 g
- Carbohydrates 1.2 g
- Sugar 0.4 g
- Protein 2.2 g
- Cholesterol 18 mg

Yummy Chicken Dip

Preparation Time: 10 minutes; Cooking Time: 20 minutes; Serve: 6

Ingredients:
- 2 cups chicken, cooked and shredded
- 3/4 cup sour cream
- 1/4 tsp onion powder
- 8 oz cream cheese, softened
- 3 tbsp hot sauce
- 1/4 tsp garlic powder

Directions:
1. Preheat the air fryer to 325 F.
2. Add all ingredients in a large bowl and mix until well combined.
3. Transfer mixture in air fryer baking dish and place in the air fryer.
4. Cook chicken dip for 20 minutes.
5. Serve and enjoy.

Nutritional Value (Amount per Serving):
- Calories 245
- Fat 17 g
- Carbohydrates 1.5 g
- Sugar 0.2 g
- Protein 16 g
- Cholesterol 85 mg

Smoked Almonds

Preparation Time: 5 minutes; Cooking Time: 6 minutes; Serve: 6

Ingredients:
- 1 cup almonds
- 1/4 tsp cumin

- 1 tsp chili powder
- 1/4 tsp smoked paprika
- 2 tsp olive oil

Directions:

1. Add almond into the bowl and remaining ingredients and toss to coat.
2. Transfer almonds into the air fryer basket and cook at 320 F for 6 minutes. Shake halfway through.
3. Serve and enjoy.

Nutritional Value (Amount per Serving):

- Calories 107
- Fat 9.6 g
- Carbohydrates 3.7 g
- Sugar 0.7 g
- Protein 3.4 g
- Cholesterol 0 mg

Parmesan Zucchini Bites

Preparation Time: 10 minutes; Cooking Time: 10 minutes; Serve: 6
Ingredients:

- 1 egg, lightly beaten
- 4 zucchinis, grated and squeeze out all liquid
- 1 cup shredded coconut
- 1 tsp Italian seasoning
- 1/2 cup parmesan cheese, grated

Directions:

1. Add all ingredients into the bowl and mix until well combined.
2. Spray air fryer basket with cooking spray.
3. Make small balls from zucchini mixture and place into the air fryer basket and cook at 400 F for 10 minutes.
4. Serve and enjoy.

Nutritional Value (Amount per Serving):

- Calories 88
- Fat 6.2 g
- Carbohydrates 6.6 g
- Sugar 3.2 g
- Protein 3.7 g
- Cholesterol 29 mg

Broccoli Pop-corn

Preparation Time: 10 minutes; Cooking Time: 6 minutes; Serve: 4
Ingredients:

- 2 cups broccoli florets
- 2 cups coconut flour
- 1/4 cup butter, melted
- 4 eggs yolks
- Pepper
- Salt

Directions:

1. In a bowl whisk egg yolk with melted butter, pepper, and salt. Add coconut flour and stir to combine.
2. Preheat the air fryer to 400 F.
3. Spray air fryer basket with cooking spray.
4. Coat each broccoli floret with egg mixture and place into the air fryer basket and cook for 6 minutes.

5. Serve and enjoy.

Nutritional Value (Amount per Serving):
- Calories 147
- Fat 12 g
- Carbohydrates 7 g
- Sugar 2 g
- Protein 2 g
- Cholesterol 31 mg

Rosemary Beans

Preparation Time: 10 minutes; Cooking Time: 5 minutes; Serve: 2

Ingredients:
- 1 cup green beans, chopped
- 2 garlic cloves, minced
- 2 tbsp rosemary, chopped
- 1 tbsp butter, melted
- 1/2 tsp salt

Directions:
1. Preheat the air fryer to 390 F.
2. Add all ingredients into the bowl and toss well.
3. Transfer green beans into the air fryer basket and cook for 5 minutes.
4. Serve and enjoy.

Nutritional Value (Amount per Serving):
- Calories 83
- Fat 6.4 g
- Carbohydrates 7 g
- Sugar 0.8 g
- Protein 1.4 g
- Cholesterol 15 mg

Cheesy Brussels sprouts

Preparation Time: 10 minutes; Cooking Time: 5 minutes; Serve: 2

Ingredients:
- 1 cup Brussels sprouts, halved
- 1/4 cup mozzarella cheese, shredded
- 1 tbsp olive oil
- 1/4 tsp salt

Directions:
1. Toss Brussels sprouts with oil and season with salt.
2. Preheat the air fryer to 375 F.
3. Transfer Brussels sprouts into the air fryer basket and top with shredded cheese.
4. Cook for 5 minutes.
5. Serve and enjoy.

Nutritional Value (Amount per Serving):
- Calories 89
- Fat 7.8 g
- Carbohydrates 4.1 g
- Sugar 1 g
- Protein 2.5 g
- Cholesterol 2 mg

Mushrooms with Sauce

Preparation Time: 10 minutes; Cooking Time: 20 minutes; Serve: 5

Ingredients:
- 1 1/2 lbs mushrooms
- 1 1/2 tbsp olive oil

- 1 1/2 tbsp vermouth
- 2 tbsp fresh lemon juice
- 1/4 tsp cayenne pepper
- 1/2 tsp turmeric
- 1/2 tbsp Tahini
- 1/4 tsp pepper
- 1 tsp kosher salt

Directions:
1. In a bowl, toss mushrooms with oil, turmeric, cayenne pepper, pepper, and salt.
2. Transfer mushrooms into the air fryer basket and cook at 350 F for 10 minutes.
3. Toss well and cook for 10 minutes more.
4. Meanwhile, in a small bowl, mix together tahini, lemon juice, and vermouth.
5. Serve cooked mushrooms with tahini sauce.

Nutritional Value (Amount per Serving):
- Calories 80
- Fat 5.5 g
- Carbohydrates 5.2 g
- Sugar 2.5 g
- Protein 4.6 g
- Cholesterol 0 mg

Cauliflower Bites

Preparation Time: 10 minutes; Cooking Time: 21 minutes; Serve: 6
Ingredients:
- 1 1/2 lbs cauliflower heads, cut into florets
- 1/3 tsp paprika
- 1 1/2 tbsp olive oil
- 1/4 cup pepper jack cheese, grated
- 1/4 tsp cumin powder
- 1 tsp pepper
- 1/3 tsp onion powder
- 1/2 tsp garlic salt

Directions:
1. Boil cauliflower into the boiling water for 5 minutes. Drain cauliflower florets well and transfer into the large bowl.
2. Add remaining ingredients over cauliflower florets and toss to coat.
3. Transfer cauliflower mixture into the air fryer basket and cook at 390 F for 16 minutes. Toss halfway through.
4. Serve and enjoy.

Nutritional Value (Amount per Serving):
- Calories 66
- Fat 4 g
- Carbohydrates 6.6 g
- Sugar 2.8 g
- Protein 2.7 g
- Cholesterol 1 mg

Cheese Artichoke Arugula Dip

Preparation Time: 10 minutes; Cooking Time: 17 minutes; Serve: 10
Ingredients:
- 1/2 cup mozzarella cheese, shredded
- 3 cups arugula leaves, chopped
- 1/2 cup mayonnaise
- 7 oz brie cheese
- 1/3 tsp dried basil
- 2 garlic cloves, minced
- 1/3 cup sour cream

- 1/3 can artichoke hearts, drained and chopped
- 1/3 tsp pepper
- 1 tsp sea salt

Directions:
1. Add all ingredients except mozzarella cheese into the air fryer baking dish and mix until well combined.
2. Spread mozzarella cheese on top and place dish in the air fryer.
3. Cook at 325 F for 17 minutes.
4. Serve and enjoy.

Nutritional Value (Amount per Serving):
- Calories 66
- Fat 4 g
- Carbohydrates 6.6 g
- Sugar 2.8 g
- Protein 2.7 g
- Cholesterol 1 mg

Thai Chili Chicken Wings

Preparation Time: 10 minutes; Cooking Time: 16 minutes; Serve: 6
Ingredients:
- 1/2 lb chicken wings
- 1 tsp paprika
- 1/3 cup Thai chili sauce
- 2 tsp garlic powder
- 2 tsp ginger powder
- 2 1/2 tbsp dry sherry
- Pepper
- Salt

Directions:
1. Toss chicken wings with dry sherry, paprika, garlic powder, ginger, powder, pepper, and salt.
2. Add chicken wings into the air fryer basket and cook at 365 F for 16 minutes.
3. Serve with Thai chili sauce and enjoy.

Nutritional Value (Amount per Serving):
- Calories 120
- Fat 2.9 g
- Carbohydrates 6 g
- Sugar 3.9 g
- Protein 11.2 g
- Cholesterol 34 mg

Pork Meatballs

Preparation Time: 10 minutes; Cooking Time: 17 minutes; Serve: 8
Ingredients:
- 1 1/2 lbs ground pork
- 2 small onions, chopped
- 4 garlic cloves, minced
- 2 tbsp brie cheese, grated
- 1 1/2 tsp mustard
- 1 tsp cayenne pepper
- Pepper
- Salt

Directions:
1. Add all ingredients into the bowl and mix until well combined.
2. Make small balls from meat mixture and place into the air fryer basket.
3. Cook at 375 F for 17 minutes.
4. Serve and enjoy.

Nutritional Value (Amount per Serving):
- Calories 142
- Fat 3.9 g
- Carbohydrates 2.5 g
- Sugar 0.8 g
- Protein 23.2 g
- Cholesterol 64 mg

Cajun Kale Chips

Preparation Time: 10 minutes; Cooking Time: 4 minutes; Serve: 4
Ingredients:
- 3 kale heads, cut into pieces
- 2 tbsp Worcestershire sauce
- 2 tbsp sesame oil
- 1 1/2 tsp Cajun spice mix
- Pepper
- Salt

Directions:
1. Add all ingredients into the large bowl and toss well.
2. Transfer kale into the air fryer basket and cook at 195 F for 4-5 minutes.
3. Serve and enjoy.

Nutritional Value (Amount per Serving):
- Calories 106
- Fat 7.1 g
- Carbohydrates 8.3 g
- Sugar 1.7 g
- Protein 2.2 g
- Cholesterol 0 mg

Spicy Habanero Chicken Wings

Preparation Time: 10 minutes; Cooking Time: 16 minutes; Serve: 6
Ingredients:
- 1 1/2 lbs chicken wings
- 1 tsp cayenne pepper
- 1/2 tbsp soy sauce
- 2 tbsp habanero hot sauce
- 2 garlic cloves, chopped
- 1 tsp pepper
- 1 tsp garlic salt

Directions:
1. Add chicken wings into the large bowl and toss with remaining ingredients.
2. Transfer chicken wings into the air fryer basket and cook at 365 F for 16 minutes.
3. Serve and enjoy.

Nutritional Value (Amount per Serving):
- Calories 226
- Fat 8.5 g
- Carbohydrates 2.2 g
- Sugar 0.2 g
- Protein 33.1 g
- Cholesterol 101 mg

Flavorful Pork Meatballs

Preparation Time: 10 minutes; Cooking Time: 10 minutes; Serve: 4
Ingredients:
- 2 eggs, lightly beaten
- 2 tbsp capers
- 1/2 lb ground pork
- 3 garlic cloves, minced
- 2 tbsp fresh mint, chopped
- 1/2 tbsp cilantro, chopped

- 2 tsp red pepper flakes, crushed
- 1 1/2 tbsp butter, melted
- 1 tsp kosher salt

Directions:

1. Preheat the air fryer to 395 F.
2. Add all ingredients into the mixing bowl and mix until well combined.
3. Spray air fryer basket with cooking spray.
4. Make small balls from meat mixture and place into the air fryer basket.
5. Cook meatballs for 10 minutes. Shake basket halfway through.
6. Serve and enjoy.

Nutritional Value (Amount per Serving):

- Calories 159
- Fat 8.7 g
- Carbohydrates 1.9 g
- Sugar 0.3 g
- Protein 18.1 g
- Cholesterol 135 mg

Crispy Onion Rings

Preparation Time: 10 minutes; Cooking Time: 10 minutes; Serve: 3
Ingredients:

- 1 egg, lightly beaten
- 1 onion, cut into slices
- 3/4 cup pork rind, crushed
- 1 cup coconut milk
- 1 tbsp baking powder
- 1 1/2 cups almond flour
- Pepper
- Salt

Directions:

1. Preheat the air fryer to 360 F.
2. In a bowl, mix together almond flour, baking powder, pepper, and salt.
3. In another bowl, whisk the egg with milk. Pour egg mixture into the almond flour mixture and stir to combine.
4. In a shallow dish, add crushed pork rinds.
5. Spray air fryer basket with cooking spray.
6. Dip onion ring in egg batter and coat with pork rind and place into the air fryer basket.
7. Cook onion rings for 10 minutes at 360 F.
8. Serve and enjoy.

Nutritional Value (Amount per Serving):

- Calories 350
- Fat 31 g
- Carbohydrates 13 g
- Sugar 4 g
- Protein 10 g
- Cholesterol 67 mg

Asparagus Fries

Preparation Time: 10 minutes; Cooking Time: 10 minutes; Serve: 5
Ingredients:

- 1 lb asparagus spears
- 1 cup pork rinds, crushed
- 1/4 cup almond flour
- 2 eggs, lightly beaten
- 1/2 cup parmesan cheese, grated
- Pepper

- Salt

Directions:
1. Preheat the air fryer to 380 F.
2. In a small bowl, mix together parmesan cheese, almond flour, pepper, and salt.
3. In a shallow bowl, whisk eggs.
4. Add crushed pork rind into the shallow dish.
5. Spray air fryer basket with cooking spray.
6. First coat asparagus with parmesan mixture then into the eggs and finally coat with crushed pork rind.
7. Place coated asparagus into the air fryer basket and cook for 10 minutes.
8. Serve and enjoy.

Nutritional Value (Amount per Serving):
- Calories 102
- Fat 6.1 g
- Carbohydrates 5 g
- Sugar 1.9 g
- Protein 8.1 g
- Cholesterol 71 mg

Zucchini Fritters

Preparation Time: 10 minutes; Cooking Time: 10 minutes; Serve: 7
Ingredients:
- 1 egg, lightly beaten
- 1/2 tsp chili flakes
- 1/4 onion, grated
- 1/2 tbsp paprika
- 1/4 cup coconut flour
- 1 zucchini, grated
- 1/2 tsp salt

Directions:
1. Preheat the air fryer to 365 F.
2. Spray air fryer baking dish with cooking spray.
3. Add all ingredients into the large bowl and mix until well combined.
4. Make small fritters from the mixture and place them in prepared baking dish.
5. Place in the air fryer and cook for 5 minutes from each side.
6. Serve and enjoy.

Nutritional Value (Amount per Serving):
- Calories 34
- Fat 1.2 g
- Carbohydrates 4.5 g
- Sugar 0.8 g
- Protein 1.8 g
- Cholesterol 23 mg

Cheese Dill Mushrooms

Preparation Time: 10 minutes; Cooking Time: 5 minutes; Serve: 6
Ingredients:
- 9 oz mushrooms, cut stems
- 1 tsp dried parsley
- 1 tsp dried dill
- 6 oz cheddar cheese, shredded
- 1 tbsp butter
- 1/2 tsp salt

Directions:

1. Chop mushrooms stem finely and place into the bowl.
2. Add parsley, dill, cheese, butter, and salt into the bowl and mix until well combined.
3. Preheat the air fryer to 400 F.
4. Stuff bowl mixture into the mushroom caps and place into the air fryer basket.
5. Cook mushrooms for 5 minutes.
6. Serve and enjoy.

Nutritional Value (Amount per Serving):
- Calories 141
- Fat 11.5 g
- Carbohydrates 1.9 g
- Sugar 0.9 g
- Protein 8.5 g
- Cholesterol 35 mg

Healthy Toasted Nuts

Preparation Time: 10 minutes; Cooking Time: 9 minutes; Serve: 4
Ingredients:
- 1/2 cup macadamia nuts
- 1/2 cup pecans
- 1 tbsp olive oil
- 1/4 cup walnuts
- 1/4 cup hazelnuts
- 1 tsp salt

Directions:
1. Preheat the air fryer to 320 F.
2. Add all nuts into the air fryer basket and cook for 8 minutes. Shake halfway through.
3. Drizzle nuts with olive oil and season with salt and toss well.
4. Cook nuts for 1 minute more.
5. Serve and enjoy.

Nutritional Value (Amount per Serving):
- Calories 240
- Fat 24.9 g
- Carbohydrates 4.1 g
- Sugar 1.1 g
- Protein 4.1 g
- Cholesterol 0 mg

Simple Radish Chips

Preparation Time: 10 minutes; Cooking Time: 15 minutes; Serve: 12
Ingredients:
- 1 lb radish, wash and slice into chips
- 2 tbsp olive oil
- 1/4 tsp pepper
- 1 tsp salt

Directions:
1. Preheat the air fryer to 375 F.
2. Add all ingredients into the large bowl and toss well.
3. Add radish slices into the air fryer basket and cook for 15 minutes. Shake basket 2-3 times while cooking.
4. Serve and enjoy.

Nutritional Value (Amount per Serving):
- Calories 26
- Fat 2.4 g
- Carbohydrates 1.3 g
- Sugar 0.7 g

- Protein 0.3 g
- Cholesterol 0 mg

Parmesan Turnip Slices

Preparation Time: 10 minutes; Cooking Time: 10 minutes; Serve: 8
Ingredients:
- 1 lb turnip, peel and cut into slices
- 1 tbsp olive oil
- 3 oz parmesan cheese, shredded
- 1 tsp garlic powder
- 1 tsp salt

Directions:
1. Preheat the air fryer to 360 F.
2. Add all ingredients into the mixing bowl and toss to coat.
3. Transfer turnip slices into the air fryer basket and cook for 10 minutes.
4. Serve and enjoy.

Nutritional Value (Amount per Serving):
- Calories 66
- Fat 4.1 g
- Carbohydrates 4.3 g
- Sugar 2.2 g
- Protein 4 g
- Cholesterol 8 mg

Chili Pepper Kale Chips

Preparation Time: 10 minutes; Cooking Time: 8 minutes; Serve: 14
Ingredients:
- 1 lb kale, wash, dry and cut into pieces
- 2 tsp olive oil
- 1 tsp chili pepper
- 1 tsp salt

Directions:
1. Preheat the air fryer to 370 F.
2. Add kale pieces into the air fryer basket. Drizzle kale with oil.
3. Sprinkle chili pepper and salt over the kale and toss well.
4. Cook kale for 5 minutes. Shake well and cook for 3 minutes more.
5. Serve and enjoy.

Nutritional Value (Amount per Serving):
- Calories 22
- Fat 0.7 g
- Carbohydrates 3.4 g
- Sugar 0 g
- Protein 1 g
- Cholesterol 0 mg

Cucumber Chips

Preparation Time: 10 minutes; Cooking Time: 11 minutes; Serve: 12
Ingredients:
- 1 lb cucumber
- 1/2 tsp garlic powder
- 1 tbsp paprika
- 1 tsp salt

Directions:
1. Wash cucumber and slice thinly using a mandolin slicer.
2. Preheat the air fryer to 370 F.

3. Add cucumber slices into the air fryer basket and sprinkle with garlic powder, paprika, and salt.
4. Toss well and cook for 11 minutes. Shake halfway through.
5. Serve and enjoy.

Nutritional Value (Amount per Serving):
- Calories 8
- Fat 0.1 g
- Carbohydrates 1.8 g
- Sugar 0.7 g
- Protein 0.4 g
- Cholesterol 0 mg

Rutabaga Fries

Preparation Time: 10 minutes; Cooking Time: 18 minutes; Serve: 8
Ingredients:
- 1 lb rutabaga, cut into fries shape
- 2 tsp olive oil
- 1 tsp garlic powder
- 1/2 tsp chili pepper
- 1/2 tsp salt

Directions:
1. Add all ingredients into the large mixing bowl and toss to coat.
2. Preheat the air fryer to 365 F.
3. Transfer rutabaga fries into the air fryer basket and cook for 18 minutes. Shake 2-3 times.
4. Serve and enjoy.

Nutritional Value (Amount per Serving):
- Calories 32
- Fat 1.3 g
- Carbohydrates 4.9 g
- Sugar 3.3 g
- Protein 0.8 g
- Cholesterol 0 mg

Kohlrabi Chips

Preparation Time: 10 minutes; Cooking Time: 20 minutes; Serve: 10
Ingredients:
- 1 lb kohlrabi, peel and slice thinly
- 1 tsp paprika
- 1 tbsp olive oil
- 1 tsp salt

Directions:
1. Preheat the air fryer to 320 F.
2. Add all ingredients into the bowl and toss to coat.
3. Transfer kohlrabi into the air fryer basket and cook for 20 minutes. Toss halfway through.
4. Serve and enjoy.

Nutritional Value (Amount per Serving):
- Calories 13
- Fat 1.4 g
- Carbohydrates 0.1 g
- Sugar 0 g
- Protein 0 g
- Cholesterol 0 mg

Daikon Chips

Preparation Time: 10 minutes; Cooking Time: 16 minutes; Serve: 6

Ingredients:

- 15 oz Daikon, slice into chips
- 1 tbsp olive oil
- 1 tsp chili powder
- 1/2 tsp pepper
- 1 tsp salt

Directions:

1. Preheat the air fryer to 375 F.
2. Add all ingredients into the bowl and toss to coat.
3. Transfer sliced the daikon into the air fryer basket and cook for 16 minutes. Toss halfway through.
4. Serve and enjoy.

Nutritional Value (Amount per Serving):

- Calories 36
- Fat 2.4 g
- Carbohydrates 3.2 g
- Sugar 1.5 g
- Protein 1.5 g
- Cholesterol 0 mg

Kale Dip

Preparation Time: 10 minutes; Cooking Time: 12 minutes; Serve: 6
Ingredients:

- 1 lb kale, wash and chopped
- 1 cup heavy cream
- 1 onion, diced
- 1 tsp butter
- 6 oz parmesan cheese, shredded
- 1/4 tsp pepper
- 1 tsp salt

Directions:

1. Add all ingredients into the air fryer baking dish and stir well.
2. Preheat the air fryer to 250 F.
3. Place dish in the air fryer and cook for 12 minutes.
4. Serve and enjoy.

Nutritional Value (Amount per Serving):

- Calories 211
- Fat 14.1 g
- Carbohydrates 11.2 g
- Sugar 0.8 g
- Protein 12 g
- Cholesterol 49 mg

Rangoon Crab Dip

Preparation Time: 10 minutes; Cooking Time: 16 minutes; Serve: 8
Ingredients:

- 2 cups crab meat
- 1 cup mozzarella cheese, shredded
- 1/2 tsp garlic powder
- 1/4 cup pimentos, drained and diced
- 1/4 tsp stevia
- 1/2 lemon juice
- 2 tsp coconut amino
- 2 tsp mayonnaise
- 8 oz cream cheese, softened
- 1 tbsp green onion
- 1/4 tsp pepper
- Salt

Directions:

1. Preheat the air fryer to 325 F.
2. Add all ingredients except half mozzarella cheese into the large bowl and mix until well combined.
3. Transfer bowl mixture into the air fryer baking dish and sprinkle with remaining mozzarella cheese.
4. Place into the air fryer and cook for 16 minutes.
5. Serve and enjoy.

Nutritional Value (Amount per Serving):
- Calories 141
- Fat 11.5 g
- Carbohydrates 4.9 g
- Sugar 1.7 g
- Protein 4.9 g
- Cholesterol 38 mg

Jalapeno Cheese Dip

Preparation Time: 10 minutes; Cooking Time: 16 minutes; Serve: 6
Ingredients:
- 1 1/2 cup Monterey jack cheese, shredded
- 1 1/2 cup cheddar cheese, shredded
- 2 jalapeno pepper, minced
- 1 tsp garlic powder
- 1/3 cup sour cream
- 1/3 cup mayonnaise
- 8 oz cream cheese, softened
- 8 bacon slices, cooked and crumbled
- Pepper
- Salt

Directions:
1. Preheat the air fryer to 325 F.
2. Add all ingredients into the bowl and mix until combined.
3. Transfer bowl mixture into the air fryer baking dish and place in the air fryer and cook for 16 minutes.
4. Serve and enjoy.

Nutritional Value (Amount per Serving):
- Calories 569
- Fat 48.7 g
- Carbohydrates 6.2 g
- Sugar 1.5 g
- Protein 26.8 g
- Cholesterol 133 mg

Garlic Mushrooms

Preparation Time: 10 minutes; Cooking Time: 20 minutes; Serve: 8
Ingredients:
- 2 lbs mushrooms, sliced
- 1/4 cup coconut amino
- 2 garlic cloves, minced
- 3 tbsp olive oil

Directions:
1. Add all ingredients into the large mixing bowl and mix well. Place in refrigerator for 2 hours.
2. Preheat the air fryer to 350 F.

3. Add Transfer marinated mushrooms into the air fryer basket and cook for 20 minutes. Toss halfway through.
4. Serve and enjoy.

Nutritional Value (Amount per Serving):

- Calories 78
- Fat 5.6 g
- Carbohydrates 5.5 g
- Sugar 2 g
- Protein 3.6 g
- Cholesterol 0 mg

Spicy Dip

Preparation Time: 5 minutes; Cooking Time: 5 minutes; Serve: 6
Ingredients:

- 12 oz hot peppers, chopped
- 1 1/2 cups apple cider vinegar
- Pepper
- Salt

Directions:

1. Add all ingredients into the air fryer baking dish and stir well.
2. Place dish in the air fryer and cook at 380 F for 5 minutes.
3. Transfer pepper mixture into the blender and blend until smooth.
4. Serve and enjoy.

Nutritional Value (Amount per Serving):

- Calories 35
- Fat 0.3 g
- Carbohydrates 5.6 g
- Sugar 3.3 g
- Protein 1.1 g
- Cholesterol 0 mg

Onion Dip

Preparation Time: 10 minutes; Cooking Time: 25 minutes; Serve: 8
Ingredients:

- 2 lbs onion, chopped
- 1/2 tsp baking soda
- 6 tbsp butter, softened
- Pepper
- Salt

Directions:

1. Melt butter in a pan over medium heat.
2. Add onion and baking soda and sauté for 5 minutes.
3. Transfer onion mixture into the air fryer baking dish.
4. Place in the air fryer and cook at 370 F for 25 minutes.
5. Serve and enjoy.

Nutritional Value (Amount per Serving):

- Calories 122
- Fat 8.8 g
- Carbohydrates 10.6 g
- Sugar 4.8 g
- Protein 1.3 g
- Cholesterol 23 mg

Easy Carrot Dip

Preparation Time: 10 minutes; Cooking Time: 15 minutes; Serve: 6

Ingredients:

- 2 cups carrots, grated
- 1/4 tsp cayenne pepper
- 4 tbsp butter, melted
- 1 tbsp chives, chopped
- Pepper
- Salt

Directions:

1. Add all ingredients into the air fryer baking dish and stir until well combined.
2. Place dish in the air fryer and cook at 380 F for 15 minutes.
3. Transfer cook carrot mixture into the blender and blend until smooth.
4. Serve and enjoy.

Nutritional Value (Amount per Serving):

- Calories 83
- Fat 7.7 g
- Carbohydrates 3.7 g
- Sugar 1.8 g
- Protein 0.4 g
- Cholesterol 20 mg

Veggie Cream Stuff Mushrooms

Preparation Time: 10 minutes; Cooking Time: 8 minutes; Serve: 12

Ingredients:

- 24 oz mushrooms, cut stems
- 1/2 cup sour cream
- 1 cup cheddar cheese, shredded
- 1 small carrot, diced
- 1/2 bell pepper, diced
- 1/2 onion, diced
- 2 bacon slices, diced

Directions:

1. Chop mushroom stems finely.
2. Spray pan with cooking spray and heat over medium heat.
3. Add chopped mushrooms, bacon, carrot, onion, and bell pepper into the pan and cook until tender.
4. Remove pan from heat. Add cheese and sour cream into the cooked vegetables and stir well.
5. Stuff vegetable mixture into the mushroom cap and place into the air fryer basket.
6. Cook mushrooms at 350 F for 8 minutes.
7. Serve and enjoy.

Nutritional Value (Amount per Serving):

- Calories 93
- Fat 6.6 g
- Carbohydrates 3.7 g
- Sugar 1.7 g
- Protein 5.7 g
- Cholesterol 18 mg

Sesame Okra

Preparation Time: 10 minutes; Cooking Time: 4 minutes; Serve: 4

Ingredients:

- 11 oz okra, wash and chop
- 1 egg, lightly beaten
- 1 tsp sesame seeds
- 1 tbsp sesame oil
- 1/4 tsp pepper
- 1/2 tsp salt

Directions:

1. In a bowl, whisk together egg, pepper, and salt.
2. Add okra into the whisked egg. Sprinkle with sesame seeds.
3. Preheat the air fryer to 400 F.
4. Stir okra well. Spray air fryer basket with cooking spray.
5. Place okra pieces into the air fryer basket and cook for 4 minutes.
6. Serve and enjoy.

Nutritional Value (Amount per Serving):

- Calories 82
- Fat 5 g
- Carbohydrates 6.2 g
- Sugar 1.2 g
- Protein 3 g
- Cholesterol 41 mg

Chapter 3: Brunch Recipes

Radish Hash Browns

Preparation Time: 10 minutes; Cooking Time: 13 minutes; Serve: 4

Ingredients:

- 1 lb radishes, washed and cut off roots
- 1 tbsp olive oil
- 1/2 tsp paprika
- 1/2 tsp onion powder
- 1/2 tsp garlic powder
- 1 medium onion
- 1/4 tsp pepper
- 3/4 tsp sea salt

Directions:

1. Slice onion and radishes using a mandolin slicer.
2. Add sliced onion and radishes in a large mixing bowl and toss with olive oil.
3. Transfer onion and radish slices in air fryer basket and cook at 360 F for 8 minutes. Shake basket twice.
4. Return onion and radish slices in a mixing bowl and toss with seasonings.
5. Again, cook onion and radish slices in air fryer basket for 5 minutes at 400 F. Shake basket halfway through.
6. Serve and enjoy.

Nutritional Value (Amount per Serving):

- Calories 62
- Fat 3.7 g
- Carbohydrates 7.1 g
- Sugar 3.5 g
- Protein 1.2 g
- Cholesterol 0 mg

Vegetable Egg Cups

Preparation Time:10 minutes; Cooking Time:20 minutes; Serve:4

Ingredients:

- 4 eggs
- 1 tbsp cilantro, chopped
- 4 tbsp half and half
- 1 cup cheddar cheese, shredded
- 1 cup vegetables, diced
- Pepper
- Salt

Directions:

1. Spray four ramekins with cooking spray and set aside.
2. In a mixing bowl, whisk eggs with cilantro, half and half, vegetables, 1/2 cup cheese, pepper, and salt.
3. Pour egg mixture into the four ramekins.
4. Place ramekins in air fryer basket and cook at 300 F for 12 minutes.
5. Top with remaining 1/2 cup cheese and cook for 2 minutes more at 400 F.
6. Serve and enjoy.

Nutritional Value (Amount per Serving):

- Calories 194
- Fat 11.5 g
- Carbohydrates 6 g
- Sugar 0.5 g
- Protein 13 g
- Cholesterol 190 mg

Spinach Frittata

Preparation Time: 5 minutes; Cooking Time: 8 minutes; Serve: 1
Ingredients:

- 3 eggs
- 1 cup spinach, chopped
- 1 small onion, minced
- 2 tbsp mozzarella cheese, grated
- Pepper
- Salt

Directions:

1. Preheat the air fryer to 350 F.
2. Spray air fryer pan with cooking spray.
3. In a bowl, whisk eggs with remaining ingredients until well combined.
4. Pour egg mixture into the prepared pan and place pan in the air fryer basket.
5. Cook frittata for 8 minutes or until set.
6. Serve and enjoy.

Nutritional Value (Amount per Serving):

- Calories 384
- Fat 23.3 g
- Carbohydrates 10.7 g
- Sugar 4.1 g
- Protein 34.3 g
- Cholesterol 521 mg

Omelette Frittata

Preparation Time: 10 minutes; Cooking Time: 6 minutes; Serve: 2
Ingredients:

- 3 eggs, lightly beaten
- 2 tbsp cheddar cheese, shredded
- 2 tbsp heavy cream
- 2 mushrooms, sliced
- 1/4 small onion, chopped
- 1/4 bell pepper, diced
- Pepper
- Salt

Directions:

1. In a bowl, whisk eggs with cream, vegetables, pepper, and salt.
2. Preheat the air fryer to 400 F.
3. Pour egg mixture into the air fryer pan. Place pan in air fryer basket and cook for 5 minutes.
4. Add shredded cheese on top of the frittata and cook for 1 minute more.
5. Serve and enjoy.

Nutritional Value (Amount per Serving):

- Calories 160
- Fat 10 g
- Carbohydrates 4 g
- Sugar 2 g
- Protein 12 g
- Cholesterol 255 mg

Cheese Soufflés

Preparation Time: 10 minutes; Cooking Time: 6 minutes; Serve: 8
Ingredients:

- 6 large eggs, separated
- 3/4 cup heavy cream

- 1/4 tsp cayenne pepper
- 1/2 tsp xanthan gum
- 1/2 tsp pepper
- 1/4 tsp cream of tartar
- 2 tbsp chives, chopped
- 2 cups cheddar cheese, shredded
- 1 tsp salt

Directions:
1. Preheat the air fryer to 325 F.
2. Spray eight ramekins with cooking spray. Set aside.
3. In a bowl, whisk together almond flour, cayenne pepper, pepper, salt, and xanthan gum.
4. Slowly add heavy cream and mix to combine.
5. Whisk in egg yolks, chives, and cheese until well combined.
6. In a large bowl, add egg whites and cream of tartar and beat until stiff peaks form.
7. Fold egg white mixture into the almond flour mixture until combined.
8. Pour mixture into the prepared ramekins. Divide ramekins in batches.
9. Place the first batch of ramekins into the air fryer basket.
10. Cook soufflé for 20 minutes.
11. Serve and enjoy.

Nutritional Value (Amount per Serving):
- Calories 210
- Fat 16 g
- Carbohydrates 1 g
- Sugar 0.5 g
- Protein 12 g
- Cholesterol 185 mg

Simple Egg Soufflé

Preparation Time: 5 minutes; Cooking Time: 8 minutes; Serve: 2
Ingredients:
- 2 eggs
- 1/4 tsp chili pepper
- 2 tbsp heavy cream
- 1/4 tsp pepper
- 1 tbsp parsley, chopped
- Salt

Directions:
1. In a bowl, whisk eggs with remaining gradients.
2. Spray two ramekins with cooking spray.
3. Pour egg mixture into the prepared ramekins and place into the air fryer basket.
4. Cook soufflé at 390 F for 8 minutes.
5. Serve and enjoy.

Nutritional Value (Amount per Serving):
- Calories 116
- Fat 10 g
- Carbohydrates 1.1 g
- Sugar 0.4 g
- Protein 6 g
- Cholesterol 184 mg

Vegetable Egg Soufflé

Preparation Time: 10 minutes; Cooking Time: 20 minutes; Serve: 4
Ingredients:
- 4 large eggs
- 1 tsp onion powder

- 1 tsp garlic powder
- 1 tsp red pepper, crushed
- 1/2 cup broccoli florets, chopped
- 1/2 cup mushrooms, chopped

Directions:
1. Spray four ramekins with cooking spray and set aside.
2. In a bowl, whisk eggs with onion powder, garlic powder, and red pepper.
3. Add mushrooms and broccoli and stir well.
4. Pour egg mixture into the prepared ramekins and place ramekins into the air fryer basket.
5. Cook at 350 F for 15 minutes. Make sure souffle is cooked if souffle is not cooked then cook for 5 minutes more.
6. Serve and enjoy.

Nutritional Value (Amount per Serving):
- Calories 91
- Fat 5.1 g
- Carbohydrates 4.7 g
- Sugar 2.6 g
- Protein 7.4 g
- Cholesterol 186 mg

Asparagus Frittata

Preparation Time: 10 minutes; Cooking Time: 10 minutes; Serve: 4
Ingredients:
- 6 eggs
- 3 mushrooms, sliced
- 10 asparagus, chopped
- 1/4 cup half and half
- 2 tsp butter, melted
- 1 cup mozzarella cheese, shredded
- 1 tsp pepper
- 1 tsp salt

Directions:
1. Toss mushrooms and asparagus with melted butter and add into the air fryer basket.
2. Cook mushrooms and asparagus at 350 F for 5 minutes. Shake basket twice.
3. Meanwhile, in a bowl, whisk together eggs, half and half, pepper, and salt.
4. Transfer cook mushrooms and asparagus into the air fryer baking dish.
5. Pour egg mixture over mushrooms and asparagus.
6. Place dish in the air fryer and cook at 350 F for 5 minutes or until eggs are set.
7. Slice and serve.

Nutritional Value (Amount per Serving):
- Calories 211
- Fat 13 g
- Carbohydrates 4 g
- Sugar 1 g
- Protein 16 g
- Cholesterol 272 mg

Spicy Cauliflower Rice

Preparation Time: 10 minutes; Cooking Time: 22 minutes; Serve: 2
Ingredients:
- 1 cauliflower head, cut into florets
- 1/2 tsp cumin
- 1/2 tsp chili powder
- 6 onion spring, chopped
- 2 jalapenos, chopped
- 4 tbsp olive oil
- 1 zucchini, trimmed and cut into cubes

- 1/2 tsp paprika
- 1/2 tsp garlic powder
- 1/2 tsp cayenne pepper
- 1/2 tsp pepper
- 1/2 tsp salt

Directions:
1. Preheat the air fryer to 370 F.
2. Add cauliflower florets into the food processor and process until it looks like rice.
3. Transfer cauliflower rice into the air fryer baking pan and drizzle with half oil.
4. Place pan in the air fryer and cook for 12 minutes, stir halfway through.
5. Heat remaining oil in a small pan over medium heat.
6. Add zucchini and cook for 5-8 minutes.
7. Add onion and jalapenos and cook for 5 minutes.
8. Add spices and stir well. Set aside.
9. Add cauliflower rice in the zucchini mixture and stir well.
10. Serve and enjoy.

Nutritional Value (Amount per Serving):
- Calories 254
- Fat 28 g
- Carbohydrates 12.3 g
- Sugar 5 g
- Protein 4.3 g
- Cholesterol 0 mg

Broccoli Stuffed Peppers

Preparation Time: 10 minutes; Cooking Time: 40 minutes; Serve: 2
Ingredients:
- 4 eggs
- 1/2 cup cheddar cheese, grated
- 2 bell peppers, cut in half and remove seeds
- 1/2 tsp garlic powder
- 1 tsp dried thyme
- 1/4 cup feta cheese, crumbled
- 1/2 cup broccoli, cooked
- 1/4 tsp pepper
- 1/2 tsp salt

Directions:
1. Preheat the air fryer to 325 F.
2. Stuff feta and broccoli into the bell peppers halved.
3. Beat egg in a bowl with seasoning and pour egg mixture into the pepper halved over feta and broccoli.
4. Place bell pepper halved into the air fryer basket and cook for 35-40 minutes.
5. Top with grated cheddar cheese and cook until cheese melted.
6. Serve and enjoy.

Nutritional Value (Amount per Serving):
- Calories 340
- Fat 22 g
- Carbohydrates 12 g
- Sugar 8.2 g
- Protein 22 g
- Cholesterol 374 mg

Zucchini Muffins

Preparation Time: 10 minutes; Cooking Time: 20 minutes; Serve: 8

Ingredients:

- 6 eggs
- 4 drops stevia
- 1/4 cup Swerve
- 1/3 cup coconut oil, melted
- 1 cup zucchini, grated
- 3/4 cup coconut flour
- 1/4 tsp ground nutmeg
- 1 tsp ground cinnamon
- 1/2 tsp baking soda

Directions:

1. Preheat the air fryer to 325 F.
2. Add all ingredients except zucchini in a bowl and mix well.
3. Add zucchini and stir well.
4. Pour batter into the silicone muffin molds and place into the air fryer basket.
5. Cook muffins for 20 minutes.
6. Serve and enjoy.

Nutritional Value (Amount per Serving):

- Calories 136
- Fat 12 g
- Carbohydrates 1 g
- Sugar 0.6 g
- Protein 4 g
- Cholesterol 123 mg

Jalapeno Breakfast Muffins

Preparation Time: 10 minutes; Cooking Time: 15 minutes; Serve: 8
Ingredients:

- 5 eggs
- 1/3 cup coconut oil, melted
- 2 tsp baking powder
- 3 tbsp erythritol
- 3 tbsp jalapenos, sliced
- 1/4 cup unsweetened coconut milk
- 2/3 cup coconut flour
- 3/4 tsp sea salt

Directions:

1. Preheat the air fryer to 325 F.
2. In a large bowl, stir together coconut flour, baking powder, erythritol, and sea salt.
3. Stir in eggs, jalapenos, coconut milk, and coconut oil until well combined.
4. Pour batter into the silicone muffin molds and place into the air fryer basket.
5. Cook muffins for 15 minutes.
6. Serve and enjoy.

Nutritional Value (Amount per Serving):

- Calories 125
- Fat 12 g
- Carbohydrates 7 g
- Sugar 6 g
- Protein 3 g
- Cholesterol 102 mg

Zucchini Noodles

Preparation Time: 10 minutes; Cooking Time: 44 minutes; Serve: 3
Ingredients:

- 1 egg
- 1/2 cup parmesan cheese, grated
- 1/2 cup feta cheese, crumbled
- 1 tbsp thyme

- 1 garlic clove, chopped
- 1 onion, chopped
- 2 medium zucchinis, trimmed and spiralized
- 2 tbsp olive oil
- 1 cup mozzarella cheese, grated
- 1/2 tsp pepper
- 1/2 tsp salt

Directions:
1. Preheat the air fryer to 350 F.
2. Add spiralized zucchini and salt in a colander and set aside for 10 minutes.
3. Wash zucchini noodles and pat dry with a paper towel.
4. Heat oil in a pan over medium heat.
5. Add garlic and onion and sauté for 3-4 minutes.
6. Add zucchini noodles and cook for 4-5 minutes or until softened.
7. Add zucchini mixture into the air fryer baking pan. Add egg, thyme, cheeses. Mix well and season.
8. Place pan in the air fryer and cook for 30-35 minutes.
9. Serve and enjoy.

Nutritional Value (Amount per Serving):
- Calories 435
- Fat 29 g
- Carbohydrates 10.4 g
- Sugar 5 g
- Protein 25 g
- Cholesterol 120 mg

Mushroom Frittata

Preparation Time: 10 minutes; Cooking Time: 13 minutes; Serve: 1
Ingredients:
- 1 cup egg whites
- 1 cup spinach, chopped
- 2 mushrooms, sliced
- 2 tbsp parmesan cheese, grated
- Salt

Directions:
1. Spray pan with cooking spray and heat over medium heat.
2. Add mushrooms and sauté for 2-3 minutes. Add spinach and cook for 1-2 minutes or until wilted.
3. Transfer mushroom spinach mixture into the air fryer pan.
4. Whisk egg whites in a mixing bowl until frothy. Season with a pinch of salt.
5. Pour egg white mixture into the spinach and mushroom mixture and sprinkle with parmesan cheese.
6. Place pan in air fryer basket and cook frittata at 350 F for 8 minutes.
7. Slice and serve.

Nutritional Value (Amount per Serving):
- Calories 176
- Fat 3 g
- Carbohydrates 4 g
- Sugar 2.5 g
- Protein 31 g
- Cholesterol 8 mg

Egg Muffins

Preparation Time: 10 minutes; Cooking Time: 15 minutes; Serve: 12
Ingredients:

- 9 eggs
- 1/2 cup onion, sliced
- 1 tbsp olive oil
- 8 oz ground sausage
- 1/4 cup coconut milk
- 1/2 tsp oregano
- 1 1/2 cups spinach
- 3/4 cup bell peppers, chopped
- Pepper
- Salt

Directions:

1. Preheat the air fryer to 325 F.
2. Add ground sausage in a pan and sauté over medium heat for 5 minutes.
3. Add olive oil, oregano, bell pepper, and onion and sauté until onion is translucent.
4. Add spinach to the pan and cook for 30 seconds.
5. Remove pan from heat and set aside.
6. In a mixing bowl, whisk together eggs, coconut milk, pepper, and salt until well beaten.
7. Add sausage and vegetable mixture into the egg mixture and mix well.
8. Pour egg mixture into the silicone muffin molds and place into the air fryer basket. (Cook in batches)
9. Cook muffins for 15 minutes.
10. Serve and enjoy.

Nutritional Value (Amount per Serving):

- Calories 135
- Fat 11 g
- Carbohydrates 1.5 g
- Sugar 1 g
- Protein 8 g
- Cholesterol 140 mg

Bacon Egg Muffins

Preparation Time: 10 minutes; Cooking Time: 20 minutes; Serve: 12
Ingredients:

- 12 eggs
- 2 tbsp fresh parsley, chopped
- 1/2 tsp mustard powder
- 1/3 cup heavy cream
- 2 green onion, chopped
- 4 oz cheddar cheese, shredded
- 8 bacon slices, cooked and crumbled
- Pepper
- Salt

Directions:

1. Preheat the air fryer to 350 F.
2. In a mixing bowl, whisk together eggs, mustard powder, heavy cream, pepper, and salt.
3. Divide cheddar cheese, onions, and bacon into the silicone muffin molds.
4. Now pour egg mixture into the silicone muffin molds and place in the air fryer basket.
5. Cook muffins for 20 minutes.
6. Serve and enjoy.

Nutritional Value (Amount per Serving):

- Calories 115
- Fat 9 g
- Carbohydrates 1 g

- Sugar 0.5 g
- Protein 8 g
- Cholesterol 178 mg

Zucchini Cheese Quiche

Preparation Time: 10 minutes; Cooking Time: 35 minutes; Serve: 6
Ingredients:
- 8 eggs
- 1 cup zucchini, shredded and squeezed
- 1 cup ham, cooked and diced
- 1/2 tsp dry mustard

- 1/2 cup heavy cream
- 1 cup cheddar cheese, shredded
- Pepper
- Salt

Directions:
1. Preheat the air fryer to 350 F.
2. Spray air fryer baking dish with cooking spray.
3. Combine ham, cheddar cheese, and zucchini in a baking dish.
4. In a bowl, whisk together eggs, heavy cream, and seasoning. Pour egg mixture over ham mixture.
5. Place dish in the air fryer and cook for 30-35 minutes.
6. Serve and enjoy.

Nutritional Value (Amount per Serving):
- Calories 234
- Fat 17 g
- Carbohydrates 2.5 g

- Sugar 1 g
- Protein 16 g
- Cholesterol 265 mg

Breakfast Casserole

Preparation Time: 10 minutes; Cooking Time: 28 minutes; Serve: 4
Ingredients:
- 2 eggs
- 4 egg whites
- 4 tsp pine nuts, minced
- 2/3 cup chicken broth
- 1 lb Italian sausage

- 1/4 cup roasted red pepper, sliced
- 1/4 cup pesto sauce
- 2/3 cup parmesan cheese, grated
- 1/8 tsp pepper
- 1/4 tsp sea salt

Directions:
1. Preheat the air fryer to 370 F.
2. Spray air fryer pan with cooking spray and set aside.
3. Heat another pan over medium heat. Add sausage in a pan and cook until golden brown.
4. Once cooked then drain excess oil and spread it into the prepared pan.
5. Whisk remaining ingredients except pine nuts in a bowl and pour over sausage.
6. Place pan in the air fryer and cook for 25-28 minutes.
7. Top with pine nuts and serve.

Nutritional Value (Amount per Serving):
- Calories 625

- Fat 49 g

- Carbohydrates 2 g
- Sugar 2.1 g
- Protein 39 g
- Cholesterol 200 mg

Egg Cups

Preparation Time: 10 minutes; Cooking Time: 18 minutes; Serve: 12
Ingredients:

- 12 eggs
- 4 oz cream cheese
- 12 bacon strips, uncooked
- 1/4 cup buffalo sauce
- 2/3 cup cheddar cheese, shredded
- Pepper
- Salt

Directions:

1. In a bowl, whisk together eggs, pepper, and salt.
2. Line each silicone muffin mold with one bacon strip.
3. Pour egg mixture into each muffin mold and place in the air fryer basket. (In batches)
4. Cook at 350 F for 8 minutes.
5. In another bowl, mix together cheddar cheese and cream cheese and microwave for 30 seconds. Add buffalo sauce and stir well.
6. Remove muffin molds from air fryer and add 2 tsp cheese mixture in the center of each egg cup.
7. Return muffin molds to the air fryer and cook for 10 minutes more.
8. Serve and enjoy.

Nutritional Value (Amount per Serving):

- Calories 225
- Fat 19 g
- Carbohydrates 1 g
- Sugar 0.4 g
- Protein 11 g
- Cholesterol 180 mg

Spinach Muffins

Preparation Time: 10 minutes; Cooking Time: 20 minutes; Serve: 8
Ingredients:

- 4 eggs
- 1/2 tsp baking powder
- 1 zucchini, grated
- 1/4 cup parmesan cheese, grated
- 1/2 cup feta cheese, crumbled
- 4 onion spring, chopped
- 1/3 cup coconut flour
- 1/4 cup butter, melted
- 4 tbsp parsley, chopped
- 1/2 tsp nutmeg
- 1/4 cup water
- 1/2 cup spinach, cooked
- 1/4 tsp pepper
- 1/4 tsp salt

Directions:

1. Preheat the air fryer to 370 F.
2. In a bowl, whisk together eggs, water, butter, and salt.
3. Add baking soda and coconut flour and mix well.
4. Add onions, nutmeg, parsley, spinach, and zucchini. Mix well.
5. Add parmesan cheese and feta cheese and stir well. Season with pepper and salt.

6. Pour batter into the silicone muffin molds and place in the air fryer basket.
7. Cook muffins for 20 minutes.
8. Serve and enjoy.

Nutritional Value (Amount per Serving):
- Calories 235
- Fat 18.1 g
- Carbohydrates 4.2 g
- Sugar 1.1 g
- Protein 16 g
- Cholesterol 135 mg

Broccoli Muffins

Preparation Time: 10 minutes; Cooking Time: 24 minutes; Serve: 6
Ingredients:
- 2 large eggs
- 1 cup broccoli florets, chopped
- 1 cup unsweetened almond milk
- 2 cups almond flour
- 1 tsp baking powder
- 2 tbsp nutritional yeast
- 1/2 tsp sea salt

Directions:
1. Preheat the air fryer to 325 F.
2. Add all ingredients into the large bowl and mix until well combined.
3. Pour mixture into the silicone muffin molds and place into the air fryer basket.
4. Cook muffins for 20-24 minutes.
5. Serve and enjoy.

Nutritional Value (Amount per Serving):
- Calories 260
- Fat 21.2 g
- Carbohydrates 11 g
- Sugar 1.7 g
- Protein 12 g
- Cholesterol 62 mg

Zucchini Gratin

Preparation Time: 10 minutes; Cooking Time: 24 minutes; Serve: 4
Ingredients:
- 1 large egg, lightly beaten
- 1 1/4 cup unsweetened almond milk
- 3 medium zucchinis, sliced
- 1 tbsp Dijon mustard
- 1/2 cup nutritional yeast
- 1 tsp sea salt

Directions:
1. Preheat the air fryer to 370 F.
2. Arrange zucchini slices in the air fryer baking dish.
3. In a saucepan, heat almond milk over low heat and stir in Dijon mustard, nutritional yeast, and sea salt. Add beaten egg and whisk well.
4. Pour sauce over zucchini slices.
5. Place dish in the air fryer and cook for 20-24 minutes.
6. Serve and enjoy.

Nutritional Value (Amount per Serving):
- Calories 120
- Fat 3.4 g

- Carbohydrates 14 g
- Sugar 2 g
- Protein 13 g
- Cholesterol 47 mg

Breakfast Egg Muffins

Preparation Time: 10 minutes; Cooking Time: 20 minutes; Serve: 12
Ingredients:
- 6 eggs
- 1 lb ground pork sausage
- 3 tbsp onion, minced
- 1/2 red pepper, diced
- 1 cup egg whites
- 1/2 cup mozzarella cheese
- 1 cup cheddar cheese

Directions:
1. Preheat the air fryer to 325 F.
2. Brown sausage over medium-high heat until meat is no pink.
3. Divide red pepper, cheese, cooked sausages, and onion into each silicone muffin mold.
4. In a large bowl, whisk together egg whites, egg, pepper, and salt.
5. Pour egg mixture into each muffin mold and place into the air fryer basket in batches.
6. Cook muffins in the air fryer for 20 minutes.
7. Serve and enjoy.

Nutritional Value (Amount per Serving):
- Calories 189
- Fat 13.6 g
- Carbohydrates 2 g
- Sugar 0.7 g
- Protein 13 g
- Cholesterol 115 mg

Cheese Pie

Preparation Time: 10 minutes; Cooking Time: 16 minutes; Serve: 4
Ingredients:
- 8 eggs
- 1 1/2 cups heavy whipping cream
- 1 lb cheddar cheese, grated
- Pepper
- Salt

Directions:
1. Preheat the air fryer to 325 F.
2. In a bowl, whisk together cheese, eggs, whipping cream, pepper, and salt.
3. Spray air fryer baking dish with cooking spray.
4. Pour egg mixture into the prepared dish and place in the air fryer basket.
5. Cook for 16 minutes or until the egg is set.
6. Serve and enjoy.

Nutritional Value (Amount per Serving):
- Calories 735
- Fat 63 g
- Carbohydrates 3 g
- Sugar 1.3 g
- Protein 40.2 g
- Cholesterol 505 mg

Parmesan Breakfast Casserole

Preparation Time: 10 minutes; Cooking Time: 20 minutes; Serve: 3
Ingredients:

- 5 eggs
- 2 tbsp heavy cream
- 3 tbsp chunky tomato sauce
- 2 tbsp parmesan cheese, grated

Directions:

1. Preheat the air fryer to 325 F.
2. In mixing bowl, combine together cream and eggs.
3. Add cheese and tomato sauce and mix well.
4. Spray air fryer baking dish with cooking spray.
5. Pour mixture into baking dish and place in the air fryer basket.
6. Cook for 20 minutes.
7. Serve and enjoy.

Nutritional Value (Amount per Serving):

- Calories 185
- Fat 14 g
- Carbohydrates 2 g
- Sugar 1.2 g
- Protein 13.6 g
- Cholesterol 290 mg

Spinach Egg Breakfast

Preparation Time: 10 minutes; Cooking Time: 20 minutes; Serve: 4
Ingredients:

- 3 eggs
- 1/4 cup coconut milk
- 1/4 cup parmesan cheese, grated
- 4 oz spinach, chopped
- 3 oz cottage cheese

Directions:

1. Preheat the air fryer to 350 F.
2. Add eggs, milk, half parmesan cheese, and cottage cheese in a bowl and whisk well. Add spinach and stir well.
3. Pour mixture into the air fryer baking dish.
4. Sprinkle remaining half parmesan cheese on top.
5. Place dish in the air fryer and cook for 20 minutes.
6. Serve and enjoy.

Nutritional Value (Amount per Serving):

- Calories 144
- Fat 8.5 g
- Carbohydrates 2.5 g
- Sugar 1.1 g
- Protein 14 g
- Cholesterol 135 mg

Vegetable Quiche

Preparation Time: 10 minutes; Cooking Time: 24 minutes; Serve: 6
Ingredients:

- 8 eggs
- 1 cup coconut milk

- 1 cup tomatoes, chopped
- 1 cup zucchini, chopped
- 1 tbsp butter
- 1 onion, chopped
- 1 cup Parmesan cheese, grated
- 1/2 tsp pepper
- 1 tsp salt

Directions:
1. Preheat the air fryer to 370 F.
2. Melt butter in a pan over medium heat then add onion and sauté until onion lightly brown.
3. Add tomatoes and zucchini to the pan and sauté for 4-5 minutes.
4. Transfer cooked vegetables into the air fryer baking dish.
5. Beat eggs with cheese, milk, pepper, and salt in a bowl.
6. Pour egg mixture over vegetables in a baking dish.
7. Place dish in the air fryer and cook for 24 minutes or until eggs are set.
8. Slice and serve.

Nutritional Value (Amount per Serving):
- Calories 255
- Fat 16 g
- Carbohydrates 8 g
- Sugar 4.2 g
- Protein 21 g
- Cholesterol 257 mg

Breakfast Egg Tomato

Preparation Time: 10 minutes; Cooking Time: 24 minutes; Serve: 2
Ingredients:
- 2 eggs
- 2 large fresh tomatoes
- 1 tsp fresh parsley
- Pepper
- Salt

Directions:
1. Preheat the air fryer to 325 F.
2. Cut off the top of a tomato and spoon out the tomato innards.
3. Break the egg in each tomato and place in air fryer basket and cook for 24 minutes.
4. Season with parsley, pepper, and salt.
5. Serve and enjoy.

Nutritional Value (Amount per Serving):
- Calories 95
- Fat 5 g
- Carbohydrates 7.5 g
- Sugar 5.1 g
- Protein 7 g
- Cholesterol 164 mg

Mushroom Leek Frittata

Preparation Time: 10 minutes; Cooking Time: 32 minutes; Serve: 4
Ingredients:
- 6 eggs
- 6 oz mushrooms, sliced
- 1 cup leeks, sliced
- Salt

Directions:

1. Preheat the air fryer to 325 F.
2. Spray air fryer baking dish with cooking spray and set aside.
3. Heat another pan over medium heat. Spray pan with cooking spray.
4. Add mushrooms, leeks, and salt in a pan sauté for 6 minutes.
5. Break eggs in a bowl and whisk well.
6. Transfer sautéed mushroom and leek mixture into the prepared baking dish.
7. Pour egg over mushroom mixture.
8. Place dish in the air fryer and cook for 32 minutes.
9. Serve and enjoy.

Nutritional Value (Amount per Serving):
- Calories 116
- Fat 7 g
- Carbohydrates 5.1 g
- Sugar 2.1 g
- Protein 10 g
- Cholesterol 245 mg

Perfect Breakfast Frittata

Preparation Time: 10 minutes; Cooking Time: 32 minutes; Serve: 2
Ingredients:
- 3 eggs
- 2 tbsp parmesan cheese, grated
- 2 tbsp sour cream
- 1/2 cup bell pepper, chopped
- 1/4 cup onion, chopped
- 1/2 tsp pepper
- 1/2 tsp salt

Directions:
1. Add eggs in a mixing bowl and whisk with remaining ingredients.
2. Spray air fryer baking dish with cooking spray.
3. Pour egg mixture into the prepared dish and place in the air fryer and cook at 350 F for 5 minutes.
4. Serve and enjoy.

Nutritional Value (Amount per Serving):
- Calories 227
- Fat 15.2 g
- Carbohydrates 6 g
- Sugar 2.6 g
- Protein 18.2 g
- Cholesterol 271 mg

Indian Cauliflower

Preparation Time: 10 minutes; Cooking Time: 20 minutes; Serve: 2
Ingredients:
- 3 cups cauliflower florets
- 2 tbsp water
- 2 tsp fresh lemon juice
- ½ tbsp ginger paste
- 1 tsp chili powder
- ¼ tsp turmeric
- ½ cup vegetable stock
- Pepper
- Salt

Directions:
1. Add all ingredients into the air fryer baking dish and mix well.

2. Place dish in the air fryer and cook at 400 F for 10 minutes.
3. Stir well and cook at 360 F for 10 minutes more.
4. Stir well and serve.

Nutritional Value (Amount per Serving):
- Calories 49
- Fat 0.5 g
- Carbohydrates 9 g
- Sugar 3 g
- Protein 3 g
- Cholesterol 0 mg

Zucchini Salad

Preparation Time: 10 minutes; Cooking Time: 25 minutes; Serve: 4

Ingredients:
- 1 lb zucchini, cut into slices
- 2 tbsp tomato paste
- ½ tbsp tarragon, chopped
- 1 yellow squash, diced
- ½ lb carrots, peeled and diced
- 1 tbsp olive oil
- Pepper
- Salt

Directions:
1. In air fryer baking dish mix together zucchini, tomato paste, tarragon, squash, carrots, pepper, and salt. Drizzle with olive oil.
2. Place in the air fryer and cook at 400 F for 25 minutes. Stir halfway through.
3. Serve and enjoy.

Nutritional Value (Amount per Serving):
- Calories 79
- Fat 3 g
- Carbohydrates 11 g
- Sugar 5 g
- Protein 2 g
- Cholesterol 0 mg

Healthy Squash

Preparation Time: 10 minutes; Cooking Time: 25 minutes; Serve: 4

Ingredients:
- 2 lbs yellow squash, cut into half-moons
- 1 tsp Italian seasoning
- ¼ tsp pepper
- 1 tbsp olive oil
- ¼ tsp salt

Directions:
1. Add all ingredients into the large bowl and toss well.
2. Preheat the air fryer to 400 F.
3. Add squash mixture into the air fryer basket and cook for 10 minutes.
4. Shake basket and cook for another 10 minutes.
5. Shake once again and cook for 5 minutes more.

Nutritional Value (Amount per Serving):
- Calories 70
- Fat 4 g
- Carbohydrates 7 g
- Sugar 4 g
- Protein 2 g
- Cholesterol 1 mg

Spinach Frittata

Preparation Time: 10 minutes; Cooking Time: 8 minutes; Serve: 6

Ingredients:

- 8 eggs
- 1 1/4 cup mushrooms, sliced
- 1 tbsp olive oil
- 2 cups spinach
- 1 tbsp curry powder
- 1/4 cup onion, diced
- Pepper
- Salt

Directions:

1. Preheat the air fryer to 325 F.
2. Heat oil in a pan over medium-high heat.
3. Add onion and mushrooms to the pan and sauté for 5-8 minutes.
4. Add spinach and cook for 2 minutes.
5. In a large bowl, whisk eggs, curry powder, pepper, and salt.
6. Transfer pan mixture into the air fryer baking dish. Pour egg mixture over vegetables and stir well.
7. Place dish in the air fryer and cook for 8 minutes or until eggs are set
8. Serve and enjoy.

Nutritional Value (Amount per Serving):

- Calories 116
- Fat 8 g
- Carbohydrates 2 g
- Sugar 1 g
- Protein 8 g
- Cholesterol 218 mg

Healthy Mix Vegetables

Preparation Time: 10 minutes; Cooking Time: 18 minutes; Serve: 4

Ingredients:

- ½ cup mushrooms, sliced
- 1 onion, sliced
- ½ cup zucchini, sliced
- ½ cup squash, sliced
- ½ cup baby carrot
- 1 cup cauliflower florets
- 1 cup broccoli florets
- ¼ cup parmesan cheese
- 1 tsp red pepper flakes
- 1 tbsp garlic, minced
- 1 tbsp olive oil
- ¼ cup vinegar
- ¼ tsp pepper
- ½ tsp sea salt

Directions:

1. Preheat the air fryer to 400 F.
2. In a bowl, mix together oil, vinegar, garlic, pepper, red pepper flakes, and salt.
3. Add vegetables into the bowl and toss to coat.
4. Transfer vegetable mixture into the air fryer basket and cook for 16 minutes. Shake basket halfway through.
5. Sprinkle with cheese and cook for 1-2 minutes more.
6. Serve and enjoy.

Nutritional Value (Amount per Serving):

- Calories 69
- Fat 3 g
- Carbohydrates 7 g
- Sugar 2 g
- Protein2 g
- Cholesterol 0 mg

Tomato Mushroom Frittata

Preparation Time: 10 minutes; Cooking Time: 15 minutes; Serve: 2
Ingredients:
- 1 cup egg whites
- 1/4 cup tomato, sliced
- 2 tbsp coconut milk
- 2 tbsp chives, chopped
- 1/4 cup mushrooms, sliced
- Pepper
- Salt

Directions:
1. Preheat the air fryer to 320 F.
2. In a bowl, whisk together all ingredients.
3. Spray air fryer baking pan with cooking spray.
4. Pour egg mixture into the prepared pan and place in the air fryer.
5. Cook frittata for 15 minutes.
6. Serve and enjoy.

Nutritional Value (Amount per Serving):
- Calories 75
- Fat 0.6 g
- Carbohydrates 3 g
- Sugar 1 g
- Protein 14.3 g
- Cholesterol 1 mg

Broccoli Frittata

Preparation Time: 10 minutes; Cooking Time: 17 minutes; Serve: 2
Ingredients:
- 3 eggs
- 1/2 cup bell pepper, chopped
- 1/2 cup broccoli florets
- 2 tbsp parmesan cheese, grated
- 1/4 tsp garlic powder
- 1/4 tsp onion powder
- 2 tbsp coconut milk
- Pepper
- Salt

Directions:
1. Spray air fryer baking dish with cooking spray.
2. Place bell peppers and broccoli in the prepared baking dish.
3. Cook broccoli and bell pepper in the air fryer at 350 F for 7 minutes.
4. In a bowl, whisk together eggs, milk, and seasoning.
5. Once veggies are cooked then pour egg mixture over vegetables and sprinkle cheese on top.
6. Cook frittata in the air fryer for 10 minutes.
7. Serve and enjoy.

Nutritional Value (Amount per Serving):
- Calories 155
- Fat 9.3 g

- Carbohydrates 5.1 g
- Sugar 3 g
- Protein 12.8 g
- Cholesterol 254 mg

Perfect Breakfast Frittata

Preparation Time: 10 minutes; Cooking Time: 10 minutes; Serve: 2

Ingredients:
- 2 large eggs
- 1 tbsp bell peppers, chopped
- 1 tbsp spring onions, chopped
- 1 sausage patty, chopped
- 1 tbsp butter, melted
- 2 tbsp cheddar cheese
- Pepper
- Salt

Directions:
1. Add sausage patty in air fryer baking dish and cook in air fryer 350 F for 5 minutes.
2. Meanwhile, in a bowl whisk together eggs, pepper, and salt.
3. Add bell peppers, onions and stir well.
4. Pour egg mixture over sausage patty and stir well.
5. Sprinkle with cheese and cook in the air fryer at 350 F for 5 minutes.
6. Serve and enjoy.

Nutritional Value (Amount per Serving):
- Calories 205
- Fat 14.7 g
- Carbohydrates 5 g
- Sugar 4 g
- Protein 12 g
- Cholesterol 221 mg

Scrambled Eggs

Preparation Time: 10 minutes; Cooking Time: 6 minutes; Serve: 2

Ingredients:
- 4 eggs
- 1/4 tsp garlic powder
- 1/4 tsp onion powder
- 1 tbsp parmesan cheese
- Pepper
- Salt

Directions:
1. Whisk eggs with garlic powder, onion powder, parmesan cheese, pepper, and salt.
2. Pour egg mixture into the air fryer baking dish.
3. Place dish in the air fryer and cook at 360 F for 2 minutes. Stir quickly and cook for 3-4 minutes more.
4. Stir well and serve.

Nutritional Value (Amount per Serving):
- Calories 149
- Fat 9.1 g
- Carbohydrates 4.5 g
- Sugar 1.1 g
- Protein 11 g
- Cholesterol 325 mg

Sausage Egg Cups

Preparation Time: 10 minutes; Cooking Time: 10 minutes; Serve: 2

Ingredients:

- 1/4 cup egg beaters
- 1/4 sausage, cooked and crumbled
- 4 tsp jack cheese, shredded
- 1/4 tsp garlic powder
- 1/4 tsp onion powder
- 4 tbsp spinach, chopped
- Pepper
- Salt

Directions:
1. In a bowl, whisk together all ingredients until well combined.
2. Pour batter into the silicone muffin molds and place in the air fryer basket.
3. Cook at 330 F for 10 minutes.
4. Serve and enjoy.

Nutritional Value (Amount per Serving):
- Calories 90
- Fat 5 g
- Carbohydrates 1 g
- Sugar 0.2 g
- Protein 7 g
- Cholesterol 14 mg

Cheese Stuff Peppers

Preparation Time: 5 minutes; Cooking Time: 8 minutes; Serve: 8
Ingredients:
- 8 small bell pepper, cut the top of peppers
- 3.5 oz feta cheese, cubed
- 1 tbsp olive oil
- 1 tsp Italian seasoning
- 1 tbsp parsley, chopped
- ¼ tsp garlic powder
- Pepper
- Salt

Directions:
1. In a bowl, toss cheese with oil and seasoning.
2. Stuff cheese in each bell peppers and place into the air fryer basket.
3. Cook at 400 F for 8 minutes.
4. Serve and enjoy.

Nutritional Value (Amount per Serving):
- Calories 88
- Fat 5 g
- Carbohydrates 9 g
- Sugar 6 g
- Protein 3 g
- Cholesterol 10 mg

Roasted Pepper Salad

Preparation Time: 10 minutes; Cooking Time: 10 minutes; Serve: 4
Ingredients:
- 4 bell peppers
- 2 oz rocket leaves
- 2 tbsp olive oil
- 4 tbsp heavy cream
- 1 lettuce head, torn
- 1 tbsp fresh lime juice
- Pepper
- Salt

Directions:
1. Add bell peppers into the air fryer basket and cook for 10 minutes at 400 F.
2. Remove peppers from air fryer and let it cool for 5 minutes.

3. Peel cooked peppers and cut into strips and place into the large bowl.
4. Add remaining ingredients into the bowl and toss well.
5. Serve and enjoy.

Nutritional Value (Amount per Serving):
- Calories 160
- Fat 13 g
- Carbohydrates 11 g
- Sugar 6 g
- Protein 2 g
- Cholesterol 20 mg

Delicious Breakfast Casserole

Preparation Time: 10 minutes; Cooking Time: 20 minutes; Serve: 4
Ingredients:
- 4 eggs
- 7 oz spinach, chopped
- 3 bacon slices, chopped
- 8 grape tomatoes, halved
- 1 garlic clove, minced
- 8 mushrooms, sliced
- Pepper
- Salt

Directions:
1. Spray air fryer baking dish with cooking spray and set aside.
2. Add all ingredients into the large bowl and whisk until well combined.
3. Pour bowl mixture into the prepared baking dish.
4. Place dish in the air fryer and cook at 400 F for 20 minutes.
5. Serve and enjoy.

Nutritional Value (Amount per Serving):
- Calories 125
- Fat 5 g
- Carbohydrates 12 g
- Sugar 7 g
- Protein 10 g
- Cholesterol 165 mg

Tomato Egg Breakfast

Preparation Time: 10 minutes; Cooking Time: 30 minutes; Serve: 2
Ingredients:
- 2 eggs
- ½ cup tomatoes, chopped
- ¼ cup coconut milk
- 2 tbsp onion, chopped
- ½ cup cheddar cheese, shredded
- Pepper
- Salt

Directions:
1. In a large bowl, add all ingredients except cheese and stir to combine.
2. Pour bowl mixture into the air fryer baking dish and sprinkle cheese on top.
3. Place in the air fryer and cook at 350 F for 30 minutes.
4. Serve and enjoy.

Nutritional Value (Amount per Serving):
- Calories 255
- Fat 21 g
- Carbohydrates 5 g
- Sugar 3 g
- Protein 13 g
- Cholesterol 192 mg

Turkey Egg Casserole

Preparation Time: 10 minutes; Cooking Time: 25 minutes; Serve: 6
Ingredients:

- 12 eggs
- 2 tomatoes, chopped
- 1 cup spinach, chopped
- ½ sweet potato, cubed
- 1 tsp chili powder
- 1 tbsp olive oil
- 1 lb ground turkey
- Pepper
- Salt

Directions:

1. In a bowl, whisk eggs with pepper, chili powder, and salt until well combined.
2. Add spinach, sweet potato, tomato, and turkey and stir well.
3. Pour egg mixture into the air fryer baking dish and place in the air fryer.
4. Cook at 350 F for 25 minutes.
5. Serve and enjoy.

Nutritional Value (Amount per Serving):

- Calories 312
- Fat 19 g
- Carbohydrates 4 g
- Sugar 2 g
- Protein 30 g
- Cholesterol 402 mg

Sausage Cheese Mix

Preparation Time: 10 minutes; Cooking Time: 20 minutes; Serve: 4
Ingredients:

- 8 eggs, lightly beaten
- 1 cup coconut milk
- 1 cup mozzarella cheese, shredded
- 1 cup cheddar cheese, shredded
- 10 oz sausage, cooked and crumbled
- Pepper
- Salt

Directions:

1. In a bowl, add all ingredients and stir until well combined.
2. Transfer bowl mixture into the air fryer baking pan and place into the air fryer.
3. Cook at 380 F for 20 minutes.
4. Serve and enjoy.

Nutritional Value (Amount per Serving):

- Calories 635
- Fat 53 g
- Carbohydrates 4 g
- Sugar 2 g
- Protein 35 g
- Cholesterol 420 mg

Tofu Omelet

Preparation Time: 10 minutes; Cooking Time: 10 minutes; Serve: 1
Ingredients:

- 3 eggs, lightly beaten
- ¼ cup onion, chopped
- 2 tbsp green onion, chopped
- 2 tbsp soy sauce

- 1 tsp cumin
- 1 tsp coriander
- 1 /4 cup tofu, cubed
- Pepper
- Salt

Directions:
1. Add all ingredients into the large bowl and stir until well combined.
2. Spray air fryer baking pan with cooking spray.
3. Pour bowl mixture into the prepared baking pan and place into the air fryer.
4. Cook at 400 F for 10 minutes.
5. Serve and enjoy.

Nutritional Value (Amount per Serving):
- Calories 273
- Fat 16 g
- Carbohydrates 9 g
- Sugar 3 g
- Protein 24 g
- Cholesterol 490 mg

Kale Omelet

Preparation Time: 10 minutes; Cooking Time: 10 minutes; Serve: 1
Ingredients:
- 3 eggs, lightly beaten
- 1 tbsp parsley, chopped
- 1 tbsp basil, chopped
- 3 tbsp kale, chopped
- 3 tbsp cottage cheese, crumbled
- Pepper
- Salt

Directions:
1. Spray air fryer baking dish with cooking spray.
2. In a bowl, whisk eggs with pepper and salt.
3. Add remaining ingredients into the egg and stir to combine.
4. Pour egg mixture into the prepared dish and place into the air fryer.
5. Cook at 330 F for10 minutes.
6. Serve and enjoy.

Nutritional Value (Amount per Serving):
- Calories 235
- Fat 14 g
- Carbohydrates 4 g
- Sugar 1 g
- Protein 23 g
- Cholesterol 495 mg

Tofu Scrambled

Preparation Time: 10 minutes; Cooking Time: 15 minutes; Serve: 4
Ingredients:
- 1 block firm tofu, cubed
- ½ cup onion, chopped
- ½ tsp garlic powder
- ½ tsp onion powder
- 1 tbsp olive oil
- 1 tsp turmeric
- 2 tbsp coconut aminos
- Pepper
- Salt

Directions:

1. Add all ingredients into the large bowl and toss well.
2. Transfer tofu mixture into the air fryer basket and cook at 350 F for 15 minutes.
3. Serve and enjoy.

Nutritional Value (Amount per Serving):
- Calories 56
- Fat 4.5 g
- Carbohydrates 2 g
- Sugar 1 g
- Protein 2 g
- Cholesterol 0 mg

Lemon Dill Scallops

Preparation Time: 10 minutes; Cooking Time: 5 minutes; Serve: 4

Ingredients:
- 1 lb scallops
- 2 tsp olive oil
- 1 tsp dill, chopped
- 1 tbsp fresh lemon juice
- Pepper
- Salt

Directions:
1. Add scallops into the bowl and toss with oil, dill, lemon juice, pepper, and salt.
2. Add scallops into the air fryer basket and cook at 360 F for 5 minutes.
3. Serve and enjoy.

Nutritional Value (Amount per Serving):
- Calories 121
- Fat 3.2 g
- Carbohydrates 2.9 g
- Sugar 0.1 g
- Protein 19 g
- Cholesterol 37 mg

Herb Mushrooms

Preparation Time: 10 minutes; Cooking Time: 12 minutes; Serve: 2

Ingredients:
- 10 mushrooms, stems remove
- 1 tbsp dill, chopped
- 1 tbsp olive oil
- 1 tbsp parmesan cheese, grated
- ½ tbsp oregano
- ½ tsp dried basil
- Pepper
- Salt

Directions:
1. Add mushrooms into the bowl and toss with oil, oregano, basil, pepper, and salt.
2. Add mushrooms into the air fryer basket and cook at 360 F for 6 minutes.
3. Add dill and cheese and toss well and cook for 6 minutes more.
4. Serve and enjoy.

Nutritional Value (Amount per Serving):
- Calories 87
- Fat 7 g
- Carbohydrates 4 g
- Sugar 1 g
- Protein 3 g
- Cholesterol 0 mg

Easy & Tasty Salsa Chicken

Preparation Time: 10 minutes; Cooking Time: 30 minutes; Serve: 4

Ingredients:
- 1 lb chicken thighs, boneless and skinless
- 1 cup salsa
- Pepper
- Salt

Directions:
1. Preheat the air fryer to 350 F.
2. Place chicken thighs into the air fryer baking dish and season with pepper and salt. Top with salsa.
3. Place in the air fryer and cook for 30 minutes.
4. Serve and enjoy.

Nutritional Value (Amount per Serving):
- Calories 233
- Fat 8 g
- Carbohydrates 4 g
- Sugar 2 g
- Protein 33 g
- Cholesterol 101 mg

Buttery Scallops

Preparation Time: 10 minutes; Cooking Time: 8 minutes; Serve: 2
Ingredients:
- 1 lb jumbo scallops
- 1 tbsp fresh lemon juice
- 2 tbsp butter, melted

Directions:
1. Preheat the air fryer to 400 F.
2. In a small bowl, mix together lemon juice and butter.
3. Brush scallops with lemon juice and butter mixture and place into the air fryer basket.
4. Cook scallops for 4 minutes. Turn halfway through.
5. Again brush scallops with lemon butter mixture and cook for 4 minutes more. Turn halfway through.
6. Serve and enjoy.

Nutritional Value (Amount per Serving):
- Calories 199
- Fat 14 g
- Carbohydrates 2 g
- Sugar 0.2 g
- Protein 17 g
- Cholesterol 111 mg

Protein Egg Cups

Preparation Time: 10 minutes; Cooking Time: 9 minutes; Serve: 4
Ingredients:
- 3 eggs, lightly beaten
- 4 tomato slices
- 4 tsp cheddar cheese, shredded
- 2 bacon slices, cooked and crumbled
- Pepper
- Salt

Directions:
1. Spray silicone muffin molds with cooking spray.
2. In a small bowl, whisk the egg with pepper and salt.

3. Preheat the air fryer to 350 F.
4. Pour eggs into the silicone muffin molds. Divide cheese and bacon into molds.
5. Top each with tomato slice and place in the air fryer basket.
6. Cook for 9 minutes.
7. Serve and enjoy.

Nutritional Value (Amount per Serving):
- Calories 67
- Fat 4 g
- Carbohydrates 1 g
- Sugar 0.7 g
- Protein 5.1 g
- Cholesterol 125 mg

Crab Cheese Frittata

Preparation Time: 10 minutes; Cooking Time: 14 minutes; Serve: 2
Ingredients:
- 5 eggs
- ¼ tsp fresh lemon juice
- 2 tbsp fresh mint, chopped
- 1/3 cup goat cheese, crumbled
- ¼ cup onion, minced
- ¼ tsp pepper
- ¼ tsp salt

Directions:
1. Preheat the air fryer to 325 F.
2. In a bowl, whisk eggs with pepper and salt. Add remaining ingredients and stir well.
3. Spray air fryer baking dish with cooking spray.
4. Pour egg mixture into the prepared dish and place in the air fryer and cook for 14 minutes.
5. Serve and enjoy.

Nutritional Value (Amount per Serving):
- Calories 325
- Fat 25 g
- Carbohydrates 2.9 g
- Sugar 1.5 g
- Protein 24 g
- Cholesterol 469 mg

Broccoli Chicken Frittata

Preparation Time: 10 minutes; Cooking Time: 14 minutes; Serve: 2
Ingredients:
- 5 large eggs
- ¼ tsp fresh lemon juice
- 1/3 cup cheddar cheese, shredded
- ¼ cup broccoli, chopped
- ¼ cup chicken, cooked and chopped
- ¼ cup bell pepper, minced
- ¼ tsp pepper
- ¼ tsp salt

Directions:
1. Preheat the air fryer to 325 F.
2. In a bowl, whisk eggs with pepper and salt.
3. Add remaining ingredients and stir well.
4. Spray air fryer baking dish with cooking spray.

5. Pour egg mixture into the prepared dish and place into the air fryer and cook for 14 minutes.
6. Serve and enjoy.

Nutritional Value (Amount per Serving):
- Calories 291
- Fat 19 g
- Carbohydrates 3.3 g
- Sugar 2 g
- Protein 26 g
- Cholesterol 498 mg

Herb Carrots

Preparation Time: 10 minutes; Cooking Time: 20 minutes; Serve: 4

Ingredients:
- 1 lb baby carrots, trimmed
- 2 tbsp fresh lime juice
- 1 tsp herb de Provence
- 2 tsp olive oil
- Pepper
- Salt

Directions:
1. Add carrots into the bowl and toss with remaining ingredients.
2. Transfer carrots into the air fryer basket and cook at 320 F for 20 minutes.
3. Serve and enjoy.

Nutritional Value (Amount per Serving):
- Calories 60
- Fat 2.5 g
- Carbohydrates 9.4 g
- Sugar 5.4 g
- Protein 0.7 g
- Cholesterol 0 mg

Tomato Mushroom Mix

Preparation Time: 10 minutes; Cooking Time: 15 minutes; Serve: 4

Ingredients:
- 6 oz tomatoes, chopped
- 2 tbsp olive oil
- ½ tsp ground nutmeg
- 1 onion, chopped
- 15 oz mushrooms, sliced
- Pepper
- Salt

Directions:
1. Add all ingredients into the air fryer baking dish and mix well.
2. Place dish in the air fryer and cook at 380 F for 15 minutes.
3. Serve and enjoy.

Nutritional Value (Amount per Serving):
- Calories 103
- Fat 7.5 g
- Carbohydrates 7.9 g
- Sugar 4 g
- Protein 4 g
- Cholesterol 0 mg

Zucchini Squash Mix

Preparation Time: 10 minutes; Cooking Time: 35 minutes; Serve: 4

Ingredients:

- 1 lb zucchini, sliced
- 1 tbsp parsley, chopped
- 1 yellow squash, halved, deseeded, and chopped
- 1 tbsp olive oil
- Pepper
- Salt

Directions:
1. Add all ingredients into the large bowl and mix well.
2. Transfer bowl mixture into the air fryer basket and cook at 400 F for 35 minutes.
3. Serve and enjoy.

Nutritional Value (Amount per Serving):
- Calories 49
- Fat 3 g
- Carbohydrates 4 g
- Sugar 2 g
- Protein 1.5 g
- Cholesterol 0 mg

Mushroom Cheese Salad

Preparation Time: 10 minutes; Cooking Time: 15 minutes; Serve: 3
Ingredients:
- 10 mushrooms, halved
- 1 tbsp fresh parsley, chopped
- 1 tbsp olive oil
- 1 tbsp mozzarella cheese, grated
- 1 tbsp cheddar cheese, grated
- 1 tbsp dried mix herbs
- Pepper
- Salt

Directions:
1. Add all ingredients into the bowl and toss well.
2. Transfer bowl mixture into the air fryer baking dish.
3. Place in the air fryer and cook at 380 F for 15 minutes.
4. Serve and enjoy.

Nutritional Value (Amount per Serving):
- Calories 90
- Fat 7 g
- Carbohydrates 2 g
- Sugar 1 g
- Protein 5 g
- Cholesterol 7 mg

Creamy Cabbage

Preparation Time: 10 minutes; Cooking Time: 20 minutes; Serve: 4
Ingredients:
- 1 cabbage head, shredded
- 1 cup heavy cream
- 4 bacon slices, chopped
- 1 onion, chopped
- Pepper
- Salt

Directions:
1. Add all ingredients into the air fryer baking dish and stir well.
2. Place dish in the air fryer and cook at 400 F for 20 minutes.
3. Serve and enjoy.

Nutritional Value (Amount per Serving):
- Calories 163
- Fat 11 g

- Carbohydrates 13 g
- Sugar 7 g
- Protein 3 g
- Cholesterol 41 mg

Greek Vegetables

Preparation Time: 10 minutes; Cooking Time: 35 minutes; Serve: 6
Ingredients:
- 1 eggplant, sliced
- 4 tomatoes, quarters
- 2 onion, chopped
- 1 thyme sprig, chopped
- 1 bay leaf
- 3 tbsp olive oil
- 3 garlic cloves, minced
- 2 bell peppers, chopped
- 1 zucchini, sliced
- Pepper
- Salt

Directions:
1. Add all ingredients into the air fryer baking pan and mix well.
2. Place pan in the air fryer and cook at 300 F for 35 minutes.
3. Serve and enjoy.

Nutritional Value (Amount per Serving):
- Calories 123
- Fat 7 g
- Carbohydrates 14 g
- Sugar 8 g
- Protein 2 g
- Cholesterol 0 mg

Lemon Butter Artichokes

Preparation Time: 10 minutes; Cooking Time: 15 minutes; Serve: 4
Ingredients:
- 2 medium artichokes, trimmed and halved
- 2 tbsp fresh lemon juice
- 1 tbsp butter, melted
- Pepper
- Salt

Directions:
1. Place artichokes into the air fryer basket. Drizzle with butter and lemon juice and season with pepper and salt.
2. Cook at 380 F for 15 minutes.
3. Serve and enjoy.

Nutritional Value (Amount per Serving):
- Calories 57
- Fat 3 g
- Carbohydrates 6.9 g
- Sugar 0.8 g
- Protein 2.2 g
- Cholesterol 8 mg

Shrimp Stuff Peppers

Preparation Time: 10 minutes; Cooking Time: 6 minutes; Serve: 6
Ingredients:
- 12 baby bell peppers, cut into halves
- 1 tbsp olive oil
- 1 tbsp fresh lemon juice
- ¼ cup basil pesto

- 1 lb shrimp, cooked
- ½ tsp red pepper flakes, crushed
- 2 tbsp parsley, chopped
- Pepper
- Salt

Directions:

1. In a bowl, mix together shrimp, parsley, red pepper flakes, basil pesto, lemon juice, oil, pepper, and salt.
2. Stuff shrimp mixture into the bell pepper halved and place into the air fryer basket.
3. Cook at 320 F for 6 minutes.
4. Serve and enjoy.

Nutritional Value (Amount per Serving):

- Calories 191
- Fat 3.7 g
- Carbohydrates 13 g
- Sugar 12 g
- Protein 19 g
- Cholesterol 159 mg

Delicious Eggplant Hash

Preparation Time: 10 minutes; Cooking Time: 14 minutes; Serve: 4
Ingredients:

- 1 eggplant, chopped
- ¼ cup fresh mint, chopped
- ¼ cup basil, chopped
- 1 tsp Tabasco sauce
- ½ lb cherry tomatoes halved
- ½ cup olive oil
- Pepper
- Salt

Directions:

1. Heat oil in a pan over medium-high heat.
2. Add eggplant into the pan and cook for 3 minutes stir well and cook for 3 minutes more.
3. Transfer eggplant into the air fryer baking dish.
4. Add tomatoes in the same pan and cook for 1-2 minutes.
5. Transfer tomatoes in eggplant dish along with remaining ingredients and stir well.
6. Place dish in the air fryer and cook at 320 F for 6 minutes.
7. Serve and enjoy.

Nutritional Value (Amount per Serving):

- Calories 258
- Fat 25 g
- Carbohydrates 9 g
- Sugar 4 g
- Protein 2 g
- Cholesterol 0 mg

Garlic Feta Asparagus

Preparation Time: 10 minutes; Cooking Time: 15 minutes; Serve: 4
Ingredients:

- 2 lbs asparagus, trimmed
- 2 tbsp fresh parsley, chopped
- 4 oz feta cheese, crumbled
- ½ tsp red pepper flakes
- ½ tsp dried oregano
- 3 garlic cloves, minced
- 1 tsp lemon zest
- ¼ cup olive oil
- 1 lemon juice
- Pepper

- Salt

Directions:
1. In a bowl, whisk together oil, oregano, red pepper flakes, garlic, and lemon zest.
2. Add asparagus, crumbled cheese, pepper, and salt and toss well.
3. Transfer asparagus mixture into the air fryer basket and cook at 350 F for 8 minutes.
4. Drizzle asparagus with lemon juice and sprinkle with parsley.
5. Serve and enjoy.

Nutritional Value (Amount per Serving):
- Calories 234
- Fat 19 g
- Carbohydrates 11 g
- Sugar 5 g
- Protein 9 g
- Cholesterol 25 mg

Chicken Meatballs

Preparation Time: 10 minutes; Cooking Time: 12 minutes; Serve: 4
Ingredients:
- 1 lb ground chicken
- 1/3 cup frozen spinach, drained and thawed
- 1/3 cup feta cheese, crumbled
- 1 tsp greek seasoning
- ½ oz pork rinds, crushed
- Pepper
- Salt

Directions:
1. Spray air fryer basket with cooking spray.
2. Add all ingredients into the large bowl and mix until well combined.
3. Make small balls from meat mixture and place into the air fryer basket and cook for 12 minutes.
4. Serve and enjoy.

Nutritional Value (Amount per Serving):
- Calories 271
- Fat 12 g
- Carbohydrates 1 g
- Sugar 0.5 g
- Protein 37 g
- Cholesterol 117 mg

Almond Crust Chicken

Preparation Time: 10 minutes; Cooking Time: 25 minutes; Serve: 2
Ingredients:
- 2 chicken breasts, skinless and boneless
- 1 tbsp Dijon mustard
- 2 tbsp mayonnaise
- ¼ cup almonds
- Pepper
- Salt

Directions:
1. Add almond into the food processor and process until finely ground. Transfer almonds on a plate and set aside.
2. Mix together mustard and mayonnaise and spread over chicken.

3. Coat chicken with almond and place into the air fryer basket and cook at 350 F for 25 minutes.
4. Serve and enjoy.

Nutritional Value (Amount per Serving):
- Calories 409
- Fat 22 g
- Carbohydrates 6 g
- Sugar 1.5 g
- Protein 45 g
- Cholesterol 134 mg

Italian Chicken

Preparation Time: 10 minutes; Cooking Time: 20 minutes; Serve: 4
Ingredients:
- 4 chicken thighs
- ¼ tsp onion powder
- ½ tsp garlic powder
- 2 ½ tsp dried Italian herbs
- 2 tbsp butter, melted

Directions:
1. Brush chicken with melted butter.
2. Mix together Italian herbs, onion powder, and garlic powder and rub over chicken.
3. Place chicken into the air fryer basket and cook at 380 F for 20 minutes.
4. Serve and enjoy.

Nutritional Value (Amount per Serving):
- Calories 330
- Fat 16 g
- Carbohydrates 0.4 g
- Sugar 0.1 g
- Protein 42 g
- Cholesterol 145 mg

Almond Pesto Salmon

Preparation Time: 10 minutes; Cooking Time: 12 minutes; Serve: 2
Ingredients:
- 2 salmon fillets
- 2 tbsp butter, melted
- ¼ cup pesto
- ¼ cup almond, ground

Directions:
1. Mix together pesto and almond.
2. Brush salmon fillets with melted butter and place into the air fryer baking dish.
3. Top salmon fillets with pesto and almond mixture.
4. Place dish in the air fryer and cook at 390 F for 12 minutes.
5. Serve and enjoy.

Nutritional Value (Amount per Serving):
- Calories 541
- Fat 41 g
- Carbohydrates 4 g
- Sugar 2.5 g
- Protein 40 g
- Cholesterol 117 mg

Chapter 4: Poultry Recipes

Chicken Popcorn

Preparation Time: 10 minutes; Cooking Time: 10 minutes; Serve: 6

Ingredients:

- 4 eggs
- 1 1/2 lbs chicken breasts, cut into small chunks
- 1 tsp paprika
- 1/2 tsp garlic powder
- 1 tsp onion powder
- 2 1/2 cups pork rind, crushed
- 1/4 cup coconut flour
- Pepper
- Salt

Directions:

1. In a small bowl, mix together coconut flour, pepper, and salt.
2. In another bowl, whisk eggs until combined.
3. Take one more bowl and mix together pork panko, paprika, garlic powder, and onion powder.
4. Add chicken pieces in a large mixing bowl. Sprinkle coconut flour mixture over chicken and toss well.
5. Dip chicken pieces in the egg mixture and coat with pork panko mixture and place on a plate.
6. Spray air fryer basket with cooking spray.
7. Preheat the air fryer to 400 F.
8. Add half prepared chicken in air fryer basket and cook for 10-12 minutes. Shake basket halfway through.
9. Cook remaining half using the same method.
10. Serve and enjoy.

Nutritional Value (Amount per Serving):

- Calories 265
- Fat 11 g
- Carbohydrates 3 g
- Sugar 0.5 g
- Protein 35 g
- Cholesterol 195 mg

Delicious Whole Chicken

Preparation Time: 10 minutes; Cooking Time: 50 minutes; Serve: 4

Ingredients:

- 3 lbs whole chicken, remove giblets and pat dry chicken
- 1 tsp Italian seasoning
- 1/2 tsp garlic powder
- 1/2 tsp onion powder
- 1/4 tsp paprika
- 1/4 tsp pepper
- 1 1/2 tsp salt

Directions:

1. In a small bowl, mix together Italian seasoning, garlic powder, onion powder, paprika, pepper, and salt.
2. Rub spice mixture from inside and outside of the chicken.

3. Place chicken breast side down in air fryer basket.
4. Roast chicken for 30 minutes at 360 F.
5. Turn chicken and roast for 20 minutes more or internal temperature of chicken reaches at 165 F.
6. Serve and enjoy.

Nutritional Value (Amount per Serving):
- Calories 356
- Fat 25 g
- Carbohydrates 1 g
- Sugar 1 g
- Protein 30 g
- Cholesterol 120 mg

Quick & Easy Meatballs

Preparation Time: 10 minutes; Cooking Time: 10 minutes; Serve: 4
Ingredients:
- 1 lb ground chicken
- 1 egg, lightly beaten
- 1/2 cup mozzarella cheese, shredded
- 1 1/2 tbsp taco seasoning
- 3 garlic cloves, minced
- 3 tbsp fresh parsley, chopped
- 1 small onion, minced
- Pepper
- Salt

Directions:
1. Add all ingredients into the large mixing bowl and mix until well combined.
2. Make small balls from mixture and place in the air fryer basket.
3. Cook meatballs for 10 minutes at 400 F.
4. Serve and enjoy.

Nutritional Value (Amount per Serving):
- Calories 253
- Fat 10 g
- Carbohydrates 2 g
- Sugar 0.9 g
- Protein 35 g
- Cholesterol 144 mg

Lemon Pepper Chicken Wings

Preparation Time: 10 minutes; Cooking Time: 16 minutes; Serve: 4
Ingredients:
- 1 lb chicken wings
- 1 tsp lemon pepper
- 1 tbsp olive oil
- 1 tsp salt

Directions:
1. Add chicken wings into the large mixing bowl.
2. Add remaining ingredients over chicken and toss well to coat.
3. Place chicken wings in the air fryer basket.
4. Cook chicken wings for 8 minutes at 400 F.
5. Turn chicken wings to another side and cook for 8 minutes more.
6. Serve and enjoy.

Nutritional Value (Amount per Serving):
- Calories 247
- Fat 11 g

- Carbohydrates 0.3 g
- Sugar 0 g
- Protein 32 g
- Cholesterol 101 mg

BBQ Chicken Wings

Preparation Time: 10 minutes; Cooking Time: 20 minutes; Serve: 4
Ingredients:
- 1 1/2 lbs chicken wings
- 2 tbsp unsweetened BBQ sauce
- 1 tsp paprika
- 1 tbsp olive oil
- 1 tsp garlic powder
- Pepper
- Salt

Directions:
1. In a large bowl, toss chicken wings with garlic powder, oil, paprika, pepper, and salt.
2. Preheat the air fryer to 360 F.
3. Add chicken wings in air fryer basket and cook for 12 minutes.
4. Turn chicken wings to another side and cook for 5 minutes more.
5. Remove chicken wings from air fryer and toss with BBQ sauce.
6. Return chicken wings in air fryer basket and cook for 2 minutes more.
7. Serve and enjoy.

Nutritional Value (Amount per Serving):
- Calories 372
- Fat 16.2 g
- Carbohydrates 4.3 g
- Sugar 3.7 g
- Protein 49.4 g
- Cholesterol 151 mg

Flavorful Fried Chicken

Preparation Time: 10 minutes; Cooking Time: 40 minutes; Serve: 10
Ingredients:
- 5 lbs chicken, about 10 pieces
- 1 tbsp coconut oil
- 2 1/2 tsp white pepper
- 1 tsp ground ginger
- 1 1/2 tsp garlic salt
- 1 tbsp paprika
- 1 tsp dried mustard
- 1 tsp pepper
- 1 tsp celery salt
- 1/3 tsp oregano
- 1/2 tsp basil
- 1/2 tsp thyme
- 2 cups pork rinds, crushed
- 1 tbsp vinegar
- 1 cup unsweetened almond milk
- 1/2 tsp salt

Directions:
1. Add chicken in a large mixing bowl.
2. Add milk and vinegar over chicken and place in the refrigerator for 2 hours.
3. I a shallow dish, mix together pork rinds, white pepper, ginger, garlic salt, paprika, mustard, pepper, celery salt, oregano, basil, thyme, and salt.
4. Coat air fryer basket with coconut oil.
5. Coat each chicken piece with pork rind mixture and place on a plate.
6. Place half coated chicken in the air fryer basket.

7. Cook chicken at 360 F for 10 minutes then turn chicken to another side and cook for 10 minutes more or until internal temperature reaches at 165 F.
8. Cook remaining chicken using the same method.
9. Serve and enjoy.

Nutritional Value (Amount per Serving):
- Calories 539
- Fat 37 g
- Carbohydrates 1 g
- Sugar 0 g
- Protein 45 g
- Cholesterol 175 mg

Yummy Chicken Nuggets

Preparation Time: 10 minutes; Cooking Time: 12 minutes; Serve: 4
Ingredients:
- 1 lb chicken breast, skinless, boneless and cut into chunks
- 6 tbsp sesame seeds, toasted
- 4 egg whites
- 1/2 tsp ground ginger
- 1/4 cup coconut flour
- 1 tsp sesame oil
- Pinch of salt

Directions:
1. Preheat the air fryer to 400 F.
2. Toss chicken with oil and salt in a bowl until well coated.
3. Add coconut flour and ginger in a zip-lock bag and shake to mix. Add chicken to the bag and shake well to coat.
4. In a large bowl, add egg whites. Add chicken in egg whites and toss until well coated.
5. Add sesame seeds in a large zip-lock bag.
6. Shake excess egg off from chicken and add chicken in sesame seed bag. Shake bag until chicken well coated with sesame seeds.
7. Spray air fryer basket with cooking spray.
8. Place chicken in air fryer basket and cook for 6 minutes.
9. Turn chicken to another side and cook for 6 minutes more.
10. Serve and enjoy.

Nutritional Value (Amount per Serving):
- Calories 265
- Fat 11.5 g
- Carbohydrates 8.6 g
- Sugar 0.3 g
- Protein 31.1 g
- Cholesterol 73 mg

Italian Seasoned Chicken Tenders

Preparation Time: 10 minutes; Cooking Time: 10 minutes; Serve: 2
Ingredients:
- 2 eggs, lightly beaten
- 1 1/2 lbs chicken tenders
- 1/2 tsp onion powder
- 1/2 tsp garlic powder
- 1 tsp paprika
- 1 tsp Italian seasoning
- 2 tbsp ground flax seed
- 1 cup almond flour
- 1/2 tsp pepper
- 1 tsp sea salt

Directions:

1. Preheat the air fryer to 400 F.
2. Season chicken with pepper and salt.
3. In a medium bowl, whisk eggs to combine.
4. In a shallow dish, mix together almond flour, all seasonings, and flaxseed.
5. Dip chicken into the egg then coats with almond flour mixture and place on a plate.
6. Spray air fryer basket with cooking spray.
7. Place half chicken tenders in air fryer basket and cook for 10 minutes. Turn halfway through.
8. Cook remaining chicken tenders using same steps.
9. Serve and enjoy.

Nutritional Value (Amount per Serving):

- Calories 315
- Fat 21 g
- Carbohydrates 12 g
- Sugar 0.6 g
- Protein 17 g
- Cholesterol 184 mg

Classic Chicken Wings

Preparation Time: 10 minutes; Cooking Time: 40 minutes; Serve: 4

Ingredients:

- 2 lbs chicken wings

For sauce:

- 1/4 tsp Tabasco
- 1/4 tsp Worcestershire sauce
- 6 tbsp butter, melted
- 12 oz hot sauce

Directions:

1. Spray air fryer basket with cooking spray.
2. Add chicken wings in air fryer basket and cook for 25 minutes at 380 F. Shake basket after every 5 minutes.
3. After 25 minutes turn temperature to 400 F and cook for 10-15 minutes more.
4. Meanwhile, in a large bowl, mix together all sauce ingredients.
5. Add cooked chicken wings in a sauce bowl and toss well to coat.
6. Serve and enjoy.

Nutritional Value (Amount per Serving):

- Calories 593
- Fat 34.4 g
- Carbohydrates 1.6 g
- Sugar 1.1 g
- Protein 66.2 g
- Cholesterol 248 mg

Simple Spice Chicken Wings

Preparation Time: 10 minutes; Cooking Time: 30 minutes; Serve: 3

Ingredients:

- 1 1/2 lbs chicken wings
- 1 tbsp baking powder, gluten-free
- 1/2 tsp onion powder
- 1/2 tsp garlic powder
- 1/2 tsp smoked paprika
- 1 tbsp olive oil

- 1/2 tsp pepper
- 1/4 tsp sea salt

Directions:
1. Add chicken wings and oil in a large mixing bowl and toss well.
2. Mix together remaining ingredients and sprinkle over chicken wings and toss to coat.
3. Spray air fryer basket with cooking spray.
4. Add chicken wings in air fryer basket and cook at 400 F for 15 minutes. Toss well.
5. Turn chicken wings to another side and cook for 15 minutes more.
6. Serve and enjoy.

Nutritional Value (Amount per Serving):
- Calories 280
- Fat 19 g
- Carbohydrates 2 g
- Sugar 0 g
- Protein 22 g
- Cholesterol 94 mg

Quick & Simple Chicken Breast

Preparation Time: 10 minutes; Cooking Time: 22 minutes; Serve: 4
Ingredients:
- 4 chicken breasts, skinless and boneless
- 1/2 tsp dried oregano
- 1/2 tsp dried basil
- 1/2 tsp dried thyme
- 1/2 tsp garlic powder
- 2 tbsp olive oil
- 1/8 tsp pepper
- 1/2 tsp salt

Directions:
1. In a small bowl, mix together olive oil, oregano, basil, thyme, garlic powder, pepper, and salt.
2. Rub herb oil mixture all over chicken breasts.
3. Spray air fryer basket with cooking spray.
4. Place chicken in air fryer basket and cook at 360 F for 10 minutes.
5. Turn chicken to another side and cook for 8-12 minutes more or until the internal temperature of chicken reaches at 165 F.
6. Serve and enjoy.

Nutritional Value (Amount per Serving):
- Calories 340
- Fat 17.9 g
- Carbohydrates 0.5 g
- Sugar 0.1 g
- Protein 42.3 g
- Cholesterol 130 mg

Easy & Crispy Chicken Wings

Preparation Time: 5 minutes; Cooking Time: 20 minutes; Serve: 8
Ingredients:
- 1 1/2 lbs chicken wings
- 2 tbsp olive oil
- Pepper
- Salt

Directions:
1. Toss chicken wings with oil and place in the air fryer basket.

2. Cook chicken wings at 370 F for 15 minutes.
3. Shake basket and cook at 400 F for 5 minutes more.
4. Season chicken wings with pepper and salt.
5. Serve and enjoy.

Nutritional Value (Amount per Serving):

- Calories 192
- Fat 9.8 g
- Carbohydrates 0 g
- Sugar 0 g
- Protein 24.6 g
- Cholesterol 76 mg

Herb Seasoned Turkey Breast

Preparation Time: 10 minutes; Cooking Time: 35 minutes; Serve: 4

Ingredients:

- 2 lbs turkey breast
- 1 tsp fresh sage, chopped
- 1 tsp fresh rosemary, chopped
- 1 tsp fresh thyme, chopped
- Pepper
- Salt

Directions:
1. Spray air fryer basket with cooking spray.
2. In a small bowl, mix together sage, rosemary, and thyme.
3. Season turkey breast with pepper and salt and rub with herb mixture.
4. Place turkey breast in air fryer basket and cook at 390 F for 30-35 minutes.
5. Slice and serve.

Nutritional Value (Amount per Serving):

- Calories 238
- Fat 3.9 g
- Carbohydrates 10 g
- Sugar 8 g
- Protein 38.8 g
- Cholesterol 98 mg

Tasty Rotisserie Chicken

Preparation Time: 10 minutes; Cooking Time: 20 minutes; Serve: 6

Ingredients:

- 3 lbs chicken, cut into eight pieces
- 1/4 tsp cayenne
- 1 tsp paprika
- 2 tsp onion powder
- 1 1/2 tsp garlic powder
- 1 1/2 tsp dried oregano
- 1/2 tbsp dried thyme
- Pepper
- Salt

Directions:
1. Season chicken with pepper and salt.
2. In a bowl, mix together spices and herbs and rub spice mixture over chicken pieces.
3. Spray air fryer basket with cooking spray.
4. Place chicken in air fryer basket and cook at 350 F for 10 minutes.
5. Turn chicken to another side and cook for 10 minutes more or until the internal temperature of chicken reaches at 165 F.
6. Serve and enjoy.

Nutritional Value (Amount per Serving):
- Calories 350
- Fat 7 g
- Carbohydrates 1.8 g
- Sugar 0.5 g
- Protein 66 g
- Cholesterol 175 mg

Spicy Asian Chicken Thighs

Preparation Time: 10 minutes; Cooking Time: 20 minutes; Serve: 4
Ingredients:
- 4 chicken thighs, skin-on, and bone-in
- 2 tsp ginger, grated
- 1 lime juice
- 2 tbsp chili garlic sauce
- 1/4 cup olive oil
- 1/3 cup soy sauce

Directions:
1. In a large bowl, whisk together ginger, lime juice, chili garlic sauce, oil, and soy sauce.
2. Add chicken in bowl and coat well with marinade and place in the refrigerator for 30 minutes.
3. Place marinated chicken in air fryer basket and cook at 400 F for 15-20 minutes or until the internal temperature of chicken reaches at 165 F. Turn chicken halfway through.
4. Serve and enjoy.

Nutritional Value (Amount per Serving):
- Calories 403
- Fat 23.5 g
- Carbohydrates 3.2 g
- Sugar 0.6 g
- Protein 43.7 g
- Cholesterol 130 mg

Chicken with Broccoli

Preparation Time: 10 minutes; Cooking Time: 20 minutes; Serve: 4
Ingredients:
- 1 lb chicken breast, skinless, boneless, and cut into chunks
- 2 cups broccoli florets
- 2 tsp hot sauce
- 2 tsp vinegar
- 1 tsp sesame oil
- 1 tbsp soy sauce
- 1 tbsp ginger, minced
- 1/2 tsp garlic powder
- 1 tbsp olive oil
- 1/2 onion, sliced
- Pepper
- Salt

Directions:
1. Add all ingredients into the large mixing bowl and toss well.
2. Spray air fryer basket with cooking spray.
3. Transfer chicken and broccoli mixture into the air fryer basket.
4. Cook at 380 F for 15-20 minutes. Shake halfway through.
5. Serve and enjoy.

Nutritional Value (Amount per Serving):
- Calories 199
- Fat 7.7 g
- Carbohydrates 5.9 g
- Sugar 1.6 g

- Protein 25.9 g
- Cholesterol 73 mg

Zaatar Chicken

Preparation Time: 10 minutes; Cooking Time: 35 minutes; Serve: 4

Ingredients:

- 4 chicken thighs
- 2 sprigs thyme
- 1 onion, cut into chunks
- 2 1/2 tbsp zaatar
- 1/2 tsp cinnamon
- 2 garlic cloves, smashed
- 1 lemon juice
- 1 lemon zest
- 1/4 cup olive oil
- 1/4 tsp pepper
- 1 tsp salt

Directions:

1. Add oil, lemon juice, lemon zest, cinnamon, garlic, pepper, 2 tbsp zaatar, and salt in a large zip-lock bag and shake well.
2. Add chicken, thyme, and onion to bag and shake well to coat. Place in refrigerator for overnight.
3. Preheat the air fryer to 380 F.
4. Add marinated chicken in air fryer basket and cook at 380 F for 15 minutes.
5. Turn chicken to another side and sprinkle with remaining za'atar spice and cook at 380 F for 15-18 minutes more.
6. Serve and enjoy.

Nutritional Value (Amount per Serving):

- Calories 415
- Fat 24.1 g
- Carbohydrates 5.2 g
- Sugar 1.5 g
- Protein 43 g
- Cholesterol 130 mg

Teriyaki Chicken

Preparation Time: 10 minutes; Cooking Time: 20 minutes; Serve: 6

Ingredients:

- 6 chicken drumsticks
- 1 cup keto teriyaki sauce
- 1 tbsp sesame seeds, toasted
- 2 tbsp green onion, sliced

Directions:

1. Add chicken and teriyaki sauce into the large zip-lock bag. Shake well and place in the refrigerator for 1 hour.
2. Preheat the air fryer to 360 F.
3. Add marinated chicken drumsticks into the air fryer basket and cook for 20 minutes. Shake basket twice.
4. Garnish with green onion and sesame seeds.
5. Serve and enjoy.

Nutritional Value (Amount per Serving):

- Calories 165
- Fat 7 g
- Carbohydrates 7 g
- Sugar 6 g

- Protein 16 g
- Cholesterol 65 mg

Crispy & Juicy Whole Chicken

Preparation Time: 10 minutes; Cooking Time: 60 minutes; Serve: 8
Ingredients:
- 5 lbs chicken, wash and remove giblets
- 1/2 tsp onion powder
- 1/2 tsp pepper
- 1 tsp paprika
- 1 tsp dried oregano
- 1 tsp dried basil
- 1 1/2 tsp salt

Directions:
1. Preheat the air fryer to 360 F.
2. Mix together all spices and rub over chicken.
3. Place chicken into the air fryer basket. Make sure the chicken breast side down.
4. Cook chicken for 30 minutes then turn to another side and cook for 30 minutes more.
5. Slice and serve.

Nutritional Value (Amount per Serving):
- Calories 430
- Fat 8.6 g
- Carbohydrates 0.5 g
- Sugar 0.1 g
- Protein 82.3 g
- Cholesterol 218 mg

Juicy Turkey Breast Tenderloin

Preparation Time: 10 minutes; Cooking Time: 25 minutes; Serve: 3
Ingredients:
- 1 turkey breast tenderloin
- 1/2 tsp sage
- 1/2 tsp smoked paprika
- 1/2 tsp pepper
- 1/2 tsp thyme
- 1/2 tsp salt

Directions:
1. Preheat the air fryer to 350 F.
2. Spray air fryer basket with cooking spray.
3. Rub turkey breast tenderloin with paprika, pepper, thyme, sage, and salt and place in the air fryer basket.
4. Cook for 25 minutes. Turn halfway through.
5. Slice and serve.

Nutritional Value (Amount per Serving):
- Calories 61
- Fat 1 g
- Carbohydrates 1 g
- Sugar 1 g
- Protein 12 g
- Cholesterol 25 mg

Flavorful Cornish Hen

Preparation Time: 10 minutes; Cooking Time: 25 minutes; Serve: 3
Ingredients:
- 1 Cornish hen, wash and pat dry
- 1 tbsp olive oil

- 1 tsp smoked paprika
- 1/2 tsp garlic powder
- Pepper
- Salt

Directions:

1. Coat Cornish hen with olive oil and rub with paprika, garlic powder, pepper, and salt.
2. Place Cornish hen in the air fryer basket.
3. Cook at 390 F for 25 minutes. Turn halfway through.
4. Slice and serve.

Nutritional Value (Amount per Serving):

- Calories 301
- Fat 5 g
- Carbohydrates 2 g
- Sugar 0.5 g
- Protein 25 g
- Cholesterol 150 mg

Chicken Vegetable Fry

Preparation Time: 10 minutes; Cooking Time: 15 minutes; Serve: 2

Ingredients:

- 6 oz chicken breast, boneless and cut into cubes
- 1/4 tsp dried thyme
- 1/2 tsp garlic powder
- 1 tsp dried oregano
- 1/4 onion, sliced
- 1/2 bell pepper, chopped
- 1/2 zucchini, chopped
- 1 tbsp olive oil

Directions:

1. Add all ingredients into the large bowl and toss well.
2. Transfer chicken mixture into the air fryer basket and cook at 375 F for 15 minutes. Shake basket halfway through.
3. Serve and enjoy.

Nutritional Value (Amount per Serving):

- Calories 185
- Fat 8 g
- Carbohydrates 5 g
- Sugar 3 g
- Protein 20 g
- Cholesterol 0 mg

Cilantro Lime Chicken

Preparation Time: 10 minutes; Cooking Time: 20 minutes; Serve: 4

Ingredients:

- 2 lbs chicken thighs, boneless
- 2 tbsp fresh cilantro, chopped
- 1 tsp Montreal chicken seasoning
- 1 tsp soy sauce
- 1/2 lime juice
- 1 tsp olive oil
- Pepper
- Salt

Directions:

1. Whisk together cilantro, seasoning, soy sauce, lime juice, olive oil, pepper, and salt in a large bowl.
2. Add chicken into the bowl and coat well with marinade and place in the refrigerator for overnight.

3. Spray air fryer basket with cooking spray.
4. Place marinated chicken into the air fryer basket and cook at 400 F for 10 minutes.
5. Turn chicken to another side and cook for 10 minutes more.
6. Serve and enjoy.

Nutritional Value (Amount per Serving):
- Calories 444
- Fat 18 g
- Carbohydrates 0.8 g
- Sugar 0.1 g
- Protein 65.8 g
- Cholesterol 202 mg

Delicious Chicken Casserole

Preparation Time: 10 minutes; Cooking Time: 32 minutes; Serve: 8
Ingredients:
- 2 lbs cooked chicken, shredded
- 6 oz cream cheese, softened
- 4 oz butter, melted
- 6 oz ham, cut into small pieces
- 5 oz Swiss cheese
- 1 oz fresh lemon juice
- 1 tbsp Dijon mustard
- 1/2 tsp salt

Directions:
1. Preheat the air fryer to 325 F.
2. Arrange chicken in the bottom of air fryer baking dish then layer ham pieces on top.
3. Add butter, lemon juice, mustard, cream cheese, and salt into the blender and blend until a thick sauce.
4. Spread sauce on top of chicken and ham mixture.
5. Arrange Swiss cheese slices on top of sauce. Place baking dish in the air fryer and cook for 30-32 minutes.
6. Serve and enjoy.

Nutritional Value (Amount per Serving):
- Calories 450
- Fat 29 g
- Carbohydrates 2.5 g
- Sugar 0.4 g
- Protein 40 g
- Cholesterol 170 mg

Chicken with Mushrooms

Preparation Time: 10 minutes; Cooking Time: 24 minutes; Serve: 4
Ingredients:
- 2 lbs chicken breasts, halved
- 1/3 cup sun-dried tomatoes
- 8 oz mushrooms, sliced
- 1/2 cup mayonnaise
- 1 tsp salt

Directions:
1. Preheat the air fryer to 370 F.
2. Spray air fryer baking dish with cooking spray.
3. Place chicken breasts into the baking dish and top with sun-dried tomatoes, mushrooms, mayonnaise, and salt. Mix well.
4. Place dish in the air fryer and cook for 24 minutes.

5. Serve and enjoy.

Nutritional Value (Amount per Serving):
- Calories 561
- Fat 26.8 g
- Carbohydrates 9 g
- Sugar 3.2 g
- Protein 65 g
- Cholesterol 209 mg

Delicious Meatloaf

Preparation Time: 10 minutes; Cooking Time: 32 minutes; Serve: 8

Ingredients:
- 2 eggs
- 1/2 cup parmesan cheese, grated
- 1/2 cup marinara sauce, without sugar
- 1 cup cottage cheese
- 1 lb mozzarella cheese, cut into cubes
- 2 lbs ground turkey
- 2 tsp Italian seasoning
- 1/4 cup basil pesto
- 1 tsp salt

Directions:
1. Preheat the air fryer to 370 F.
2. Add all ingredients into the large bowl and mix until well combined.
3. Transfer bowl mixture to the silicone loaf pan and place in the air fryer.
4. Cook for 32 minutes.
5. Serve and enjoy.

Nutritional Value (Amount per Serving):
- Calories 350
- Fat 19.5 g
- Carbohydrates 4 g
- Sugar 2 g
- Protein 43 g
- Cholesterol 175 mg

Greek Chicken

Preparation Time: 10 minutes; Cooking Time: 24 minutes; Serve: 4

Ingredients:
- 2 lbs chicken tenders
- 1 cup cherry tomatoes
- 2 tbsp olive oil
- 3 dill sprigs
- 1 large zucchini
- For topping:
- 2 tbsp feta cheese, crumbled
- 1 tbsp fresh dill, chopped
- 1 tbsp olive oil
- 1 tbsp fresh lemon juice

Directions:
1. Preheat the air fryer to 370 F.
2. Spray air fryer basket with cooking spray.
3. Add chicken, zucchini, dill, and tomatoes into the air fryer basket. Drizzle with olive oil and season with salt.
4. Cook chicken for 24 minutes.
5. Meanwhile, in a small bowl, stir together all topping ingredients.
6. Place chicken on the serving plate then top with veggies and discard dill sprigs.
7. Sprinkle topping mixture on top of chicken and vegetables.

8. Serve and enjoy.

Nutritional Value (Amount per Serving):
- Calories 555
- Fat 28 g
- Carbohydrates 5.2 g
- Sugar 3 g
- Protein 68 g
- Cholesterol 205 mg

Meatloaf

Preparation Time: 10 minutes; Cooking Time: 28 minutes; Serve: 8
Ingredients:
- 1 egg
- 1 tsp chili powder
- 1 tsp garlic powder
- 1 tsp garlic, minced
- 2 lbs ground turkey
- 2 oz BBQ sauce, sugar-free
- 1 tsp ground mustard
- 1 tbsp onion, minced
- 1 cup cheddar cheese, shredded
- 1 tsp salt

Directions:
1. Preheat the air fryer to 370 F.
2. In a large bowl, combine together all ingredients then transfer into the silicon loaf pan.
3. Place loaf pan in the air fryer and cook for 25-28 minutes.
4. Serve and enjoy.

Nutritional Value (Amount per Serving):
- Calories 301
- Fat 17 g
- Carbohydrates 3 g
- Sugar 2.2 g
- Protein 35.5 g
- Cholesterol 150 mg

Chili Garlic Chicken Wings

Preparation Time: 10 minutes; Cooking Time: 35 minutes; Serve: 4
Ingredients:
- 2 lbs chicken wings
- 1/8 tsp paprika
- 2 tsp seasoned salt
- 1/2 cup coconut flour
- 1/4 tsp garlic powder
- 1/4 tsp chili powder

Directions:
1. Preheat the air fryer to 370 F.
2. In a large bowl, add all ingredients except chicken wings and mix well.
3. Add chicken wings into the bowl coat well.
4. Spray air fryer basket with cooking spray.
5. Add chicken wings into the air fryer basket. (In batches)
6. Cook for 35-40 minutes. Shake halfway through.
7. Serve and enjoy.

Nutritional Value (Amount per Serving):
- Calories 440
- Fat 17.1 g
- Carbohydrates 1 g
- Sugar 0.2 g
- Protein 65 g
- Cholesterol 200 mg

Garlic Chicken

Preparation Time: 10 minutes; Cooking Time: 32 minutes; Serve: 4

Ingredients:

- 2 lbs chicken drumsticks
- 1 fresh lemon juice
- 9 garlic cloves, sliced
- 4 tbsp butter, melted
- 2 tbsp parsley, chopped
- 2 tbsp olive oil
- Pepper
- Salt

Directions:

1. Preheat the air fryer to 400 F.
2. Add all ingredients into the large mixing bowl and toss well.
3. Transfer chicken wings into the air fryer basket and cook for 32 minutes. Toss halfway through.
4. Serve and enjoy.

Nutritional Value (Amount per Serving):

- Calories 560
- Fat 31 g
- Carbohydrates 3 g
- Sugar 0.4 g
- Protein 63 g
- Cholesterol 230 mg

Cumin Chicken Wings

Preparation Time: 10 minutes; Cooking Time: 31 minutes; Serve: 6

Ingredients:

- 12 chicken wings
- 1/2 tsp turmeric
- 2 tsp cumin seeds
- 1 garlic clove, minced
- 3 tbsp ghee
- 1/2 tsp pepper
- 1/2 tsp salt

Directions:

1. Preheat the air fryer to 400 F.
2. In a large bowl, mix together 1 teaspoon cumin, 1 tbsp ghee, turmeric, pepper, and salt.
3. Add chicken wings to the bowl and toss until well coated.
4. Add chicken wings into the air fryer basket and cook for 24 minutes. Shake basket halfway through.
5. Turn chicken wings to another side and cook for 5 minutes more.
6. Meanwhile, heat remaining ghee in a pan over medium heat.
7. Once the ghee is melted add garlic and cumin and cook for a minute. Remove pan from heat and set aside.
8. Remove chicken wings from air fryer and spoon ghee mixture over each chicken wing.
9. Cook chicken wings 2-3 minutes more.
10. Serve and enjoy.

Nutritional Value (Amount per Serving):

- Calories 375
- Fat 27.9 g
- Carbohydrates 11 g
- Sugar 0 g

- Protein 19 g
- Cholesterol 94 mg

Chicken Fajita Casserole

Preparation Time: 10 minutes; Cooking Time: 12 minutes; Serve: 4
Ingredients:

- 1 lb cooked chicken, shredded
- 1 onion, sliced
- 1 bell pepper, sliced
- 1/3 cup mayonnaise
- 7 oz cream cheese
- 7 oz cheese, shredded
- 2 tbsp tex-mex seasoning
- Pepper
- Salt

Directions:

1. Preheat the air fryer to 370 F.
2. Spray air fryer baking dish with cooking spray.
3. Mix all ingredients except 2 oz shredded cheese in a prepared dish.
4. Spread remaining cheese on top.
5. Place dish in the air fryer and cook for 12 minutes.
6. Serve and enjoy.

Nutritional Value (Amount per Serving):

- Calories 640
- Fat 43.8 g
- Carbohydrates 11 g
- Sugar 4.3 g
- Protein 50 g
- Cholesterol 200 mg

Dry Rub Chicken Wings

Preparation Time: 10 minutes; Cooking Time: 20 minutes; Serve: 2
Ingredients:

- 8 chicken wings
- ¼ tsp onion powder
- 1/2 tsp chili powder
- 1/2 tsp garlic powder
- 1/4 tsp pepper
- 1/4 tsp salt

Directions:

1. In a bowl, mix together chili powder, onion powder, garlic powder, pepper, and salt.
2. Add chicken wings to the bowl and coat well with spice mixture.
3. Add chicken wings into the air fryer basket and cook at 350 F for 20 minutes. Shake halfway through.
4. Serve and enjoy.

Nutritional Value (Amount per Serving):

- Calories 85
- Fat 5.5 g
- Carbohydrates 3 g
- Sugar 0.2 g
- Protein 6 g
- Cholesterol 20 mg

Chicken Cheese Wings

Preparation Time: 10 minutes; Cooking Time: 25 minutes; Serve: 2
Ingredients:

- 1 lb chicken wings
- 1 garlic clove, minced
- 2 tbsp butter
- 2 tbsp parmesan cheese, grated
- 1/8 tsp paprika
- 1/2 tsp oregano
- 1/2 tsp rosemary
- 1/4 tsp salt

Directions:
1. Preheat the air fryer to 390 F.
2. Add chicken wings into the air fryer basket and cook for 24 minutes. Shake basket 2-3 times while cooking.
3. Meanwhile, for sauce melt butter in a pan over medium heat. Add garlic and sauté for 30 seconds.
4. Mix together herb and spices and add to the pan.
5. Toss chicken wings with pan sauce and top with cheese.
6. Serve and enjoy.

Nutritional Value (Amount per Serving):
- Calories 568
- Fat 30.5 g
- Carbohydrates 2 g
- Sugar 0.1 g
- Protein 68.4 g
- Cholesterol 240 mg

Spicy Chicken Wings

Preparation Time: 10 minutes; Cooking Time: 20 minutes; Serve: 2
Ingredients:
- 6 chicken wings
- 1 tbsp olive oil
- 1 tsp hot paprika
- Pepper
- Salt

Directions:
1. Preheat the air fryer to 390 F.
2. In a bowl, mix together chicken, paprika, olive oil, pepper, and salt. Place in refrigerator for 1 hour.
3. Add marinated chicken wings into the air fryer basket and cook for 12 minutes.
4. Toss well and cook for 8 minutes more.
5. Serve and enjoy.

Nutritional Value (Amount per Serving):
- Calories 540
- Fat 39.2 g
- Carbohydrates 14 g
- Sugar 0.1 g
- Protein 30 g
- Cholesterol 115 mg

Tasty Southwest Chicken

Preparation Time: 10 minutes; Cooking Time: 25 minutes; Serve: 2
Ingredients:
- 1/2 lb chicken breasts, skinless and boneless
- 1/2 tsp chili powder
- 1 tbsp olive oil
- 1 tbsp lime juice
- 1/8 tsp garlic powder

- 1/8 tsp onion powder
- 1/4 tsp cumin
- 1/8 tsp salt

Directions:
1. Add all ingredients into the zip-lock bag and shake well to coat and place in the refrigerator for 1 hour.
2. Add a marinated chicken wing to the air fryer basket and cook at 400 F for 25 minutes. Shake halfway through.
3. Serve and enjoy.

Nutritional Value (Amount per Serving):
- Calories 250
- Fat 12 g
- Carbohydrates 0.6 g
- Sugar 0.1 g
- Protein 33 g
- Cholesterol 100 mg

Easy & Spicy Chicken Wings

Preparation Time: 10 minutes; Cooking Time: 25 minutes; Serve: 2
Ingredients:
- 1 lb chicken wings
- 1/2 tsp pepper
- 1/2 tsp salt
- For sauce:
- 1/2 tbsp sesame oil
- 1/2 tbsp mayonnaise
- 1 tbsp gochujang
- 1/2 tbsp garlic, minced
- 1.2 tbsp ginger, minced

Directions:
1. Preheat the air fryer to 400 F.
2. Add chicken wings into the air fryer basket and season with pepper and salt and cook for 20 minutes.
3. Meanwhile, in a bowl mix together all sauce ingredients.
4. Toss chicken wings with sauce and cook for 5 minutes more.
5. Serve and enjoy.

Nutritional Value (Amount per Serving):
- Calories 505
- Fat 22 g
- Carbohydrates 7 g
- Sugar 4 g
- Protein 66.1 g
- Cholesterol 200 mg

Yummy Shredded Chicken

Preparation Time: 10 minutes; Cooking Time: 15 minutes; Serve: 2
Ingredients:
- 2 large chicken breasts
- ¼ tsp Pepper
- 1 tsp garlic puree
- 1 tsp mustard
- Salt

Directions:
1. Add all ingredients to the bowl and toss well.
2. Transfer chicken into the air fryer basket and cook at 360 F for 15 minutes.

3. Remove chicken from air fryer and shred using a fork.
4. Serve and enjoy.

Nutritional Value (Amount per Serving):
- Calories 295
- Fat 11 g
- Carbohydrates 4 g
- Sugar 3 g
- Protein 42 g
- Cholesterol 130 mg

Perfect Grill Chicken Breast

Preparation Time: 10 minutes; Cooking Time: 12 minutes; Serve: 2

Ingredients:
- 2 chicken breast, skinless and boneless
- 2 tsp olive oil
- Pepper
- Salt

Directions:
1. Remove air fryer basket and replace it with air fryer grill pan.
2. Place chicken breast to the grill pan. Season chicken with pepper and salt. Drizzle with oil.
3. Cook chicken for 375 F for 12 minutes.
4. Serve and enjoy.

Nutritional Value (Amount per Serving):
- Calories 165
- Fat 7 g
- Carbohydrates 0 g
- Sugar 0 g
- Protein 24 g
- Cholesterol 70 mg

Fennel Chicken

Preparation Time: 10 minutes; Cooking Time: 15 minutes; Serve: 2

Ingredients:
- 1/2 lb chicken thighs, skinless, boneless, and cut each thigh into 3 pieces
- 1/2 tsp paprika
- 1 tsp garlic, minced
- 1 tsp ginger, minced
- 1/2 tbsp olive oil
- 1/4 tsp cayenne pepper
- 1/2 tsp turmeric
- 1/4 tsp garam masala
- 1/2 tsp ground fennel seeds
- 1/2 onion, sliced
- 1/2 tsp salt

Directions:
1. Add chicken into the bowl and toss with remaining ingredients to coat. Place in refrigerator for overnight.
2. Place marinated chicken into the air fryer basket and cook at 360 F for 15 minutes. Turn halfway through.
3. Serve and enjoy.

Nutritional Value (Amount per Serving):
- Calories 305
- Fat 19 g
- Carbohydrates 6 g
- Sugar 0.7 g
- Protein 25 g
- Cholesterol 80 mg

Pesto Chicken

Preparation Time: 10 minutes; Cooking Time: 20 minutes; Serve: 2
Ingredients:

- 4 chicken drumsticks
- 6 garlic cloves
- 1/2 jalapeno pepper
- 2 tbsp lemon juice
- 2 tbsp olive oil
- 1 tbsp ginger, sliced
- 1/2 cup cilantro
- 1 tsp salt

Directions:

1. Add all the ingredients except chicken into the blender and blend until smooth.
2. Pour blended mixture into the large bowl.
3. Add chicken and stir well to coat. Place in refrigerator for 2 hours.
4. Spray air fryer basket with cooking spray.
5. Place marinated chicken into the air fryer basket and cook at 390 F for 20 minutes. Turn halfway through.
6. Serve and enjoy.

Nutritional Value (Amount per Serving):

- Calories 305
- Fat 19 g
- Carbohydrates 5 g
- Sugar 0.7 g
- Protein 25 g
- Cholesterol 80 mg

Herb Chicken Roast

Preparation Time: 10 minutes; Cooking Time: 25 minutes; Serve: 2
Ingredients:

- 10 oz chicken breast
- 1/4 tsp dried thyme
- 1/2 tsp paprika
- 1 tbsp butter
- 1/4 tsp black pepper
- 1/4 tsp garlic powder
- 1/4 tsp dried rosemary
- 1/4 tsp salt

Directions:

1. In a small bowl, combine together butter, black pepper, garlic powder, rosemary, thyme, paprika, and salt.
2. Rub chicken with butter spice herb mixture and place into the air fryer basket.
3. Cook at 375 F for 25 minutes.
4. Serve and enjoy.

Nutritional Value (Amount per Serving):

- Calories 325
- Fat 15 g
- Carbohydrates 0.7 g
- Sugar 0.1 g
- Protein 41 g
- Cholesterol 140 mg

Thyme Butter Turkey Breast

Preparation Time: 10 minutes; Cooking Time: 60 minutes; Serve: 8
Ingredients:

- 2 lbs turkey breast
- ½ tsp thyme leaves, chopped
- ¼ tsp pepper
- ½ tsp sage leaves, chopped
- 1 tbsp butter
- 1 tsp salt

Directions:
1. Spray air fryer basket with cooking spray.
2. Rub butter all over the turkey breast and season with pepper, sage, thyme, and salt.
3. Place turkey breast into the air fryer basket and cook at 25 F for 60 minutes. Turn turkey breast to another side halfway through.
4. Slice and serve.

Nutritional Value (Amount per Serving):
- Calories 130
- Fat 3 g
- Carbohydrates 5 g
- Sugar 4 g
- Protein 19 g
- Cholesterol 145 mg

Meatballs

Preparation Time: 10 minutes; Cooking Time: 10 minutes; Serve: 6
Ingredients:
- 2 lbs ground chicken breast
- ½ cup ricotta cheese
- 2 eggs, lightly beaten
- ¼ cup fresh parsley, chopped
- ½ cup almond flour
- 1/2 tsp pepper
- 2 tsp salt

Directions:
1. Spray air fryer basket with cooking spray.
2. Add all ingredients into the large bowl and mix until well combined.
3. Make small balls from meat mixture and place in the air fryer basket and cook at 380 F for 10 minutes. Shake basket twice while cooking.
4. Serve and enjoy.

Nutritional Value (Amount per Serving):
- Calories 225
- Fat 5 g
- Carbohydrates 2 g
- Sugar 0.5 g
- Protein 42 g
- Cholesterol 143 mg

Turkey Meatballs

Preparation Time: 10 minutes; Cooking Time: 12 minutes; Serve: 4
Ingredients:
- 1 lb ground turkey
- 2 garlic cloves, minced
- ¼ cup carrots, grated
- 1 egg, lightly beaten
- 2 tbsp coconut flour
- 2 green onion, chopped
- ¼ cup celery, chopped
- Pepper
- Salt

Directions:
1. Spray air fryer basket with cooking spray.

2. Preheat the air fryer to 400 F.
3. Add all ingredients into the large bowl and mix until well combined.
4. Make balls from meat mixture and place into the air fryer basket and cook for 12 minutes. Turn halfway through.
5. Serve and enjoy.

Nutritional Value (Amount per Serving):
- Calories 275
- Fat 13 g
- Carbohydrates 6 g
- Sugar 1 g
- Protein 34 g
- Cholesterol 125 mg

Chicken Tenders

Preparation Time: 10 minutes; Cooking Time: 12 minutes; Serve: 4
Ingredients:
- 1 lb chicken tenders
- 1 egg, lightly beaten
- 3/4 cup pecans, crushed
- ¼ cup ground mustard
- ½ tsp paprika
- ¼ tsp garlic powder
- ¼ tsp onion powder
- 1/4 tsp pepper
- 1 tsp salt

Directions:
1. Spray air fryer basket with cooking spray.
2. Add chicken into the large bowl. Season with paprika, pepper, garlic powder, onion powder, and salt. Add mustard mix well.
3. In a separate bowl, add egg and whisk well.
4. In a shallow bowl, add crushed pecans.
5. Dip chicken into the egg then coats with pecans and place into the air fryer basket.
6. Cook at 350 F for 12 minutes.
7. Serve and enjoy.

Nutritional Value (Amount per Serving):
- Calories 481
- Fat 31 g
- Carbohydrates 7 g
- Sugar 2 g
- Protein 40 g
- Cholesterol 145 mg

Chicken Coconut Meatballs

Preparation Time: 10 minutes; Cooking Time: 10 minutes; Serve: 4
Ingredients:
- 1 lb ground chicken
- 1 ½ tsp sriracha
- 1/2 tbsp soy sauce
- 1/2 tbsp hoisin sauce
- ¼ cup shredded coconut
- 1 tsp sesame oil
- ½ cup fresh cilantro, chopped
- 2 green onions, chopped
- Pepper
- Salt

Directions:
1. Spray air fryer basket with cooking spray.

2. Add all ingredients into the large bowl and mix until well combined.
3. Make small balls from meat mixture and place into the air fryer basket.
4. Cook at 350 F for 10 minutes. Turn halfway through.
5. Serve and enjoy.

Nutritional Value (Amount per Serving):
- Calories 255
- Fat 11 g
- Carbohydrates 3 g
- Sugar 1 g
- Protein 32 g
- Cholesterol 145 mg

Cheese Herb Chicken Wings

Preparation Time: 10 minutes; Cooking Time: 15 minutes; Serve: 4
Ingredients:
- 2 lbs chicken wings
- 1 tsp herb de Provence
- ½ cup parmesan cheese, grated
- 1 tsp paprika
- Salt

Directions:
1. Preheat the air fryer to 350 F.
2. In a small bowl, mix together cheese, herb de Provence, paprika, and salt.
3. Spray air fryer basket with cooking spray.
4. Toss chicken wings with cheese mixture and place into the air fryer basket and cook for 15 minutes. Turn halfway through.
5. Serve and enjoy.

Nutritional Value (Amount per Serving):
- Calories 505
- Fat 20 g
- Carbohydrates 0.4 g
- Sugar 0.2 g
- Protein 70 g
- Cholesterol 132 mg

Delicious Chicken Tenderloins

Preparation Time: 10 minutes; Cooking Time: 15 minutes; Serve: 6
Ingredients:
- 1 egg, lightly beaten
- ¼ cup heavy whipping cream
- 8 oz chicken breast tenderloins
- 1 cup almond flour
- ¼ tsp garlic powder
- ¼ tsp onion powder
- 1 tsp pepper
- 1 tsp salt

Directions:
1. Whisk egg, with garlic powder, onion powder, cream, pepper, and salt in a bowl.
2. In a shallow dish, add the almond flour.
3. Dip chicken in egg mixture then coats with almond flour mixture.
4. Spray air fryer basket with cooking spray.
5. Place chicken into the air fryer basket and cook at 450 F for 15 minutes.
6. Serve and enjoy.

Nutritional Value (Amount per Serving):

- Calories 255
- Fat 6 g
- Carbohydrates 2 g

- Sugar 0.5 g
- Protein 45 g
- Cholesterol 125 mg

Garlic Herb Chicken Breasts

Preparation Time: 10 minutes; Cooking Time: 15 minutes; Serve: 5
Ingredients:
- 2 lbs chicken breasts, skinless and boneless
- 4 garlic cloves, minced
- ¼ cup yogurt

- ¼ cup mayonnaise
- 2 tsp garlic herb seasoning
- 1/2 tsp onion powder
- ¼ tsp salt

Directions:
1. Preheat the air fryer to 380 F.
2. In a small bowl, mix together mayonnaise, seasoning, onion powder, garlic, and yogurt.
3. Brush chicken with mayo mixture and season with salt.
4. Spray air fryer basket with cooking spray.
5. Place chicken into the air fryer basket and cook for 15 minutes.
6. Serve and enjoy.

Nutritional Value (Amount per Serving):
- Calories 410
- Fat 16 g
- Carbohydrates 5 g

- Sugar 2 g
- Protein 55 g
- Cholesterol 146 mg

Tasty Caribbean Chicken

Preparation Time: 10 minutes; Cooking Time: 10 minutes; Serve: 8
Ingredients:
- 3 lbs chicken thigh, skinless and boneless
- 1 tbsp coriander powder
- 3 tbsp coconut oil, melted
- ½ tsp ground nutmeg

- ½ tsp ground ginger
- 1 tbsp cayenne
- 1 tbsp cinnamon
- Pepper
- Salt

Directions:
1. In a small bowl, mix together all spices and rub all over the chicken.
2. Spray air fryer basket with cooking spray.
3. Place chicken into the air fryer basket and cook at 390 F for 10 minutes.
4. Serve and enjoy.

Nutritional Value (Amount per Serving):
- Calories 375
- Fat 18 g
- Carbohydrates 1 g

- Sugar 0.2 g
- Protein 50 g
- Cholesterol 142 mg

Chicken Kabab

Preparation Time: 10 minutes; Cooking Time: 6 minutes; Serve: 3

Ingredients:

- 1 lb ground chicken
- 1 tbsp fresh lemon juice
- ¼ cup almond flour
- 2 green onion, chopped
- 1 egg, lightly beaten
- 1/3 cup fresh parsley, chopped
- 3 garlic cloves
- 4 oz onion, chopped
- ¼ tsp turmeric powder
- ½ tsp pepper

Directions:

1. Add all ingredients into the food processor and process until well combined.
2. Transfer chicken mixture to the bowl and place in the refrigerator for 1 hour.
3. Divide mixture into the 6 equal portions and roll around the soaked wooden skewers.
4. Spray air fryer basket with cooking spray.
5. Place skewers into the air fryer basket and cooks at 400 F for 6 minutes.
6. Serve and enjoy.

Nutritional Value (Amount per Serving):

- Calories 290
- Fat 7 g
- Carbohydrates 6 g
- Sugar 2 g
- Protein 48 g
- Cholesterol 123 mg

Mediterranean Chicken

Preparation Time: 10 minutes; Cooking Time: 35 minutes; Serve: 6

Ingredients:

- 4 lbs whole chicken, cut into pieces
- 2 tsp ground sumac
- 2 garlic cloves, minced
- 2 lemons, sliced
- 2 tbsp olive oil
- 1 tsp lemon zest
- 2 tsp kosher salt

Directions:

1. Rub chicken with oil, sumac, lemon zest, and salt. Place in the refrigerator for 2-3 hours.
2. Add lemon sliced into the air fryer basket top with marinated chicken.
3. Cook at 350 for 35 minutes.
4. Serve and enjoy.

Nutritional Value (Amount per Serving):

- Calories 616
- Fat 27 g
- Carbohydrates 0.4 g
- Sugar 0 g
- Protein 87 g
- Cholesterol 269 mg

Asain Chicken Wings

Preparation Time: 10 minutes; Cooking Time: 30 minutes; Serve: 2

Ingredients:

- 4 chicken wings
- 3/4 tbsp Chinese spice

- 1 tbsp soy sauce
- 1 tsp mixed spice
- Pepper
- Salt

Directions:
1. Add chicken wings into the bowl. Add remaining ingredients and toss to coat.
2. Transfer chicken wings into the air fryer basket.
3. Cook at 350 f for 15 minutes.
4. Turn chicken to another side and cook for 15 minutes more.
5. Serve and enjoy.

Nutritional Value (Amount per Serving):
- Calories 560
- Fat 21 g
- Carbohydrates 0.5 g
- Sugar 0.2 g
- Protein 86 g
- Cholesterol 134 mg

Delicious Chicken Fajitas

Preparation Time: 10 minutes; Cooking Time: 15 minutes; Serve: 4
Ingredients:
- 4 chicken breasts
- 1 onion, sliced
- 1 bell pepper, sliced
- 1 1/2 tbsp fajita seasoning
- 2 tbsp olive oil
- 3/4 cup cheddar cheese, shredded

Directions:
1. Preheat the air fryer at 380 F.
2. Coat chicken with oil and rub with seasoning.
3. Place chicken into the air fryer baking dish and top with bell peppers and onion.
4. Cook for 15 minutes.
5. Top with shredded cheese and cook for 1-2 minutes until cheese is melted.
6. Serve and enjoy.

Nutritional Value (Amount per Serving):
- Calories 425
- Fat 23 g
- Carbohydrates 7 g
- Sugar 2 g
- Protein 45 g
- Cholesterol 142 mg

Juicy & Spicy Chicken Wings

Preparation Time: 10 minutes; Cooking Time: 25 minutes; Serve: 4
Ingredients:
- 2 lbs chicken wings
- 12 oz hot sauce
- 1 tsp Worcestershire sauce
- 1 tsp Tabasco
- 6 tbsp butter, melted

Directions:
1. Spray air fryer basket with cooking spray.
2. Add chicken wings into the air fryer basket and cook at 380 F for 25 minutes. Shake basket after every 5 minutes.

3. Meanwhile, in a bowl, mix together hot sauce, Worcestershire sauce, and butter. Set aside.
4. Add chicken wings into the sauce and toss well.
5. Serve and enjoy.

Nutritional Value (Amount per Serving):

- Calories 595
- Fat 35 g
- Carbohydrates 1 g
- Sugar 1 g
- Protein 65 g
- Cholesterol 142 mg

Indian Chicken Tenders

Preparation Time: 10 minutes; Cooking Time: 15 minutes; Serve: 4

Ingredients:

- 1 lb chicken tenders, cut in half
- ¼ cup parsley, chopped
- 1/2 tbsp garlic, minced
- 1/2 tbsp ginger, minced
- ¼ cup yogurt
- 3/4 tsp paprika
- 1 tsp garam masala
- 1 tsp turmeric
- 1/2 tsp cayenne pepper
- 1 tsp salt

Directions:

1. Preheat the air fryer to 350 F.
2. Add all ingredients into the large bowl and mix well. Place in refrigerator for 30 minutes.
3. Spray air fryer basket with cooking spray.
4. Add marinated chicken into the air fryer basket and cook for 10 minutes.
5. Turn chicken to another side and cook for 5 minutes more.
6. Serve and enjoy.

Nutritional Value (Amount per Serving):

- Calories 241
- Fat 10 g
- Carbohydrates 4 g
- Sugar 1 g
- Protein 35 g
- Cholesterol 24 mg

Dijon Turkey Drumstick

Preparation Time: 10 minutes; Cooking Time: 28 minutes; Serve: 2

Ingredients:

- 4 turkey drumsticks
- 1/3 tsp paprika
- 1/3 cup sherry wine
- 1/3 cup coconut milk
- 1/2 tbsp ginger, minced
- 2 tbsp Dijon mustard
- Pepper
- Salt

Directions:

1. Add all ingredients into the large bowl and stir to coat. Place in refrigerator for 2 hours.
2. Spray air fryer basket with cooking spray.
3. Place marinated turkey drumsticks into the air fryer basket and cook at 380 F for 28 minutes. Turn halfway through.
4. Serve and enjoy.

Nutritional Value (Amount per Serving):

- Calories 365
- Fat 18 g
- Carbohydrates 5 g
- Sugar 2 g
- Protein 40 g
- Cholesterol 0 mg

Curried Drumsticks

Preparation Time: 10 minutes; Cooking Time: 22 minutes; Serve: 2
Ingredients:

- 2 turkey drumsticks
- 1/3 cup coconut milk
- 1 1/2 tbsp ginger, minced
- 1/4 tsp cayenne pepper
- 2 tbsp red curry paste
- 1/4 tsp pepper
- 1 tsp kosher salt

Directions:

1. Add all ingredients into the bowl and stir to coat. Place in refrigerator for overnight.
2. Spray air fryer basket with cooking spray.
3. Place marinated drumsticks into the air fryer basket and cook at 390 F for 22 minutes.
4. Serve and enjoy.

Nutritional Value (Amount per Serving):

- Calories 279
- Fat 18 g
- Carbohydrates 8 g
- Sugar 1.5 g
- Protein 20 g
- Cholesterol 0 mg

Korean Chicken Tenders

Preparation Time: 10 minutes; Cooking Time: 10 minutes; Serve: 3
Ingredients:

- 12 oz chicken tenders, skinless and boneless
- 2 tbsp green onion, chopped
- 3 garlic cloves, chopped
- 2 tsp sesame seeds, toasted
- 1 tbsp ginger, grated
- 1/4 cup sesame oil
- 1/2 cup soy sauce
- 1/4 tsp pepper

Directions:

1. Slide chicken tenders onto the skewers.
2. In a large bowl, mix together green onion, garlic, sesame seeds, ginger, sesame oil, soy sauce, and pepper.
3. Add chicken skewers into the bowl and coat well with marinade. Place in refrigerator for overnight.
4. Preheat the air fryer to 390 F.
5. Place marinated chicken skewers into the air fryer basket and cook for 10 minutes.

Nutritional Value (Amount per Serving):

- Calories 423
- Fat 27 g
- Carbohydrates 6 g
- Sugar 1 g
- Protein 36 g
- Cholesterol 101 mg

Chapter 5: Beef Pork & Lamb Recipes

Crisp Pork Chops

Preparation Time: 10 minutes; Cooking Time: 12 minutes; Serve: 6
Ingredients:
- 1 1/2 lbs pork chops, boneless
- 1 tsp paprika
- 1 tsp creole seasoning
- 1 tsp garlic powder
- 1/4 cup parmesan cheese, grated
- 1/3 cup almond flour

Directions:
1. Preheat the air fryer to 360 F.
2. Add all ingredients except pork chops in a zip-lock bag.
3. Add pork chops in the bag. Seal bag and shake well to coat pork chops.
4. Remove pork chops from zip-lock bag and place in the air fryer basket.
5. Cook pork chops for 10-12 minutes.
6. Serve and enjoy.

Nutritional Value (Amount per Serving):
- Calories 230
- Fat 11 g
- Carbohydrates 2 g
- Sugar 0.2 g
- Protein 27 g
- Cholesterol 79 mg

Parmesan Pork Chops

Preparation Time: 10 minutes; Cooking Time: 15 minutes; Serve: 4
Ingredients:
- 4 pork chops, boneless
- 4 tbsp parmesan cheese, grated
- 1 cup pork rind
- 2 eggs, lightly beaten
- 1/2 tsp chili powder
- 1/2 tsp onion powder
- 1 tsp paprika
- 1/4 tsp pepper
- 1/2 tsp salt

Directions:
1. Preheat the air fryer to 400 F.
2. Season pork chops with pepper and salt.
3. Add pork rind in food processor and process until crumbs form.
4. Mix together pork rind crumbs and seasoning in a large bowl.
5. Place egg in a separate bowl.
6. Dip pork chops in egg mixture then coat with pork crumb mixture and place in the air fryer basket.
7. Cook pork chops for 12-15 minutes.
8. Serve and enjoy.

Nutritional Value (Amount per Serving):
- Calories 329
- Fat 24 g
- Carbohydrates 1 g
- Sugar 0.4 g

- Protein 23 g
- Cholesterol 158 mg

Meatloaf Sliders

Preparation Time: 10 minutes; Cooking Time: 10 minutes; Serve: 8
Ingredients:
- 1 lb ground beef
- 1/2 tsp dried tarragon
- 1 tsp Italian seasoning
- 1 tbsp Worcestershire sauce
- 1/4 cup ketchup
- 1/4 cup coconut flour
- 1/2 cup almond flour
- 1 garlic clove, minced
- 1/4 cup onion, chopped
- 2 eggs, lightly beaten
- 1/4 tsp pepper
- 1/2 tsp sea salt

Directions:
1. Add all ingredients into the mixing bowl and mix until well combined.
2. Make the equal shape of patties from mixture and place on a plate. Place in refrigerator for 10 minutes.
3. Spray air fryer basket with cooking spray.
4. Preheat the air fryer to 360 F.
5. Place prepared patties in air fryer basket and cook for 10 minutes.
6. Serve and enjoy.

Nutritional Value (Amount per Serving):
- Calories 228
- Fat 16 g
- Carbohydrates 6 g
- Sugar 2 g
- Protein 13 g
- Cholesterol 80 mg

Quick & Easy Steak

Preparation Time: 10 minutes; Cooking Time: 7 minutes; Serve: 2
Ingredients:
- 12 oz steaks
- 1/2 tbsp unsweetened cocoa powder
- 1 tbsp Montreal steak seasoning
- 1 tsp liquid smoke
- 1 tbsp soy sauce
- Pepper
- Salt

Directions:
1. Add steak, liquid smoke, and soy sauce in a zip-lock bag and shake well.
2. Season steak with seasonings and place in the refrigerator for overnight.
3. Place marinated steak in air fryer basket and cook at 375 F for 5 minutes.
4. Turn steak to another side and cook for 2 minutes more.
5. Serve and enjoy.

Nutritional Value (Amount per Serving):
- Calories 356
- Fat 8.7 g
- Carbohydrates 1.4 g
- Sugar 0.2 g
- Protein 62.2 g
- Cholesterol 153 mg

Perfect Cheeseburger

Preparation Time: 5 minutes; Cooking Time: 12 minutes; Serve: 2

Ingredients:

- 1/2 lb ground beef
- 1/4 tsp onion powder
- 2 cheese slices
- 1/4 tsp pepper
- 1/8 tsp salt

Directions:

1. In a bowl, mix together ground beef, onion powder, pepper, and salt.
2. Make two equal shapes of patties from meat mixture and place in the air fryer basket.
3. Cook patties at 370 F for 12 minutes. Turn patties halfway through.
4. Once air fryer timer goes off then place cheese slices on top of each patty and close the air fryer basket for 1 minute.
5. Serve and enjoy.

Nutritional Value (Amount per Serving):

- Calories 325
- Fat 16.4 g
- Carbohydrates 0.8 g
- Sugar 0.3 g
- Protein 41.4 g
- Cholesterol 131 mg

Steak Bites with Mushrooms

Preparation Time: 10 minutes; Cooking Time: 18 minutes; Serve: 3

Ingredients:

- 1 lb steaks, cut into 1/2-inch cubes
- 1/2 tsp garlic powder
- 1 tsp Worcestershire sauce
- 2 tbsp butter, melted
- 8 oz mushrooms, sliced
- Pepper
- Salt

Directions:

1. Add all ingredients into the large mixing bowl and toss well.
2. Spray air fryer basket with cooking spray.
3. Preheat the air fryer to 400 F.
4. Add steak mushroom mixture into the air fryer basket and cook at 400 F for 15-18 minutes. Shake basket twice.
5. Serve and enjoy.

Nutritional Value (Amount per Serving):

- Calories 388
- Fat 15.5 g
- Carbohydrates 3.2 g
- Sugar 1.8 g
- Protein 57.1 g
- Cholesterol 156 mg

Simple & Tasty Pork Chops

Preparation Time: 10 minutes; Cooking Time: 9 minutes; Serve:4

Ingredients:

- 4 pork chops, boneless
- 1 tsp onion powder

- 1 tsp smoked paprika
- 1/2 cup parmesan cheese, grated
- 2 tbsp olive oil
- 1/2 tsp pepper
- 1 tsp kosher salt

Directions:

1. Brush pork chops with olive oil.
2. In a bowl, mix together parmesan cheese and spices.
3. Spray air fryer basket with cooking spray.
4. Coat pork chops with parmesan cheese mixture and place in the air fryer basket.
5. Cook pork chops at 375 F for 9 minutes. Turn halfway through.
6. Serve and enjoy.

Nutritional Value (Amount per Serving):

- Calories 332
- Carbohydrates 1.1 g
- Sugar 0.3 g
- Protein 19.3 g
- Cholesterol 71 mg

Simple Air Fryer Steak

Preparation Time: 10 minutes; Cooking Time: 18 minutes; Serve: 2
Ingredients:

- 12 oz steaks, 3/4-inch thick
- 1 tsp garlic powder
- 1 tsp olive oil
- Pepper
- Salt

Directions:

- Coat steaks with oil and season with garlic powder, pepper, and salt.
- Preheat the air fryer to 400 F.
- Place steaks in air fryer basket and cook for 15-18 minutes. Turn halfway through.
- Serve and enjoy.

Nutritional Value (Amount per Serving):

- Calories 363
- Carbohydrates 1.1 g
- Sugar 0.3 g
- Protein 61.7 g
- Cholesterol 153 mg

Quick & Tender Pork Chops

Preparation Time: 5 minutes; Cooking Time: 14 minutes; Serve: 3
Ingredients:

- 3 pork chops, rinsed and pat dry
- 1/4 tsp smoked paprika
- 1/2 tsp garlic powder
- 2 tsp olive oil
- Pepper
- Salt

Directions:

1. Coat pork chops with olive oil and season with paprika, garlic powder, pepper, and salt.
2. Place pork chops in air fryer basket and cook at 380 F for 10-14 minutes. Turn halfway through.
3. Serve and enjoy.

Nutritional Value (Amount per Serving):
- Calories 285
- Carbohydrates 0.5 g
- Sugar 0.1 g
- Protein 18.1 g
- Cholesterol 69 mg

Pork with Mushrooms

Preparation Time: 10 minutes; Cooking Time: 18 minutes; Serve: 4

Ingredients:
- 1 lb pork chops, rinsed and pat dry
- 1/2 tsp garlic powder
- 1 tsp soy sauce
- 2 tbsp butter, melted
- 8 oz mushrooms, halved
- Pepper
- Salt

Directions:
1. Preheat the air fryer to 400 F.
2. Cut pork chops into the 3/4-inch cubes and place in a large mixing bowl.
3. Add remaining ingredients into the bowl and toss well.
4. Transfer pork and mushroom mixture into the air fryer basket and cook for 15-18 minutes. Shake basket halfway through.
5. Serve and enjoy.

Nutritional Value (Amount per Serving):
- Calories 428
- Carbohydrates 2.2 g
- Sugar 1.1 g
- Protein 27.5 g
- Cholesterol 113 mg

Quick & Simple Bratwurst with Vegetables

Preparation Time: 10 minutes; Cooking Time: 20 minutes; Serve: 6

Ingredients:
- 1 package bratwurst, sliced 1/2-inch rounds
- 1/2 tbsp Cajun seasoning
- 1/4 cup onion, diced
- 2 bell pepper, sliced

Directions:
1. Add all ingredients into the large mixing bowl and toss well.
2. Line air fryer basket with foil.
3. Add vegetable and bratwurst mixture into the air fryer basket and cook at 390 F for 10 minutes.
4. Toss well and cook for 10 minutes more.
5. Serve and enjoy.

Nutritional Value (Amount per Serving):
- Calories 63
- Fat 4 g
- Carbohydrates 4 g
- Sugar 2 g
- Protein 2 g
- Cholesterol 10 mg

Steak Fajitas

Preparation Time: 10 minutes; Cooking Time: 15 minutes; Serve: 6

Ingredients:
- 1 lb steak, sliced
- 1 tbsp olive oil
- 1 tbsp fajita seasoning, gluten-free
- 1/2 cup onion, sliced
- 3 bell peppers, sliced

Directions:
1. Line air fryer basket with aluminum foil.
2. Add all ingredients large bowl and toss until well coated.
3. Transfer fajita mixture into the air fryer basket and cook at 390 F for 5 minutes.
4. Toss well and cook for 5-10 minutes more.
5. Serve and enjoy.

Nutritional Value (Amount per Serving):
- Calories 304
- Fat 17 g
- Carbohydrates 15 g
- Sugar 4 g
- Protein 22 g
- Cholesterol 73 mg

Beef Roast

Preparation Time: 10 minutes; Cooking Time: 35 minutes; Serve: 7

Ingredients:
- 2 lbs beef roast
- 1 tbsp olive oil
- 1 tsp thyme
- 2 tsp garlic powder
- 1/4 tsp pepper
- 1 tbsp kosher salt

Directions:
1. Coat roast with olive oil.
2. Mix together thyme, garlic powder, pepper, and salt and rub all over roast.
3. Place roast into the air fryer basket and cook at 400 F for 20 minutes.
4. Spray roast with cooking spray and cook for 15 minutes more.
5. Slice and serve.

Nutritional Value (Amount per Serving):
- Calories 238
- Fat 13 g
- Carbohydrates 1 g
- Sugar 0.5 g
- Protein 25 g
- Cholesterol 89 mg

Delicious Cheeseburgers

Preparation Time: 10 minutes; Cooking Time: 12 minutes; Serve: 4

Ingredients:
- 1 lb ground beef
- 4 cheddar cheese slices
- 1/2 tsp Italian seasoning
- Pepper
- Salt

Directions:

1. Spray air fryer basket with cooking spray.
2. In a bowl, mix together ground beef, Italian seasoning, pepper, and salt.
3. Make four equal shapes of patties from meat mixture and place into the air fryer basket.
4. Cook at 375 F for 5 minutes. Turn patties to another side and cook for 5 minutes more.
5. Place cheese slices on top of each patty and cook for 2 minutes more.
6. Serve and enjoy.

Nutritional Value (Amount per Serving):
- Calories 325
- Fat 16.5 g
- Carbohydrates 0.4 g
- Sugar 0.2 g
- Protein 41.4 g
- Cholesterol 131 mg

Asian Sirloin Steaks

Preparation Time: 10 minutes; Cooking Time: 20 minutes; Serve: 2
Ingredients:
- 12 oz sirloin steaks
- 1 tbsp garlic, minced
- 1 tbsp ginger, grated
- 1/2 tbsp Worcestershire sauce
- 1 1/2 tbsp soy sauce
- 2 tbsp erythritol
- Pepper
- Salt

Directions:
1. Add steaks in a large zip-lock bag along with remaining ingredients. Shake well and place in the refrigerator for overnight.
2. Spray air fryer basket with cooking spray.
3. Place marinated steaks in air fryer basket and cook at 400 F for 10 minutes.
4. Turn steaks to another side and cook for 10-15 minutes more.
5. Serve and enjoy.

Nutritional Value (Amount per Serving):
- Calories 342
- Fat 10 g
- Carbohydrates 5 g
- Sugar 1 g
- Protein 52 g
- Cholesterol 152 mg

Soft & Juicy Beef Kabobs

Preparation Time: 10 minutes; Cooking Time: 10 minutes; Serve: 4
Ingredients:
- 1 lb beef, cut into chunks
- 1 bell pepper, cut into 1-inch pieces
- 2 tbsp soy sauce
- 1/3 cup sour cream
- 1/2 onion, cut into 1-inch pieces

Directions:
1. In a medium bowl, mix together soy sauce and sour cream.
2. Add beef into the bowl and coat well and place in the refrigerator for overnight.
3. Thread marinated beef, bell peppers, and onions onto the soaked wooden skewers.
4. Place in air fryer basket and cook at 400 F for 10 minutes. Turn halfway through.
5. Serve and enjoy.

Nutritional Value (Amount per Serving):
- Calories 251
- Fat 15 g
- Carbohydrates 4 g
- Sugar 2 g
- Protein 23 g
- Cholesterol 85 mg

Asian Flavors Beef Broccoli

Preparation Time: 10 minutes; Cooking Time: 15 minutes; Serve: 3

Ingredients:
- 1/2 lb steak, cut into strips
- 1 tsp garlic, minced
- 1 tsp ginger, minced
- 2 tbsp sesame oil
- 2 tbsp soy sauce
- 4 tbsp oyster sauce
- 1 lb broccoli florets
- 1 tbsp sesame seeds, toasted

Directions:
1. Add all ingredients except sesame seeds into the large mixing bowl and toss well. Place bowl in the refrigerator for 1 hour.
2. Add marinated steak and broccoli into the air fryer basket and cook at 350 F for 15 minutes.
3. Shake basket 2-3 times while cooking.
4. Garnish with sesame seeds and serve.

Nutritional Value (Amount per Serving):
- Calories 265
- Fat 14 g
- Carbohydrates 12.5 g
- Sugar 2 g
- Protein 21 g
- Cholesterol 45 mg

Juicy Rib Eye Steak

Preparation Time: 10 minutes; Cooking Time: 14 minutes; Serve: 2

Ingredients:
- 2 medium rib-eye steaks
- 1/4 tsp garlic powder
- 1/4 tsp onion powder
- 1 tsp olive oil
- Pepper
- Salt

Directions:
1. Coat steaks with oil and season with garlic powder, onion powder, pepper, and salt.
2. Preheat the air fryer to 400 F.
3. Place steaks into the air fryer basket and cook for 14 minutes. Turn halfway through.
4. Serve and enjoy.

Nutritional Value (Amount per Serving):
- Calories 469
- Fat 31 g
- Carbohydrates 3 g
- Sugar 0.5 g
- Protein 44 g
- Cholesterol 135 mg

Cheesy & Juicy Pork Chops

Preparation Time: 10 minutes; Cooking Time: 8 minutes; Serve: 2

Ingredients:
- 4 pork chops
- 1/4 cup cheddar cheese, shredded
- 1/2 tsp garlic powder
- 1/2 tsp salt

Directions:
1. Preheat the air fryer to 350 F.
2. Rub pork chops with garlic powder and salt and place in the air fryer basket.
3. Cook pork chops for 4 minutes.
4. Turn pork chops to another side and cook for 2 minutes.
5. Add cheese on top of pork chops and cook for 2 minutes more.
6. Serve and enjoy.

Nutritional Value (Amount per Serving):
- Calories 465
- Fat 22 g
- Carbohydrates 2 g
- Sugar 0.6 g
- Protein 61 g
- Cholesterol 190 mg

Stuffed Peppers

Preparation Time: 10 minutes; Cooking Time: 8 minutes; Serve: 2
Ingredients:
- 2 bell peppers, remove stems and seeds
- 4 oz cheddar cheese, shredded
- 1 1/2 tsp Worcestershire sauce
- 1/2 cup tomato sauce
- 8 oz ground beef
- 1 tsp olive oil
- 1 garlic clove, minced
- 1/2 onion, chopped
- 1/2 tsp pepper
- 1/2 tsp salt

Directions:
1. Preheat the air fryer to 390 F.
2. Sauté garlic and onion in the olive oil in a small pan until softened.
3. Add meat, 1/4 cup tomato sauce, Worcestershire sauce, half cheese, pepper, and salt and stir well to combine.
4. Stuff meat mixture into each pepper and top with remaining cheese and tomato sauce.
5. Spray air fryer basket with cooking spray.
6. Place stuffed peppers into the air fryer basket and cook for 15-20 minutes.
7. Serve and enjoy.

Nutritional Value (Amount per Serving):
- Calories 530
- Fat 28.7 g
- Carbohydrates 14 g
- Sugar 10.8 g
- Protein 51 g
- Cholesterol 161 mg

Lamb Patties

Preparation Time: 10 minutes; Cooking Time: 20 minutes; Serve: 4
Ingredients:
- 1 1/2 lbs ground lamb
- 1/3 cup feta cheese, crumbled
- 1 tsp oregano
- 1/4 tsp pepper

- 1/2 tsp salt

Directions:
1. Preheat the air fryer to 375 F.
2. Add all ingredients into the bowl and mix until well combined.
3. Spray air fryer basket with cooking spray.
4. Make the equal shape of patties from meat mixture and place into the air fryer basket.
5. Cook lamb patties for 10 minutes then turn to another side and cook for 10 minutes more.
6. Serve and enjoy.

Nutritional Value (Amount per Serving):
- Calories 351
- Fat 15.2 g
- Carbohydrates 0.8 g
- Sugar 0.5 g
- Protein 49.6 g
- Cholesterol 164 mg

Lemon Mustard Lamb Chops

Preparation Time: 10 minutes; Cooking Time: 15 minutes; Serve: 4

Ingredients:
- 8 lamb chops
- 1 tbsp lemon juice
- 1 tsp tarragon
- 1/2 tsp olive oil
- 2 tbsp Dijon mustard
- Pepper
- Salt

Directions:
1. Preheat the air fryer to 390 F.
2. In a small bowl, mix together mustard, lemon juice, tarragon, and olive oil.
3. Brush mustard mixture over lamb chops.
4. Place lamb chops in air fryer basket and cook for 15 minutes. Turn halfway through.
5. Serve and enjoy.

Nutritional Value (Amount per Serving):
- Calories 328
- Fat 13.4 g
- Carbohydrates 0.6 g
- Sugar 0.2 g
- Protein 48.1 g
- Cholesterol 153 mg

Italian Sausage Meatballs

Preparation Time: 10 minutes; Cooking Time: 15 minutes; Serve: 8

Ingredients:
- 1 lb Italian sausage
- 1 lb ground beef
- 1/2 tsp Italian seasoning
- 1/2 tsp red pepper flakes
- 1 1/2 cups parmesan cheese, grated
- 2 egg, lightly beaten
- 2 tbsp parsley, chopped
- 2 garlic cloves, minced
- 1/4 cup onion, minced
- Pepper
- Salt

Directions:

1. Add all ingredients into the large mixing bowl and mix until well combined.
2. Spray air fryer basket with cooking spray.
3. Make meatballs from bowl mixture and place into the air fryer basket.
4. Cook at 350 F for 15 minutes.
5. Serve and enjoy.

Nutritional Value (Amount per Serving):
- Calories 334
- Fat 21.9 g
- Carbohydrates 1 g
- Sugar 0.3 g
- Protein 31.4 g
- Cholesterol 143 mg

Yummy Meatballs

Preparation Time: 10 minutes; Cooking Time: 20 minutes; Serve: 8
Ingredients:
- 2 lbs ground beef
- 3 eggs, lightly
- 1/2 cup fresh parsley, minced
- 1 tsp cinnamon
- 2 tsp dried oregano
- 2 tsp cumin
- 1 cup almond flour
- 4 garlic cloves, minced
- 1 onion, grated
- 1 tsp pepper
- 2 tsp salt

Directions:
1. Preheat the air fryer to 370 F.
2. Spray air fryer basket with cooking spray.
3. Add all ingredients into the large bowl and mix until well combined.
4. Make small balls from mixture and place into the air fryer basket and cook for 20 minutes.
5. Serve and enjoy.

Nutritional Value (Amount per Serving):
- Calories 325
- Fat 16 g
- Carbohydrates 6 g
- Sugar 1 g
- Protein 40 g
- Cholesterol 125 mg

Stuffed Pork Chops

Preparation Time: 10 minutes; Cooking Time: 28 minutes; Serve: 4
Ingredients:
- 4 pork chops, boneless and thick-cut
- 2 tbsp olives, chopped
- 2 tbsp sun-dried tomatoes, chopped
- 1/2 cup feta cheese, crumbled
- 2 garlic cloves, minced
- 2 tbsp fresh parsley, chopped

Directions:
1. Preheat the air fryer to 350 F.
2. In a bowl, combine together feta cheese, garlic, parsley, olives, and sun-dried tomatoes.
3. Stuff cheese mixture all the pork chops.
4. Season pork chops with pepper and salt and place into the air fryer basket.

5. Cook for 28 minutes.
6. Serve and enjoy.

Nutritional Value (Amount per Serving):

- Calories 314
- Fat 10 g
- Carbohydrates 2 g
- Sugar 1 g
- Protein 19 g
- Cholesterol 130 mg

Tasty Pork Bites

Preparation Time: 10 minutes; Cooking Time: 21 minutes; Serve: 6
Ingredients:

- 2 eggs, lightly beaten
- 1 lb pork tenderloin, cut into cubes
- ¼ cup almond flour
- ½ tsp ground coriander
- ½ tsp paprika
- ½ tsp lemon zest
- ½ tsp kosher salt

Directions:

1. In a shallow bowl, whisk eggs.
2. In a shallow dish, mix together almond flour, coriander, paprika, lemon zest, and salt.
3. Dip each pork cube in egg then coat with almond flour mixture.
4. Preheat the air fryer to 365 F.
5. Spray air fryer basket with cooking spray.
6. Add coated pork cubes into the air fryer basket and cook for 14 minutes.
7. Turn pork cubes to another side and cook for 7 minutes more.
8. Serve and enjoy.

Nutritional Value (Amount per Serving):

- Calories 135
- Fat 4 g
- Carbohydrates 0.2 g
- Sugar 0.1 g
- Protein 21 g
- Cholesterol 111 mg

Lamb Meatballs

Preparation Time: 10 minutes; Cooking Time: 14 minutes; Serve: 8
Ingredients:

- 1 egg, lightly beaten
- 1 lb ground lamb
- ¼ tsp bay leaf, crushed
- 1 tsp ground coriander
- ¼ tsp cayenne pepper
- ¼ tsp turmeric
- 1 onion, chopped
- 2 garlic cloves, minced
- ¼ tsp pepper
- 1 tsp salt

Directions:

1. Preheat the air fryer to 400 F.
2. Spray air fryer basket with cooking spray.
3. Add all ingredients into the large bowl and mix until well combined.
4. Make small balls from meat mixture and place into the air fryer basket and cook for 14 minutes. Shake basket twice while cooking.

5. Serve and enjoy.

Nutritional Value (Amount per Serving):
- Calories 121
- Fat 4 g
- Carbohydrates 2 g
- Sugar 0.5 g
- Protein 16 g
- Cholesterol 70 mg

Flavorful Pork Tenderloin

Preparation Time: 10 minutes; Cooking Time: 15 minutes; Serve: 3

Ingredients:
- 1 lb pork tenderloin
- 1 tbsp vinegar
- 2 garlic cloves, minced
- 3 tbsp butter
- ½ tsp onion powder
- ½ tsp garlic powder
- ½ tsp cinnamon
- 1 tsp sage
- ½ tsp saffron

Directions:
1. In a small bowl, mix together saffron, onion powder, garlic powder, cinnamon, and sage.
2. Rub pork tenderloin with the saffron mixture.
3. Now rub pork tenderloin with garlic and vinegar and let sit for 10 minutes.
4. Preheat the air fryer to 320 F.
5. Place pork tenderloin into the air fryer and top with butter.
6. Cook for 15 minutes.
7. Slice and serve.

Nutritional Value (Amount per Serving):
- Calories 327
- Fat 16 g
- Carbohydrates 2 g
- Sugar 0.3 g
- Protein 40 g
- Cholesterol 140 mg

Spicy Lamb Chops

Preparation Time: 10 minutes; Cooking Time: 10 minutes; Serve: 6

Ingredients:
- 1 ½ lbs lamb chops
- 1 tbsp butter, melted
- 1 tbsp olive oil
- 1 ½ tsp cayenne pepper
- 1 tsp garlic powder
- 1 tsp onion powder
- ½ tsp red chili flakes
- 1 tsp chili pepper
- ½ tsp lime zest

Directions:
1. In a large bowl, mix together oil, butter, lime zest, chili pepper, chili flakes, onion powder, garlic powder, and cayenne pepper.
2. Add lamb chops to the bowl and coat well with marinade and place in the refrigerator for 30 minutes.
3. Spray air fryer basket with cooking spray.

4. Place marinated pork chops into the air fryer basket and cook for 10 minutes. Turn pork chops halfway through.
5. Serve and enjoy.

Nutritional Value (Amount per Serving):
- Calories 253
- Fat 12 g
- Carbohydrates 1 g
- Sugar 0.4 g
- Protein 32 g
- Cholesterol 105 mg

Quick & Easy Meatballs

Preparation Time: 10 minutes; Cooking Time: 12 minutes; Serve: 4
Ingredients:
- 4 oz lamb meat, minced
- 1 tbsp oregano, chopped
- ½ tbsp lemon zest
- 1 egg, lightly beaten
- Pepper
- Salt

Directions:
1. Add all ingredients into the bowl and mix until well combined.
2. Spray air fryer basket with cooking spray.
3. Make balls from bowl mixture and place into the air fryer basket and cook at 400 F for 12 minutes.
4. Serve and enjoy.

Nutritional Value (Amount per Serving):
- Calories 72
- Fat 3 g
- Carbohydrates 1 g
- Sugar 0.2 g
- Protein 10 g
- Cholesterol 66 mg

Meatloaf

Preparation Time: 10 minutes; Cooking Time: 20 minutes; Serve: 4
Ingredients:
- 1 egg, lightly beaten
- 1 onion, chopped
- 1 tbsp thyme, chopped
- 1 oz chorizo, chopped
- 3 tbsp almond flour
- 1 lb ground pork
- Pepper
- Salt

Directions:
1. Add all ingredients into the bowl and mix until well combined.
2. Transfer bowl mixture into the air fryer silicone meatloaf pan and place into the air fryer.
3. Cook at 390 F for 20 minutes.
4. Slice and serve.

Nutritional Value (Amount per Serving):
- Calories 223
- Fat 8 g
- Carbohydrates 3 g
- Sugar 1 g
- Protein 33 g
- Cholesterol 130 mg

Easy Pesto Pork Chops

Preparation Time: 10 minutes; Cooking Time: 18 minutes; Serve: 5

Ingredients:

- 5 pork chops
- 3 tbsp basil pesto
- 2 tbsp almond flour
- 1 tbsp olive oil

Directions:

1. Spray pork chops with cooking spray.
2. Coat pork chops with pesto and sprinkles with almond flour.
3. Place pork chops into the air fryer basket and cook at 350 F for 18 minutes.
4. Serve and enjoy.

Nutritional Value (Amount per Serving):

- Calories 321
- Fat 26 g
- Carbohydrates 3 g
- Sugar 0.5 g
- Protein 21 g
- Cholesterol 241 mg

Moist Lamb Roast

Preparation Time: 5 minutes; Cooking Time: 1 hour 30 minutes; Serve: 4

Ingredients:

- 2 1/2 lbs lamb leg roast
- 1 tbsp dried rosemary
- 3 garlic cloves, sliced
- 1 tbsp olive oil
- Pepper
- Salt

Directions:

1. Make small cuts on meat using a sharp knife.
2. Poke garlic slices into the cuts. Season meat with pepper and salt.
3. Mix together oil and rosemary and rub over the meat.
4. Place meat into the air fryer and cook at 400 F for 15 minutes.
5. Turn temperature to 320 F for 1 hour 15 minutes.
6. Serve and enjoy.

Nutritional Value (Amount per Serving):

- Calories 595
- Fat 25 g
- Carbohydrates 2 g
- Sugar 0 g
- Protein 85 g
- Cholesterol 423 mg

Dried Herbs Lamb Chops

Preparation Time: 10 minutes; Cooking Time: 20 minutes; Serve: 4

Ingredients:

- 1 lb lamb chops
- 1 tsp oregano
- 1 tsp thyme
- 1 tsp rosemary
- 2 tbsp fresh lemon juice
- 2 tbsp olive oil
- 1 tsp coriander
- 1/4 tsp pepper
- 1 tsp salt

Directions:

1. Add all ingredients except lamb chops into the zip-lock bag.
2. Add lamb chops to the bag. Seal bag and shake well and place in the fridge for overnight.
3. Place marinated lamb chops into the air fryer.
4. Cook at 390 F for 3 minutes. Turn lamb chops to another side and cook for 4 minutes more.
5. Serve and enjoy.

Nutritional Value (Amount per Serving):

- Calories 275
- Fat 16 g
- Carbohydrates 1 g
- Sugar 0.5 g
- Protein 30 g
- Cholesterol 124 mg

Crispy Pork Chops

Preparation Time: 10 minutes; Cooking Time: 20 minutes; Serve: 4
Ingredients:

- 4 pork chops, boneless
- 2 eggs, lightly beaten
- 1 cup almond flour
- 1/4 cup parmesan cheese, grated
- 1 tbsp onion powder
- 1/2 tbsp garlic powder
- 1/2 tbsp pepper
- 1/2 tsp sea salt

Directions:

1. Preheat the air fryer to 350 F.
2. Spray air fryer basket with cooking spray.
3. In a bowl, mix together almond flour, parmesan cheese, onion powder, garlic powder, pepper, and salt.
4. Whisk eggs in a shallow bowl.
5. Dip pork chops into the egg then coat with almond mixture and place into the air fryer basket.
6. Cook pork chops for 10 minutes. Turn pork chops to another side and cook for 10 minutes more.
7. Serve and enjoy.

Nutritional Value (Amount per Serving):

- Calories 450
- Fat 35 g
- Carbohydrates 9 g
- Sugar 3 g
- Protein 28 g
- Cholesterol 231 mg

Garlic Thyme Pork Chops

Preparation Time: 10 minutes; Cooking Time: 15 minutes; Serve: 8
Ingredients:

- 8 pork chops, boneless
- 5 garlic cloves, minced
- 1 cup parmesan cheese
- 2 tbsp butter, melted
- 1 tsp thyme
- 1 tbsp parsley
- 2 tbsp coconut oil
- 1/4 tsp pepper

- 1/2 tsp sea salt

Directions:
1. Preheat the air fryer to 400 F.
2. Spray air fryer basket with cooking spray.
3. In a bowl, mix together butter, spices, cheese, and coconut oil.
4. Rub butter mixture on top of pork chops and place into the air fryer basket.
5. Cook for 10 minutes. Turn to another side and cook for 10 minutes more.
6. Serve and enjoy.

Nutritional Value (Amount per Serving):
- Calories 355
- Fat 29 g
- Carbohydrates 2 g
- Sugar 0 g
- Protein 23 g
- Cholesterol 125 mg

Pork Strips

Preparation Time: 10 minutes; Cooking Time: 10 minutes; Serve: 2
Ingredients:
- 4 pork loin chops
- 1 tbsp swerve
- 1 tbsp soy sauce
- 1/8 tsp ground ginger
- 1 garlic clove, chopped
- 1/2 tsp balsamic vinegar

Directions:
1. Tenderize meat and season with pepper and salt.
2. In a bowl, mix together sweetener, soy sauce, and vinegar. Add ginger and garlic and set aside.
3. Add pork chops into the marinade mixture and marinate for 2 hours.
4. Preheat the air fryer to 350 F.
5. Add marinated meat into the air fryer and cook for 5 minutes on each side.
6. Cut into strips and serve.

Nutritional Value (Amount per Serving):
- Calories 551
- Fat 39.8 g
- Carbohydrates 9.9 g
- Sugar 8.8 g
- Protein 36.6 g
- Cholesterol 138 mg

BBQ Ribs

Preparation Time: 10 minutes; Cooking Time: 30 minutes; Serve: 2
Ingredients:
- 1 lb pork ribs
- 1/2 tsp five-spice powder
- 1 tbsp swerve
- 4 tbsp BBQ sauce, sugar-free
- 3 garlic cloves, chopped
- 1 tsp soy sauce
- 1 tsp pepper
- 1 tsp sesame oil
- 1 tsp salt

Directions:
1. Preheat the air fryer to 350 F.

2. Add all ingredients into the large bowl and mix well to coat. Place into the fridge for 1 hour.
3. Add marinated ribs into the air fryer basket and cook for 15 minutes.
4. Turn ribs to another side and cook for 15 minutes more.
5. Serve and enjoy.

Nutritional Value (Amount per Serving):
- Calories 697
- Fat 42 g
- Carbohydrates 12 g
- Sugar 8 g
- Protein 60 g
- Cholesterol 235 mg

Mushrooms Meatballs

Preparation Time: 10 minutes; Cooking Time: 20 minutes; Serve: 2
Ingredients:
- 1/2 lb ground beef
- 2 tbsp onion, chopped
- 2 mushrooms, diced
- 1/4 tsp pepper
- 1 tbsp parsley, chopped
- 1/4 cup almond flour
- 1/2 tsp salt

Directions:
1. In a mixing bowl, combine together all ingredients until well combined.
2. Make small balls from meat mixture and place into the air fryer basket.
3. Cook at 350 F for 20 minutes.
4. Serve and enjoy.

Nutritional Value (Amount per Serving):
- Calories 269
- Fat 8 g
- Carbohydrates 10 g
- Sugar 2 g
- Protein 34 g
- Cholesterol 105 mg

Meatloaf

Preparation Time: 10 minutes; Cooking Time: 25 minutes; Serve: 2
Ingredients:
- 1/2 lb ground beef
- 1 tbsp chorizo, chopped
- 1 1/2 tbsp almond flour
- 1 egg, lightly beaten
- 2 mushrooms, sliced
- 1/2 tbsp fresh thyme
- 1/2 small onion, chopped
- Pepper
- Salt

Directions:
1. Preheat the air fryer to 400 F.
2. In a large bowl, mix together all ingredients until well combined.
3. Transfer meat mixture into the small silicone loaf pan.
4. Place pan into the air fryer and cook for 25 minutes.
5. Slice and serve.

Nutritional Value (Amount per Serving):

- Calories 273
- Fat 9.6 g
- Carbohydrates 6.2 g
- Sugar 1.4 g
- Protein 38.4 g
- Cholesterol 183 mg

Flavorful Kabab

Preparation Time: 10 minutes; Cooking Time: 10 minutes; Serve: 2
Ingredients:
- 1/2 lb ground beef
- 1 tbsp parsley, chopped
- 1/2 tbsp olive oil
- 1 1/2 tbsp kabab spice mix
- 1/2 tbsp garlic, minced
- 1/2 tsp salt

Directions:
1. Add all ingredients into the bowl and mix well combined.
2. Divide mixture into the two equal portions and give it to kabab shape.
3. Place kababs into the air fryer basket and cook at 370 F for 10 minutes.
4. Serve and enjoy.

Nutritional Value (Amount per Serving):
- Calories 245
- Fat 11 g
- Carbohydrates 1 g
- Sugar 0 g
- Protein 35 g
- Cholesterol 103 mg

Grilled Pork Shoulder

Preparation Time: 10 minutes; Cooking Time: 15 minutes; Serve: 2
Ingredients:
- 1/2 lb pork shoulder, cut into 1/2-inch slices
- 1/2 tsp Swerve
- 1/2 tbsp sesame oil
- 1/2 tbsp rice wine
- 1/2 tbsp soy sauce
- 1 tbsp green onion, sliced
- 1/2 tbsp sesame seeds
- 1/4 tsp cayenne pepper
- 1/2 tbsp garlic, minced
- 1/2 tbsp ginger, minced
- 1 tbsp gochujang
- 1/2 onion, sliced

Directions:
1. In a large bowl, mix together all ingredients and place in the refrigerator for 60 minutes.
2. Place air fryer grill pan into the air fryer.
3. Add pork mixture into the air fryer and cook at 400 F for 15 minutes. Turn halfway through.
4. Serve and enjoy.

Nutritional Value (Amount per Serving):
- Calories 405
- Fat 30 g
- Carbohydrates 7 g
- Sugar 3 g
- Protein 28 g
- Cholesterol 105 mg

Beef Satay

Preparation Time: 10 minutes; Cooking Time: 8 minutes; Serve: 2

Ingredients:

- 1 lb beef flank steak, sliced into long strips
- 1 tsp hot sauce
- 1 tbsp Swerve
- 1 tbsp garlic, minced
- 1 tbsp ginger, minced
- 1 tbsp soy sauce
- 1/2 cup cilantro, chopped
- 1 tsp ground coriander
- 1 tbsp fish sauce
- 2 tbsp olive oil

Directions:

1. Add all ingredients into the zip-lock bag and shake well. Place into the fridge for 1 hour.
2. Add marinated meat into the air fryer basket and cook at 400 F for 8 minutes. Turn halfway through.
3. Serve and enjoy.

Nutritional Value (Amount per Serving):

- Calories 690
- Fat 36 g
- Carbohydrates 10 g
- Sugar 6 g
- Protein 74 g
- Cholesterol 205 mg

Meatloaf

Preparation Time: 10 minutes; Cooking Time: 15 minutes; Serve: 2

Ingredients:

- 1 egg, lightly beaten
- 1/2 lb ground beef
- 1/2 tsp cayenne
- 1/2 tsp turmeric
- 1 tsp garam masala
- 1/2 tbsp garlic, minced
- 1/2 tbsp ginger, minced
- 1 tbsp cilantro, chopped
- 1/2 cup onion, chopped
- 1/8 tsp ground cardamom
- 1/4 tsp ground cinnamon
- 1/2 tsp salt

Directions:

1. In a large bowl, mix together all the ingredients until well combined.
2. Place meat mixture into silicon meatloaf pan and place in the air fryer basket.
3. Cook at 360 F for 15 minutes.
4. Slice and serve.

Nutritional Value (Amount per Serving):

- Calories 265
- Fat 10 g
- Carbohydrates 5 g
- Sugar 2 g
- Protein 38 g
- Cholesterol 180 mg

Delicious Burger

Preparation Time: 10 minutes; Cooking Time: 10 minutes; Serve: 2

Ingredients:

- 1/2 lb ground beef
- 1 tsp swerve
- 1 tsp ginger, minced
- 1/2 tbsp soy sauce
- 1 tbsp gochujang
- 1 tbsp green onion, chopped
- 1/2 tbsp sesame oil
- 1/4 tsp salt

Directions:
1. In a large bowl, mix together all ingredients until well combined. Place in refrigerator for 1 hour.
2. Make patties from beef mixture and place into the air fryer basket.
3. Cook at 360 F for 10 minutes.
4. Serve and enjoy.

Nutritional Value (Amount per Serving):
- Calories 324
- Fat 16 g
- Carbohydrates 6 g
- Sugar 3 g
- Protein 36 g
- Cholesterol 102 mg

Coconut Butter Pork Chops

Preparation Time: 10 minutes; Cooking Time: 15 minutes; Serve: 2
Ingredients:
- 4 pork chops
- 1 tbsp coconut oil
- 1 tbsp coconut butter
- 1 tsp dried parsley
- 1/4 tsp dried basil
- 1/4 tsp rosemary
- 3 garlic cloves, minced
- Pepper
- Salt

Directions:
1. Preheat the air fryer to 350 F.
2. In a large bowl, mix together garlic, coconut butter, coconut oil, parsley, basil, rosemary, pepper, and salt.
3. Rub garlic mixture over pork chops. Place in the refrigerator for 2 hours.
4. Place marinated pork chops into the air fryer basket and cook for 7 minutes.
5. Turn pork chops to another side and cook for 8 minutes.
6. Serve and enjoy.

Nutritional Value (Amount per Serving):
- Calories 620
- Fat 53 g
- Carbohydrates 3.5 g
- Sugar 1 g
- Protein 37 g
- Cholesterol 140 mg

Easy Garlic Butter Steak

Preparation Time: 5 minutes; Cooking Time: 6 minutes; Serve: 2
Ingredients:
- 2 steaks
- 2 tsp garlic butter
- 1/4 tsp Italian seasoning
- Pepper
- Salt

Directions:

1. Season steaks with Italian seasoning, pepper, and salt.
2. Rub steaks with garlic butter and place into the air fryer basket and cook at 350 F for 6 minutes.
3. Serve and enjoy.

Nutritional Value (Amount per Serving):

- Calories 120
- Fat 8 g
- Carbohydrates 0 g
- Sugar 0 g
- Protein 10 g
- Cholesterol 6 mg

Beef Patties

Preparation Time: 10 minutes; Cooking Time: 10 minutes; Serve: 2

Ingredients:

- 1/2 lb ground beef
- 1/4 tsp garlic powder
- 2 drops liquid smoke
- 1/2 tsp hot sauce
- 1/2 tbsp Worcestershire sauce
- 1/2 tsp dried parsley
- 1/4 tsp pepper
- 1/4 tsp onion powder
- 1/4 tsp cayenne
- 1/2 tsp chili powder
- 1/4 tsp salt

Directions:

1. Spray air fryer basket with cooking spray.
2. Add all ingredients into the large bowl and mix until well combined.
3. Make small patties from mixture and place into the air fryer basket.
4. Cook at 350 F for 10 minutes.
5. Serve and enjoy.

Nutritional Value (Amount per Serving):

- Calories 220
- Fat 7 g
- Carbohydrates 2 g
- Sugar 1 g
- Protein 35 g
- Cholesterol 100 mg

BBQ Chops

Preparation Time: 10 minutes; Cooking Time: 10 minutes; Serve: 2

Ingredients:

- 2 pork loin chops
- 1 tbsp swerve
- 1/2 tsp balsamic vinegar
- 1/8 tsp ground ginger
- 1 tbsp soy sauce
- 1 garlic clove
- Pepper
- Salt

Directions:

1. Preheat the air fryer to 350 F for 5 minutes.
2. Season pork chops with pepper and salt.
3. In a bowl, combine together swerve, soy sauce, garlic, ground ginger, and vinegar.
4. Add pork chops in a bowl and coat well and place in the refrigerator for 2 hours.

5. Place marinated pork chops in air fryer basket and cook for 10 minutes. Turn pork chops to another side halfway through.
6. Serve and enjoy.

Nutritional Value (Amount per Serving):
- Calories 295
- Fat 19.9 g
- Carbohydrates 10 g
- Sugar 8 g
- Protein 19 g
- Cholesterol 70 mg

Meatballs

Preparation Time: 10 minutes; Cooking Time: 15 minutes; Serve: 2

Ingredients:
- 1/2 lb ground lamb
- 1 egg white, lightly beaten
- 1/2 tbsp olive oil
- 1 garlic cloves, minced
- 1/2 tbsp coriander, chopped
- 1 tbsp mint, chopped
- 1 tbsp parsley, chopped
- 2 oz ground turkey
- 1/2 tsp salt

Directions
1. Preheat the air fryer to 320 F.
2. Add all ingredients into the mixing bowl and mix well to combine.
3. Make small balls from meat mixture and place in the air fryer basket.
4. Cook meatballs for 15 minutes.
5. Serve and enjoy.

Nutritional Value (Amount per Serving):
- Calories 300
- Fat 14 g
- Carbohydrates 1 g
- Sugar 0.5 g
- Protein 41 g
- Cholesterol 125 mg

Meatballs

Preparation Time: 10 minutes; Cooking Time: 15 minutes; Serve: 2

Ingredients:
- 5 oz pork minced
- 1/2 tbsp cheddar cheese, grated
- 1/2 tsp erythritol
- 1/2 tsp garlic, minced
- 1 tbsp fresh basil, chopped
- 1/2 onion, diced
- 1/2 tsp mustard
- Pepper
- Salt

Directions:
1. Add all ingredients into the large bowl and mix well to combine.
2. Make small balls from meat mixture and place in the air fryer basket.
3. Cook at 390 F for 15 minutes.
4. Serve and enjoy.

Nutritional Value (Amount per Serving):
- Calories 146
- Fat 7 g

- Carbohydrates 5 g
- Sugar 3 g
- Protein 15 g
- Cholesterol 2 mg

Coconut Pork Chops

Preparation Time: 5 minutes; Cooking Time: 15 minutes; Serve: 2
Ingredients:

- 4 pork chops
- 1 tbsp coconut oil
- 1 tbsp coconut butter
- 1 tbsp fresh parsley, chopped
- 3 garlic cloves, grated
- Pepper
- Salt

Directions:

1. Preheat the air fryer to 350 F.
2. In a small bowl, mix together coconut butter, coconut oil, garlic, parsley, pepper, and salt.
3. Rub coconut butter mixture over pork chops and place in the refrigerator for 1 hour.
4. Place grill pan in the air fryer.
5. Place marinated chops into the air fryer and cook for 7 minutes.
6. Turn pork chops to another side and cook for 8 minutes.
7. Serve and enjoy.

Nutritional Value (Amount per Serving):

- Calories 629
- Fat 50 g
- Carbohydrates 3 g
- Sugar 0.4 g
- Protein 35 g
- Cholesterol 140 mg

Simple Pork Chops

Preparation Time: 5 minutes; Cooking Time: 20 minutes; Serve: 4
Ingredients:

- 4 pork chops, boneless
- 1 1/2 tbsp Mr. Dash seasoning
- Pepper
- Salt

Directions:

1. Coat pork chops with Mr. dash seasoning, pepper, and salt.
2. Place pork chops in the air fryer and cook at 360 F for 10 minutes.
3. Turn pork chops to another side and cook for 10 minutes more.
4. Serve and enjoy.

Nutritional Value (Amount per Serving):

- Calories 255
- Fat 20 g
- Carbohydrates 0 g
- Sugar 0 g
- Protein 20 g
- Cholesterol 70 mg

Easy Pork Loin

Preparation Time: 5 minutes; Cooking Time: 40 minutes; Serve: 6
Ingredients:

- 3 lbs pork loin cut in half
- 1/2 tsp garlic salt

- 1/4 tsp pepper
- 1 1/2 tsp herbs de Provence
- 1 tbsp olive oil

Directions:
1. Coat meat with olive oil, pepper, garlic salt, and herb de Provence.
2. Place in the air fryer and cook at 360 F for 25 minutes.
3. Turn to another side and cook for 15 minutes more.
4. Serve and enjoy.

Nutritional Value (Amount per Serving):
- Calories 569
- Fat 34 g
- Carbohydrates 0.5 g
- Sugar 0.5 g
- Protein 60 g
- Cholesterol 180 mg

Mustard Pork Tenderloin

Preparation Time: 10 minutes; Cooking Time: 15 minutes; Serve: 2
Ingredients:
- 1 pork tenderloin, cut into pieces
- 1/2 tbsp mustard
- 1 onion, sliced
- 1 bell pepper, cut into strips
- 1 tbsp oil
- 2 tsp herb de Provence
- Pepper
- Salt

Directions:
1. Preheat the air fryer to 390 F.
2. In a bowl, mix together bell pepper strips, herb de Provence, onion, pepper, and salt. Add 1/2 tbsp oil and mix well.
3. Season pork tenderloin with mustard, pepper, and salt.
4. Coat pork tenderloin with remaining oil.
5. Place pork tenderloin pieces into the air fryer pan and top with bell pepper mixture.
6. Place pan in the air fryer and cook for 15 minutes. Stir halfway through.
7. Serve and enjoy.

Nutritional Value (Amount per Serving):
- Calories 275
- Fat 12 g
- Carbohydrates 10 g
- Sugar 4 g
- Protein 31 g
- Cholesterol 83 mg

McCornick Pork Chops

Preparation Time: 10 minutes; Cooking Time: 15 minutes; Serve: 2
Ingredients:
- 2 pork chops
- 1/2 tsp McCormick Montreal chicken seasoning
- 2 tbsp arrowroot flour
- 1 1/2 tbsp coconut milk
- Salt

Directions:
1. Season pork chops with pepper and salt.
2. Drizzle milk over the pork chops.

3. Place pork chops in a zip-lock bag with flour and shake well to coat. Marinate pork chops for 30 minutes.
4. Place marinated pork chops into the air fryer basket and cook at 380 F for 15 minutes. Turn halfway through.
5. Serve and enjoy.

Nutritional Value (Amount per Serving):

- Calories 290
- Fat 19 g
- Carbohydrates 7 g
- Sugar 0.5 g
- Protein 20 g
- Cholesterol 70 mg

Sweet Mustard Pork Chops

Preparation Time: 10 minutes; Cooking Time: 12 minutes; Serve: 2
Ingredients:

- 1/2 lb pork chops, boneless
- 1 tbsp Swerve
- 1/2 tsp steak seasoning blend
- 1/2 tbsp mustard

Directions:
1. In a small bowl, mix together steak seasoning, swerve, and mustard.
2. Rub steak seasoning mixture over pork chops and place into the air fryer basket.
3. Cook at 350 F for 12 minutes. Turn halfway through.
4. Serve and enjoy.

Nutritional Value (Amount per Serving):

- Calories 395
- Fat 27 g
- Carbohydrates 9 g
- Sugar 8 g
- Protein 24 g
- Cholesterol 95 mg

BBQ Ribs

Preparation Time: 10 minutes; Cooking Time: 35 minutes; Serve: 4
Ingredients:

- 1 lb pork ribs
- 4 tbsp BBQ sauce, sugar-free
- 3 garlic cloves, chopped
- 1 tsp olive oil
- 1/2 tsp allspice
- 1 tsp pepper
- 1 tsp salt

Directions:
1. Add all ingredients into the bowl and mix until well coated. Place in the fridge for 4 hours.
2. Preheat the air fryer to 350 F.
3. Place marinated pork ribs into the air fryer and cook for 15 minutes.
4. Turn pork ribs to another side and cook for 15 minutes more.
5. Serve and enjoy.

Nutritional Value (Amount per Serving):

- Calories 348
- Fat 22 g
- Carbohydrates 7 g
- Sugar 4 g

- Protein 30 g
- Cholesterol 117 mg

Vietnamese Pork Chop

Preparation Time: 10 minutes; Cooking Time: 15 minutes; Serve: 2
Ingredients:
- 2 pork chops
- 1 tbsp olive oil
- 1 tbsp soy sauce
- 1 tsp pepper
- 2 1/2 tbsp lemongrass, chopped
- 1 tbsp onion, chopped
- 3 garlic cloves, chopped

Directions:
1. Add all ingredients into the bowl and coat well. Place in refrigerator for 2 hours.
2. Preheat the air fryer to 400 F.
3. Place marinated pork chops into the air fryer and cook for 7 minutes.
4. Turn pork chops to another side and cook for 5 minutes more.
5. Serve and enjoy.

Nutritional Value (Amount per Serving):
- Calories 340
- Fat 28 g
- Carbohydrates 6 g
- Sugar 0.5 g
- Protein 20 g
- Cholesterol 70 mg

Veggie Pork Tenderloin

Preparation Time: 10 minutes; Cooking Time: 15 minutes; Serve: 2
Ingredients:
- 10 oz pork tenderloin, cut into small pieces
- 1/2 tbsp mustard
- 1 onion, sliced
- 1/2 red bell pepper, cut into strips
- 1/2 yellow bell pepper, cut into strips
- 1/4 tsp garlic powder
- 1/4 tsp onion powder
- 1/4 tsp pepper
- 1 tbsp olive oil
- 2 tsp herb de Provence

Directions:
1. Preheat the air fryer to 390 F.
2. In air fryer baking dish mix together 1/2 tablespoon olive oil, herb de Provence, bell pepper, onion, garlic powder, onion powder, and salt.
3. Season meat with pepper, mustard, and salt. Drizzle with remaining oil and place in the dish on top of onion and pepper mixture.
4. Place the dish in the air fryer and cook for 8 minutes.
5. Stir everything well and cook for 7 minutes more.
6. Serve and enjoy.

Nutritional Value (Amount per Serving):
- Calories 325
- Fat 14 g
- Carbohydrates 11 g
- Sugar 6 g
- Protein 41 g
- Cholesterol 110 mg

Lemon Herb Lamb Chops

Preparation Time: 5 minutes; Cooking Time: 7 minutes; Serve: 4
Ingredients:

- 1 lb lamb chops
- 1 tsp oregano
- 1 tsp thyme
- 1 tsp rosemary
- 2 tbsp lemon juice
- 2 tbsp olive oil
- 1/4 tsp basil
- 1/4 tsp tarragon
- 1 tsp coriander
- 1 tsp salt

Directions:

1. Preheat the air fryer to 390 F.
2. Add all ingredients except lamb chops in a zip-lock bag and shake well to mix.
3. Add lamb chops and coat well with herb mixture and place in the refrigerator for 1 hour.
4. Place marinated lamb chops into the air fryer and cook for 3 minutes.
5. Turn lamb chops to another side and cook for 4 minutes more.
6. Serve and enjoy.

Nutritional Value (Amount per Serving):

- Calories 275
- Fat 15 g
- Carbohydrates 1 g
- Sugar 0.5 g
- Protein 33 g
- Cholesterol 105 mg

Lamb Rack

Preparation Time: 10 minutes; Cooking Time: 30 minutes; Serve: 6
Ingredients:

- 1 egg, lightly beaten
- 1 tbsp fresh thyme, chopped
- 1 3/4 lbs rack of lamb
- 1 tbsp fresh rosemary, chopped
- 1 tbsp olive oil
- 2 garlic cloves, chopped
- Pepper
- Salt

Directions:

1. Mix together oil and garlic.
2. Brush oil and garlic mixture over the rack of lamb. Season with pepper and salt.
3. Preheat the air fryer to 210 F.
4. Mix together thyme and rosemary.
5. Coat lamb with egg then with herb mixture.
6. Place lamb rack in the air fryer basket and cook for 25 minutes.
7. Turn temperature to 390 F and cook for 5 minutes more.
8. Serve and enjoy.

Nutritional Value (Amount per Serving):

- Calories 255
- Fat 15 g
- Carbohydrates 1 g
- Sugar 0.3 g
- Protein 29 g
- Cholesterol 114 mg

Cayenne Cumin Lamb

Preparation Time: 10 minutes; Cooking Time: 10 minutes; Serve: 4
Ingredients:
- 1 lb lamb, cut into 1-inch pieces
- 2 tbsp olive oil
- 1 tsp cayenne
- 2 tbsp ground cumin
- 2 chili peppers, chopped
- 1 tbsp garlic, minced
- 1 tsp salt

Directions:
1. In a bowl, mix together ground cumin, chili peppers, garlic, olive oil, cayenne, and salt.
2. Add meat to the bowl and coat well. Place in refrigerator for 1 hour.
3. Place marinated meat into the air fryer and cook at 360 F for 10 minutes.
4. Serve and enjoy.

Nutritional Value (Amount per Serving):
- Calories 285
- Fat 15 g
- Carbohydrates 2 g
- Sugar 0.5 g
- Protein 33 g
- Cholesterol 105 mg

Asian Pork

Preparation Time: 10 minutes; Cooking Time: 15 minutes; Serve: 4
Ingredients:
- 1 lb pork shoulder, boneless and cut into 1/2 inch sliced
- 3 tbsp green onions, sliced
- 3 garlic cloves, minced
- 1 tbsp ginger, minced
- 2 tbsp red pepper paste
- 1 onion, sliced
- 1 tbsp sesame seeds
- 3/4 tsp cayenne pepper
- 1 tbsp sesame oil
- 1 tbsp rice wine

Directions:
1. Add all ingredients into the bowl and mix well and place in the refrigerator for 1 hour.
2. Place marinated meat and onion slices into the air fryer.
3. Cook at 400 F for 15 minutes. Toss halfway through.
4. Serve and enjoy.

Nutritional Value (Amount per Serving):
- Calories 405
- Fat 30 g
- Carbohydrates 8 g
- Sugar 3 g
- Protein 30 g
- Cholesterol 105 mg

Classic Pork

Preparation Time: 10 minutes; Cooking Time: 10 minutes; Serve: 4
Ingredients:
- 1 lb pork shoulder, thinly sliced
- 1 tbsp fish sauce
- 3 garlic cloves, minced
- 1 tbsp Swerve

- 2 tbsp olive oil
- 1/4 cup onion, minced
- 1/2 tsp pepper
- 1 tbsp lemongrass paste

Directions:
1. In a bowl, whisk together onion, pepper, lemongrass paste, fish sauce, garlic, sweetener, and oil.
2. Add meat slices into the bowl and coat well. Place in the fridge for 1 hour.
3. Place marinated meat in the air fryer basket and cook at 400 F for 10 minutes. Turn halfway through.
4. Serve and enjoy.

Nutritional Value (Amount per Serving):
- Calories 415
- Fat 32 g
- Carbohydrates 5 g
- Sugar 4 g
- Protein 27 g
- Cholesterol 105 mg

Sirloin Steaks

Preparation Time: 10 minutes; Cooking Time: 15 minutes; Serve: 4
Ingredients:
- 1 lb lamb sirloin steaks, boneless
- 1 tsp garam masala
- 4 garlic cloves
- 3/4 tbsp ginger
- 1/2 onion
- 1 tsp cayenne
- 1/2 tsp ground cardamom
- 1 tsp ground cinnamon
- 1 tsp ground fennel
- 1 tsp salt

Directions:
1. Add all ingredients except steak into the blender and blend until smooth.
2. Place meat into the bowl and pour the blended mixture over meat and coat well. Place in refrigerator for 1 hour.
3. Place marinated meat into the air fryer and cook for 15 minutes at 330 F. Turn meat halfway through.
4. Serve and enjoy.

Nutritional Value (Amount per Serving):
- Calories 150
- Fat 4 g
- Carbohydrates 6 g
- Sugar 1 g
- Protein 25 g
- Cholesterol 45 mg

Meatballs

Preparation Time: 10 minutes; Cooking Time: 15 minutes; Serve: 4
Ingredients:
- 1 lb minced pork
- 2 tsp curry paste
- 1 tbsp Worcestershire sauce
- 1 1/2 tsp garlic paste
- 1 small onion, chopped
- 1 tsp coriander
- 1 tsp Chinese spice
- 1 tsp mixed spice
- 1/2 fresh lime juice
- Pepper

- Salt

Directions:
1. Add all ingredients into the bowl and mix until combined.
2. Make small balls from the meat mixture and place into the air fryer basket.
3. Cook for 15 minutes at 350 F.
4. Serve and enjoy.

Nutritional Value (Amount per Serving):
- Calories 175
- Fat 5 g
- Carbohydrates 4 g
- Sugar 2 g
- Protein 31 g
- Cholesterol 85 mg

Spicy & Tender Pork Chops

Preparation Time: 5 minutes; Cooking Time: 10 minutes; Serve: 4

Ingredients:
- 4 pork chops
- 2 tsp olive oil
- 1/2 tsp dried sage
- 1/2 tsp cayenne pepper
- 1/4 tsp pepper
- 1 tsp ground cumin
- 1 tsp paprika
- 1/2 tsp garlic salt

Directions:
1. Preheat the air fryer to 400 F.
2. In a small bowl, mix together paprika, garlic salt, sage, pepper, cayenne pepper, and cumin.
3. Rub pork chops with spice mixture and place into the air fryer and cook for 10 minutes. Turn halfway through.
4. Serve and enjoy.

Nutritional Value (Amount per Serving):
- Calories 275
- Fat 20 g
- Carbohydrates 1 g
- Sugar 0.4 g
- Protein 20 g
- Cholesterol 153 mg

Air Fried Thyme Garlic Lamb Chops

Preparation Time: 5 minutes; Cooking Time: 12 minutes; Serve: 4

Ingredients:
- 4 lamb chops
- 4 garlic cloves, minced
- 3 tbsp olive oil
- 1 tbsp dried thyme
- Pepper
- Salt

Directions:
1. Preheat the air fryer to 390 F.
2. Season lamb chops with pepper and salt.
3. In a small bowl, mix together thyme, oil, and garlic and rub over lamb chops.
4. Place lamb chops into the air fryer and cook for 12 minutes. Turn halfway through.
5. Serve and enjoy.

Nutritional Value (Amount per Serving):
- Calories 415
- Fat 35 g
- Carbohydrates 1 g
- Sugar 0.5 g
- Protein 20 g
- Cholesterol 124 mg

Steak with Cheese Butter

Preparation Time: 10 minutes; Cooking Time: 8 minutes; Serve: 2
Ingredients:
- 2 rib-eye steaks
- 2 tsp garlic powder
- 2 1/2 tbsp blue cheese butter
- 1 tsp pepper
- 2 tsp kosher salt

Directions:
1. Preheat the air fryer to 400 F.
2. Mix together garlic powder, pepper, and salt and rub over the steaks.
3. Spray air fryer basket with cooking spray.
4. Place steak in the air fryer basket and cook for 4-5 minutes on each side.
5. Top with blue butter cheese.
6. Serve and enjoy.

Nutritional Value (Amount per Serving):
- Calories 830
- Fat 60 g
- Carbohydrates 3 g
- Sugar 0 g
- Protein 70g
- Cholesterol 123 mg

Beef Roast

Preparation Time: 10 minutes; Cooking Time: 45 minutes; Serve: 8
Ingredients:
- 2 1/2 lbs beef roast
- 1 tsp onion powder
- 1 tsp rosemary
- 1 tsp dill
- 2 tbsp olive oil
- 1/4 tsp pepper
- 1 tsp garlic powder

Directions:
1. Preheat the air fryer to 360 F.
2. Mix together pepper, garlic powder, onion powder, rosemary, dill, and oil. Rub all over the beef roast.
3. Place roast in the air fryer and cook for 45 minutes.
4. Serve and enjoy.

Nutritional Value (Amount per Serving):
- Calories 294
- Fat 12 g
- Carbohydrates 0.5 g
- Sugar 0 g
- Protein 43 g
- Cholesterol 85 mg

Montreal Steak

Preparation Time: 5 minutes; Cooking Time: 7 minutes; Serve: 2

Ingredients:

- 12 oz steak
- 1/2 tsp liquid smoke
- 1 tbsp soy sauce
- 1/2 tbsp cocoa powder
- 1 tbsp Montreal steak seasoning
- Pepper
- Salt

Directions:

1. Add steak, liquid smoke, soy sauce, and steak seasonings into the large zip-lock bag. Coat well and place in the refrigerator for overnight.
2. Spray air fryer basket with cooking spray.
3. Place marinated steaks into the air fryer
4. Cook at 375 F for 7 minutes. Turn after 5 minutes to another side.
5. Serve and enjoy.

Nutritional Value (Amount per Serving):

- Calories 355
- Fat 9 g
- Carbohydrates 1 g
- Sugar 0.3 g
- Protein 62 g
- Cholesterol 80 mg

Garlic Pork Chops

Preparation Time: 5 minutes; Cooking Time: 20 minutes; Serve: 5

Ingredients:

- 2 lbs pork chops
- 2 tbsp garlic, minced
- 1 tbsp fresh parsley
- 2 tbsp olive oil
- 2 tbsp fresh lemon juice
- Pepper
- Salt

Directions:

1. In a small bowl, mix together garlic, parsley, oil, and lemon juice.
2. Season pork chops with pepper and salt.
3. Rub garlic mixture over the pork chops and allow to marinate for 30 minutes.
4. Add marinated pork chops into the air fryer and cook at 400 F for 10 minutes.
5. Turn pork chops to another side and cook for 10 minutes more.
6. Serve and enjoy.

Nutritional Value (Amount per Serving):

- Calories 625
- Fat 50 g
- Carbohydrates 2 g
- Sugar 0.5 g
- Protein 40 g
- Cholesterol 124 mg

Cheese Herb Pork Chops

Preparation Time: 5 minutes; Cooking Time: 9 minutes; Serve: 2

Ingredients:

- 2 pork chops, boneless
- 1 tsp herb de Provence
- 1 tsp paprika
- 4 tbsp parmesan cheese, grated
- 1/3 cup almond flour
- 1/2 tsp Cajun seasoning

Directions:

1. Preheat the air fryer to 350 F.
2. Mix together almond flour, Cajun seasoning, herb de Provence, paprika, and cheese.
3. Spray pork chops with cooking spray and coat pork chops with almond flour mixture and place into the air fryer basket.
4. Cook for 9 minutes.
5. Serve and enjoy.

Nutritional Value (Amount per Serving):

- Calories 340
- Fat 26 g
- Carbohydrates 2 g
- Sugar 0.5 g
- Protein 24 g
- Cholesterol 124 mg

Creole Pork Chops

Preparation Time: 10 minutes; Cooking Time: 12 minutes; Serve: 6

Ingredients:

- 1 1/2 lbs pork chops, boneless
- 1 tsp garlic powder
- 5 tbsp parmesan cheese, grated
- 1/3 cup almond flour
- 1 1/2 tsp paprika
- 1 tsp Creole seasoning

Directions:

1. Preheat the air fryer to 360 F.
2. Add all ingredients except pork chops into the zip-lock bag. Mix well.
3. Add pork chops into the bag. Seal bag and shake until well coated.
4. Spray air fryer basket with cooking spray.
5. Place pork chops into the air fryer basket and cook for 12 minutes.
6. Serve and enjoy.

Nutritional Value (Amount per Serving):

- Calories 400
- Fat 31 g
- Carbohydrates 1 g
- Sugar 0.4 g
- Protein 28 g
- Cholesterol 243 mg

Jerk Pork

Preparation Time: 10 minutes; Cooking Time: 20 minutes; Serve: 4

Ingredients:

- 1 1/2 lbs pork butt, chopped into pieces
- 3 tbsp jerk paste

Directions:

1. Add meat and jerk paste into the bowl and coat well. Place in the fridge for overnight.
2. Spray air fryer basket with cooking spray.
3. Preheat the air fryer to 390 F.

4. Add marinated meat into the air fryer and cook for 20 minutes. Turn halfway through.
5. Serve and enjoy.

Nutritional Value (Amount per Serving):
- Calories 325
- Fat 12 g
- Carbohydrates 0.5 g
- Sugar 0 g
- Protein 52 g
- Cholesterol 124 mg

Cumin Lamb

Preparation Time: 10 minutes; Cooking Time: 10 minutes; Serve: 4
Ingredients:
- 1 lb lamb, cut into 2-inch pieces
- 1/4 tsp liquid stevia
- 2 tbsp olive oil
- 1/2 tsp cayenne
- 2 tbsp ground cumin
- 2 red chili peppers, chopped
- 1 tbsp garlic, minced
- 1 tbsp soy sauce
- 1 tsp salt

Directions:
1. In a small bowl, mix together cumin and cayenne.
2. Rub meat with cumin mixture and place in a large bowl.
3. Add oil, soy sauce, garlic, chili peppers, stevia, and salt over the meat. Coat well and place in the refrigerator for overnight.
4. Add marinated meat to the air fryer and cook at 360 F for 10 minutes.
5. Serve and enjoy.

Nutritional Value (Amount per Serving):
- Calories 285
- Fat 16 g
- Carbohydrates 2 g
- Sugar 0.5 g
- Protein 33 g
- Cholesterol 123 mg

Juicy & Tender Steak

Preparation Time: 10 minutes; Cooking Time: 12 minutes; Serve: 2
Ingredients:
- 2 rib-eye steak
- 3 tbsp fresh parsley, chopped
- 1 stick butter, softened
- 1 1/2 tsp Worcestershire sauce
- 3 garlic cloves, minced
- Pepper
- Salt

Directions:
1. In a bowl, mix together butter, Worcestershire sauce, garlic, parsley, and salt and place in the refrigerator.
2. Preheat the air fryer to 400 F.
3. Season steak with pepper and salt.
4. Place seasoned steak in the air fryer and cook for 12 minutes. Turn halfway through.
5. Remove steak from air fryer and top with butter mixture.
6. Serve and enjoy.

Nutritional Value (Amount per Serving):
- Calories 590
- Fat 57 g
- Carbohydrates 3 g
- Sugar 0.5 g
- Protein 16 g
- Cholesterol 423 mg

Rosemary Beef Roast

Preparation Time: 10 minutes; Cooking Time: 45 minutes; Serve: 6
Ingredients:
- 2 lbs beef roast
- 1 tbsp olive oil
- 1 tsp rosemary
- 1 tsp thyme
- 1/4 tsp pepper
- 1 tsp salt

Directions:
1. Preheat the air fryer to 360 F.
2. Mix together oil, rosemary, thyme, pepper, and salt and rub over the meat.
3. Place meat in the air fryer and cook for 45 minutes.
4. Serve and enjoy.

Nutritional Value (Amount per Serving):
- Calories 300
- Fat 12 g
- Carbohydrates 0.5 g
- Sugar 0 g
- Protein 46 g
- Cholesterol 123 mg

Air Fried Steak

Preparation Time: 10 minutes; Cooking Time: 10 minutes; Serve: 2
Ingredients:
- 2 sirloin steaks
- 2 tsp olive oil
- 2 tbsp steak seasoning
- Pepper
- Salt

Directions:
1. Preheat the air fryer to 350 F.
2. Coat steak with olive oil and season with steak seasoning, pepper, and salt.
3. Spray air fryer basket with cooking spray and place steak in the air fryer basket.
4. Cook for 10 minutes. Turn halfway through.
5. Slice and serve.

Nutritional Value (Amount per Serving):
- Calories 260
- Fat 13 g
- Carbohydrates 1 g
- Sugar 0 g
- Protein 35 g
- Cholesterol 142 mg

Easy Beef Broccoli

Preparation Time: 10 minutes; Cooking Time: 10 minutes; Serve: 4
Ingredients:
- 1 lb round beef cubes
- 1/2 medium onion, diced

- 1 tbsp Worcestershire sauce
- 1/2 lb broccoli florets, steamed
- 1 tsp olive oil
- 1 tsp onion powder
- 1 tsp garlic powder
- Pepper
- Salt

Directions:
1. Spray air fryer basket with cooking spray.
2. Add all ingredients except broccoli into the large bowl and toss well.
3. Add bowl mixture into the air fryer basket and cook at 360 F for 10 minutes.
4. Serve with broccoli and enjoy.

Nutritional Value (Amount per Serving):
- Calories 230
- Fat 5 g
- Carbohydrates 7 g
- Sugar 3 g
- Protein 36 g
- Cholesterol 125 mg

Meatballs

Preparation Time: 10 minutes; Cooking Time: 20 minutes; Serve: 4
Ingredients:
- 1/2 lb ground beef
- 1/2 lb Italian sausage
- 1/2 cup cheddar cheese, shredded
- 1/3 tsp pepper
- 1/2 tsp garlic powder
- 1 tsp onion powder

Directions:
1. Spray air fryer basket with cooking spray.
2. Add all ingredients into the large bowl and mix until combined.
3. Make small balls from meat mixture and place in the air fryer basket.
4. Cook at 370 F for 15 minutes. Turn to another side and cook for 5 minutes more.
5. Serve and enjoy.

Nutritional Value (Amount per Serving):
- Calories 356
- Fat 25 g
- Carbohydrates 1 g
- Sugar 0.5 g
- Protein 32 g
- Cholesterol 158 mg

Yummy Kabab

Preparation Time: 10 minutes; Cooking Time: 10 minutes; Serve: 4
Ingredients:
- 1 lb ground beef
- 1/4 cup fresh parsley, chopped
- 1 tbsp olive oil
- 2 tbsp kabab spice mix
- 1 tbsp garlic, minced
- 1 tsp salt

Directions:
1. Add all ingredients into the bowl and mix until combined. Place in the fridge for 60 minutes.
2. Divide meat mixture into four sections and wrap around four soaked wooden skewers.
3. Spray air fryer basket with cooking spray.

4. Place kabab into the air fryer and cook at 370 F for 10 minutes.
5. Serve and enjoy.

Nutritional Value (Amount per Serving):
- Calories 246
- Fat 11 g
- Carbohydrates 1 g
- Sugar 0.5 g
- Protein 35 g
- Cholesterol 125 mg

Meatloaf

Preparation Time: 10 minutes; Cooking Time: 15 minutes; Serve: 4
Ingredients:
- 1 lb ground beef
- 1/4 tsp cinnamon
- 1 tbsp ginger, minced
- 1/4 cup fresh cilantro, chopped
- 1 cup onion, diced
- 2 eggs, lightly beaten
- 1 tsp cayenne
- 1 tsp turmeric
- 1 tsp garam masala
- 1 tbsp garlic, minced
- 1 tsp salt

Directions:
1. Add all ingredients into the large bowl and mix until combined.
2. Transfer meat mixture into the silicone meatloaf pan.
3. Place in the air fryer and cook at 360 F for 15 minutes.
4. Slice and serve.

Nutritional Value (Amount per Serving):
- Calories 260
- Fat 10 g
- Carbohydrates 4 g
- Sugar 2 g
- Protein 38 g
- Cholesterol 25 mg

Broccoli Beef

Preparation Time: 10 minutes; Cooking Time: 12 minutes; Serve: 5
Ingredients:
- 1 lb round steak, cut into strips
- 1 lb broccoli florets
- 5 drops liquid stevia
- 1 tsp soy sauce
- 1/3 cup sherry
- 2 tsp sesame oil
- 1/3 cup oyster sauce
- 1 garlic clove, minced
- 1 tbsp ginger, sliced
- 1 tsp arrowroot powder
- 1 tbsp olive oil

Directions:
1. In a small bowl, combine together oyster sauce, stevia, soy sauce, sherry, arrowroot, and sesame oil.
2. Add broccoli and meat in a large bowl.
3. Pour oyster sauce mixture over meat and broccoli and toss well. Place in the fridge for 60 minutes.

4. Add marinated meat broccoli to the air fryer basket. Drizzle with olive oil and sprinkle with ginger and garlic.
5. Cook at 360 F for 12 minutes.
6. Serve and enjoy.

Nutritional Value (Amount per Serving):

- Calories 302
- Fat 20 g
- Carbohydrates 8 g
- Sugar 2 g
- Protein 24 g
- Cholesterol 142 mg

Spiced Steak

Preparation Time: 10 minutes; Cooking Time: 9 minutes; Serve: 3

Ingredients:

- 1 lb rib eye steak
- 1/2 tsp chipotle powder
- 1/4 tsp paprika
- 1/4 tsp onion powder
- 1/2 tsp garlic powder
- 1 tsp chili powder
- 1/4 tsp black pepper
- 1 tsp coffee powder
- 1/8 tsp cocoa powder
- 1/8 tsp coriander powder
- 1 1/2 tsp sea salt

Directions:

1. In a small bowl, mix together all ingredients except steak.
2. Rub spice mixture over the steak and let marinate the steak for 20 minutes.
3. Spray air fryer basket with cooking spray.
4. Preheat the air fryer to 390 F.
5. Place marinated steak in the air fryer and cook for 9 minutes.
6. Serve and enjoy.

Nutritional Value (Amount per Serving):

- Calories 304
- Fat 6 g
- Carbohydrates 1 g
- Sugar 0.5 g
- Protein 54 g
- Cholesterol 152 mg

Meatballs

Preparation Time: 10 minutes; Cooking Time: 8 minutes; Serve: 10

Ingredients:

- 5 oz ground beef
- 1 tbsp fresh oregano, chopped
- 2 oz feta cheese, crumbled
- 2 tbsp almond flour
- 1/4 tsp garlic powder
- 1/4 tsp paprika
- Pepper
- Salt

Directions:

1. Preheat the air fryer to 390 F.
2. Add all ingredients into the bowl and mix until well combined.
3. Make small balls from meat mixture and place into the air fryer basket.
4. Cook for 8 minutes.

5. Serve and enjoy.

Nutritional Value (Amount per Serving):
- Calories 75
- Fat 4 g
- Carbohydrates 2 g
- Sugar 0.6 g
- Protein 7 g
- Cholesterol 65 mg

Meatloaf

Preparation Time: 10 minutes; Cooking Time: 25 minutes; Serve: 4

Ingredients:
- 1 lb ground beef
- 2 oz chorizo sausage, chopped
- 3 tbsp almond flour
- 1 egg, lightly beaten
- 2 mushrooms, sliced
- 1 tbsp thyme, chopped
- 1/2 tsp onion powder
- 1/4 tsp garlic powder
- 1 onion, chopped
- Pepper
- Salt

Directions:
1. Preheat the air fryer to 390 F.
2. Add all ingredients into the large bowl and mix until well combined.
3. Transfer meat mixture into the silicone meatloaf pan place into the air fryer basket.
4. Cook in for 25 minutes.
5. Serve and enjoy.

Nutritional Value (Amount per Serving):
- Calories 405
- Fat 20 g
- Carbohydrates 8 g
- Sugar 3 g
- Protein 43 g
- Cholesterol 152 mg

Easy Burger Patties

Preparation Time: 10 minutes; Cooking Time: 45 minutes; Serve: 4

Ingredients:
- 10 oz ground beef
- 1 tsp dried basil
- 1 tsp mustard
- 1 tsp tomato paste
- 1 oz cheddar cheese
- 1 tsp mixed herbs
- 1 tsp garlic puree
- Pepper
- Salt

Directions:
1. Add all ingredients into the large bowl and mix until combined.
2. Spray air fryer basket with cooking spray.
3. Make patties from meat mixture and place into the air fryer basket.
4. Cook at 390 F for 25 minutes then turn patties to another side and cook at 350 F for 20 minutes more.
5. Serve and enjoy.

Nutritional Value (Amount per Serving):

- Calories 175
- Fat 7 g
- Carbohydrates 1 g

- Sugar 2 g
- Protein 25 g
- Cholesterol 125 mg

Asian Beef

Preparation Time: 10 minutes; Cooking Time: 20 minutes; Serve: 4

Ingredients:

- 1 lb beef tips, sliced
- 1/4 cup green onion, chopped
- 2 tbsp garlic, minced
- 2 tbsp sesame oil
- 1 tbsp fish sauce

- 2 tbsp coconut aminos
- 1 tsp xanthan gum
- 2 red chili peppers, sliced
- 2 tbsp water
- 1 tbsp ginger, sliced

Directions:

1. Spray air fryer basket with cooking spray.
2. Toss beef and xanthan gum together.
3. Add beef into the air fryer basket and cook at 390F for 20 minutes. Toss halfway through.
4. Meanwhile, in a saucepan add remaining ingredients except for green onion and heat over low heat.
5. When sauce begins to boiling then remove from heat.
6. Add cooked meat into the saucepan and stir to coat. Let sit in for 5 minutes.
7. Garnish with green onion and serve.

Nutritional Value (Amount per Serving):

- Calories 295
- Fat 15 g
- Carbohydrates 6 g

- Sugar 0.4 g
- Protein 35 g
- Cholesterol 42 mg

Chapter 6: Seafood & Fish Recipes

Delicious Crab Cakes

Preparation Time: 10 minutes; Cooking Time: 10 minutes; Serve: 4
Ingredients:
- 8 oz crab meat
- 2 tbsp butter, melted
- 2 tsp Dijon mustard
- 1 tbsp mayonnaise
- 1 egg, lightly beaten
- 1/2 tsp old bay seasoning
- 1 green onion, sliced
- 2 tbsp parsley, chopped
- 1/4 cup almond flour
- 1/4 tsp pepper
- 1/2 tsp salt

Directions:
1. Add all ingredients except butter in a mixing bowl and mix until well combined.
2. Make four equal shapes of patties from mixture and place on parchment lined plate.
3. Place plate in the fridge for 30 minutes.
4. Spray air fryer basket with cooking spray.
5. Brush melted butter on both sides of crab patties.
6. Place crab patties in air fryer basket and cook for 10 minutes at 350 F.
7. Turn patties halfway through.
8. Serve and enjoy.

Nutritional Value (Amount per Serving):
- Calories 136
- Fat 12.6 g
- Carbohydrates 4.1 g
- Sugar 0.5 g
- Protein 10.3 g
- Cholesterol 88 mg

Tuna Patties

Preparation Time: 10 minutes; Cooking Time: 10 minutes; Serve: 2
Ingredients:
- 2 cans tuna
- 1/2 lemon juice
- 1/2 tsp onion powder
- 1 tsp garlic powder
- 1/2 tsp dried dill
- 1 1/2 tbsp mayonnaise
- 1 1/2 tbsp almond flour
- 1/4 tsp pepper
- 1/4 tsp salt

Directions:
1. Preheat the air fryer to 400 F.
2. Add all ingredients in a mixing bowl and mix until well combined.
3. Spray air fryer basket with cooking spray.
4. Make four patties from mixture and place in the air fryer basket.
5. Cook patties for 10 minutes at 400 F if you want crispier patties then cook for 3 minutes more.
6. Serve and enjoy.

Nutritional Value (Amount per Serving):
- Calories 414
- Fat 20.6 g
- Carbohydrates 5.6 g
- Sugar 1.3 g
- Protein 48.8 g
- Cholesterol 58 mg

Crispy Fish Sticks

Preparation Time: 10 minutes; Cooking Time: 10 minutes; Serve: 4
Ingredients:
- 1 lb white fish, cut into pieces
- 3/4 tsp Cajun seasoning
- 1 1/2 cups pork rind, crushed
- 2 tbsp water
- 2 tbsp Dijon mustard
- 1/4 cup mayonnaise
- Pepper
- Salt

Directions:
1. Spray air fryer basket with cooking spray.
2. In a small bowl, whisk together mayonnaise, water, and mustard.
3. In a shallow bowl, mix together pork rind, pepper, Cajun seasoning, and salt.
4. Dip fish pieces in mayo mixture and coat with pork rind mixture and place in the air fryer basket.
5. Cook at 400 F for 5 minutes. Turn fish sticks to another side and cook for 5 minutes more.
6. Serve and enjoy.

Nutritional Value (Amount per Serving):
- Calories 397
- Fat 36.4 g
- Carbohydrates 4 g
- Sugar 1 g
- Protein 14.7 g
- Cholesterol 4 mg

Flavorful Parmesan Shrimp

Preparation Time: 10 minutes; Cooking Time: 10 minutes; Serve: 6
Ingredients:
- 2 lbs cooked shrimp, peeled and deveined
- 2 tbsp olive oil
- 1/2 tsp onion powder
- 1 tsp basil
- 1/2 tsp oregano
- 2/3 cup parmesan cheese, grated
- 3 garlic cloves, minced
- 1/4 tsp pepper

Directions:
1. In a large mixing bowl, combine together garlic, oil, onion powder, oregano, pepper, and cheese.
2. Add shrimp in a bowl and toss until well coated.
3. Spray air fryer basket with cooking spray.
4. Add shrimp into the air fryer basket and cook at 350 F for 8-10 minutes.
5. Serve and enjoy.

Nutritional Value (Amount per Serving):

- Calories 233
- Fat 7.9 g
- Carbohydrates 3.2 g

- Sugar 0.1 g
- Protein 35.6 g
- Cholesterol 32 mg

Simple Air Fryer Salmon

Preparation Time: 5 minutes; Cooking Time: 10 minutes; Serve: 2
Ingredients:

- 2 salmon fillets, skinless and boneless
- 1 tsp olive oil

- Pepper
- Salt

Directions:

1. Coat salmon fillets with olive oil and season with pepper and salt.
2. Place salmon fillets in air fryer basket and cook at 360 F for 8-10 minutes.
3. Serve and enjoy.

Nutritional Value (Amount per Serving):

- Calories 256
- Fat 13.3 g
- Carbohydrates 0 g

- Sugar 0 g
- Protein 34.5 g
- Cholesterol 78 mg

Delicious White Fish

Preparation Time: 10 minutes; Cooking Time: 10 minutes; Serve: 2
Ingredients:

- 12 oz white fish fillets
- 1/2 tsp onion powder
- 1/2 tsp lemon pepper seasoning
- 1/2 tsp garlic powder

- 1 tbsp olive oil
- Pepper
- Salt

Directions:

1. Spray air fryer basket with cooking spray.
2. Preheat the air fryer to 360 F.
3. Coat fish fillets with olive oil and season with onion powder, lemon pepper seasoning, garlic powder, pepper, and salt.
4. Place fish fillets in air fryer basket and cook for 10-12 minutes.
5. Serve and enjoy.

Nutritional Value (Amount per Serving):

- Calories 358
- Fat 19.8 g
- Carbohydrates 1.3 g

- Sugar 0.4 g
- Protein 41.9 g
- Cholesterol 131 mg

Shrimp with Veggie

Preparation Time: 10 minutes; Cooking Time: 20 minutes; Serve: 4
Ingredients:

- 50 small shrimp
- 1 tbsp Cajun seasoning

- 1 bag of frozen mix vegetables
- 1 tbsp olive oil

Directions:
1. Line air fryer basket with aluminum foil.
2. Add all ingredients into the large mixing bowl and toss well.
3. Transfer shrimp and vegetable mixture into the air fryer basket and cook at 350 F for 10 minutes.
4. Toss well and cook for 10 minutes more.
5. Serve and enjoy.

Nutritional Value (Amount per Serving):
- Calories 101
- Fat 4 g
- Carbohydrates 14 g
- Sugar 1 g
- Protein 2 g
- Cholesterol 3 mg

Salmon Patties

Preparation Time: 10 minutes; Cooking Time: 7 minutes; Serve: 2
Ingredients:
- 8 oz salmon fillet, minced
- 1 lemon, sliced
- 1/2 tsp garlic powder
- 1 egg, lightly beaten
- 1/8 tsp salt

Directions:
1. Add all ingredients except lemon slices into the bowl and mix until well combined.
2. Spray air fryer basket with cooking spray.
3. Place lemon slice into the air fryer basket.
4. Make the equal shape of patties from salmon mixture and place on top of lemon slices into the air fryer basket.
5. Cook at 390 F for 7 minutes.
6. Serve and enjoy.

Nutritional Value (Amount per Serving):
- Calories 184
- Fat 9.2 g
- Carbohydrates 1 g
- Sugar 0.4 g
- Protein 24.9 g
- Cholesterol 132 mg

Perfect Salmon Fillets

Preparation Time: 10 minutes; Cooking Time: 15 minutes; Serve: 2
Ingredients:
- 2 salmon fillets
- 1/2 tsp garlic powder
- 1/4 cup plain yogurt
- 1 tsp fresh lemon juice
- 1 tbsp fresh dill, chopped
- 1 lemon, sliced
- Pepper
- Salt

Directions:
1. Place lemon slices into the air fryer basket.
2. Season salmon with pepper and salt and place on top of lemon slices into the air fryer basket.

3. Cook salmon at 330 F for 15 minutes.
4. Meanwhile, in a bowl, mix together yogurt, garlic powder, lemon juice, dill, pepper, and salt.
5. Place salmon on serving plate and top with yogurt mixture.
6. Serve and enjoy.

Nutritional Value (Amount per Serving):
- Calories 195
- Fat 7 g
- Carbohydrates 6 g
- Sugar 2 g
- Protein 24 g
- Cholesterol 65 mg

Nutritious Salmon

Preparation Time: 10 minutes; Cooking Time: 10 minutes; Serve: 2
Ingredients:
- 2 salmon fillets
- 1 tbsp olive oil
- 1/4 tsp ground cardamom
- 1/2 tsp paprika
- Salt

Directions:
1. Preheat the air fryer to 350 F.
2. Coat salmon fillets with olive oil and season with paprika, cardamom, and salt and place into the air fryer basket.
3. Cook salmon for 10-12 minutes. Turn halfway through.
4. Serve and enjoy.

Nutritional Value (Amount per Serving):
- Calories 160
- Fat 1 g
- Carbohydrates 1 g
- Sugar 0.5 g
- Protein 22 g
- Cholesterol 60 mg

Shrimp Scampi

Preparation Time: 10 minutes; Cooking Time: 10 minutes; Serve: 4
Ingredients:
- 1 lb shrimp, peeled and deveined
- 10 garlic cloves, peeled
- 2 tbsp olive oil
- 1 fresh lemon, cut into wedges
- 1/4 cup parmesan cheese, grated
- 2 tbsp butter, melted

Directions:
1. Preheat the air fryer to 370 F.
2. Mix together shrimp, lemon wedges, olive oil, and garlic cloves in a bowl.
3. Pour shrimp mixture into the air fryer pan and place into the air fryer and cook for 10 minutes.
4. Drizzle with melted butter and sprinkle with parmesan cheese.
5. Serve and enjoy.

Nutritional Value (Amount per Serving):
- Calories 295
- Fat 17 g

- Carbohydrates 4 g
- Sugar 0.1 g
- Protein 29 g
- Cholesterol 260 mg

Lemon Chili Salmon

Preparation Time: 10 minutes; Cooking Time: 17 minutes; Serve: 4
Ingredients:

- 2 lbs salmon fillet, skinless and boneless
- 2 lemon juice
- 1 orange juice
- 1 tbsp olive oil
- 1 bunch fresh dill
- 1 chili, sliced
- Pepper
- Salt

Directions:

1. Preheat the air fryer to 325 F.
2. Place salmon fillets in air fryer baking pan and drizzle with olive oil, lemon juice, and orange juice.
3. Sprinkle chili slices over salmon and season with pepper and salt.
4. Place pan in the air fryer and cook for 15-17 minutes.
5. Garnish with dill and serve.

Nutritional Value (Amount per Serving):

- Calories 339
- Fat 17.5 g
- Carbohydrates 2 g
- Sugar 2 g
- Protein 44 g
- Cholesterol 100 mg

Pesto Salmon

Preparation Time: 10 minutes; Cooking Time: 16 minutes; Serve: 4
Ingredients:

- 25 oz salmon fillet
- 1 tbsp green pesto
- 1 cup mayonnaise
- 1/2 oz olive oil
- 1 lb fresh spinach
- 2 oz parmesan cheese, grated
- Pepper
- Salt

Directions:

1. Preheat the air fryer to 370 F.
2. Spray air fryer basket with cooking spray.
3. Season salmon fillet with pepper and salt and place into the air fryer basket.
4. In a bowl, mix together mayonnaise, parmesan cheese, and pesto and spread over the salmon fillet.
5. Cook salmon for 14-16 minutes.
6. Meanwhile, in a pan sauté spinach with olive oil until spinach is wilted, about 2-3 minutes. Season with pepper and salt.
7. Transfer spinach in serving plate and top with cooked salmon.
8. Serve and enjoy.

Nutritional Value (Amount per Serving):

- Calories 545
- Fat 39.6 g
- Carbohydrates 9.5 g
- Sugar 3.1 g
- Protein 43 g
- Cholesterol 110 mg

Parmesan Walnut Salmon

Preparation Time: 10 minutes; Cooking Time: 12 minutes; Serve: 4
Ingredients:

- 4 salmon fillets
- 1/4 cup parmesan cheese, grated
- 1/2 cup walnuts
- 1 tsp olive oil
- 1 tbsp lemon rind

Directions:

1. Preheat the air fryer to 370 F.
2. Spray an air fryer baking dish with cooking spray.
3. Place salmon on a baking dish.
4. Add walnuts into the food processor and process until finely ground.
5. Mix ground walnuts with parmesan cheese, oil, and lemon rind. Stir well.
6. Spoon walnut mixture over the salmon and press gently.
7. Place in the air fryer and cook for 12 minutes.
8. Serve and enjoy.

Nutritional Value (Amount per Serving):

- Calories 420
- Fat 27.4 g
- Carbohydrates 2 g
- Sugar 0.3 g
- Protein 46.3 g
- Cholesterol 98 mg

Pesto Salmon

Preparation Time: 10 minutes; Cooking Time: 16 minutes; Serve: 2
Ingredients:

- 2 salmon fillets
- 1/4 cup parmesan cheese, grated
- For pesto:
- 1/4 cup pine nuts
- 1/4 cup olive oil
- 1 1/2 cups fresh basil leaves
- 2 garlic cloves, peeled and chopped
- 1/4 cup parmesan cheese, grated
- 1/2 tsp pepper
- 1/2 tsp salt

Directions:

1. Add all pesto ingredients to the blender and blend until smooth.
2. Preheat the air fryer to 370 F.
3. Spray air fryer basket with cooking spray.
4. Place salmon fillet into the air fryer basket and spread 2 tablespoons of the pesto on each salmon fillet.
5. Sprinkle grated cheese on top of the pesto.
6. Cook salmon for 16 minutes.
7. Serve and enjoy.

Nutritional Value (Amount per Serving):

- Calories 725
- Fat 57 g
- Carbohydrates 4 g

- Sugar 0.7 g
- Protein 49 g
- Cholesterol 108 mg

Lemon Shrimp

Preparation Time: 10 minutes; Cooking Time: 8 minutes; Serve: 2

Ingredients:

- 12 oz shrimp, peeled and deveined
- 1 lemon sliced
- 1/4 tsp garlic powder
- 1/4 tsp paprika

- 1 tsp lemon pepper
- 1 lemon juice
- 1 tbsp olive oil

Directions:

1. In a bowl, mix together oil, lemon juice, garlic powder, paprika, and lemon pepper.
2. Add shrimp to the bowl and toss well to coat.
3. Spray air fryer basket with cooking spray.
4. Transfer shrimp into the air fryer basket and cook at 400 F for 8 minutes.
5. Garnish with lemon slices and serve.

Nutritional Value (Amount per Serving):

- Calories 381
- Fat 17.1 g
- Carbohydrates 4.1 g

- Sugar 0.6 g
- Protein 50.6 g
- Cho10sterol 358 mg

Cajun Shrimp

Preparation Time: 10 minutes; Cooking Time: 8 minutes; Serve: 4

Ingredients:

- 1 lb shrimp, peeled and deveined
- 1 lime, cut into wedges
- 1/2 tbsp chipotle chili in adobo, minced

- 1 tbsp Cajun seasoning
- 2 tbsp olive oil
- Pepper
- Salt

Directions:

1. Add all ingredients into the large bowl and toss well to coat. Place in the fridge for 1 hour.
2. Spray air fryer basket with cooking spray.
3. Add marinated shrimp into the air fryer basket and cook at 400 F for 8 minutes.
4. Serve and enjoy.

Nutritional Value (Amount per Serving):

- Calories 201
- Fat 9.1 g
- Carbohydrates 3.6 g

- Sugar 0.3 g
- Protein 26.1 g
- Cho10sterol 239 mg

Miso Fish

Preparation Time: 10 minutes; Cooking Time: 10 minutes; Serve: 2

Ingredients:

- 2 cod fish fillets
- 1 tbsp garlic, chopped
- 2 tsp swerve
- 2 tbsp miso

Directions:

1. Add all ingredients to the zip-lock bag. Shake well place in the refrigerator for overnight.
2. Place marinated fish fillets into the air fryer basket and cook at 350 F for 10 minutes.
3. Serve and enjoy.

Nutritional Value (Amount per Serving):

- Calories 229
- Fat 2.6 g
- Carbohydrates 10.9 g
- Sugar 6.1 g
- Protein 43.4 g
- Cholesterol 99 mg

Tilapia Fish Fillets

Preparation Time: 10 minutes; Cooking Time: 7 minutes; Serve: 2

Ingredients:

- 2 tilapia fillets
- 1 tsp old bay seasoning
- 1/2 tsp butter
- 1/4 tsp lemon pepper
- Pepper
- Salt

Directions:

1. Spray air fryer basket with cooking spray.
2. Place fish fillets into the air fryer basket and season with lemon pepper, old bay seasoning, pepper, and salt.
3. Spray fish fillets with cooking spray and cook at 400 F for 7 minutes.
4. Serve and enjoy.

Nutritional Value (Amount per Serving):

- Calories 80
- Fat 2 g
- Carbohydrates 0.2 g
- Sugar 0 g
- Protein 15 g
- Cholesterol 45 mg

Garlic Mayo Shrimp

Preparation Time: 10 minutes; Cooking Time: 8 minutes; Serve: 2

Ingredients:

- 1/2 lb shrimp, peeled
- 1/2 tbsp ketchup
- 1 1/2 tbsp mayonnaise
- 1/4 tsp paprika
- 1/2 tsp sriracha
- 1/2 tbsp garlic, minced
- 1/4 tsp salt

Directions:

1. In a bowl, mix together mayonnaise, paprika, sriracha, garlic, ketchup, and salt.
2. Add shrimp into the bowl and coat well.
3. Spray air fryer basket with cooking spray.
4. Transfer shrimp into the air fryer basket and cook at 325 F for 8 minutes. Shake halfway through.

5. Serve and enjoy.

Nutritional Value (Amount per Serving):
- Calories 185
- Fat 5.7 g
- Carbohydrates 6 g
- Sugar 1.6 g
- Protein 25 g
- Cholesterol 240 mg

Creamy Crab Dip

Preparation Time: 10 minutes; Cooking Time: 7 minutes; Serve: 2
Ingredients:
- 1/2 cup crabmeat, cooked
- 1/2 tsp pepper
- 1 tbsp hot sauce
- 1/4 cup scallions
- 1 cup cheese, grated
- 1 tbsp mayonnaise
- 1 tbsp parsley, chopped
- 1 tbsp lemon juice
- 1/4 tsp salt

Directions:
1. In an air fryer baking dish, mix together crabmeat, hot sauce, scallions, cheese, mayonnaise, pepper, and salt.
2. Place dish into the air fryer basket and cook at 400 F for 7 minutes.
3. Add parsley and lemon juice. Stir well.
4. Serve and enjoy.

Nutritional Value (Amount per Serving):
- Calories 295
- Fat 21 g
- Carbohydrates 4 g
- Sugar 1.3 g
- Protein 20 g
- Cholesterol 90 mg

Fish Packets

Preparation Time: 10 minutes; Cooking Time: 15 minutes; Serve: 2
Ingredients:
- 2 cod fish fillets
- 1/2 tsp dried tarragon
- 1/2 cup bell peppers, sliced
- 1/4 cup celery, cut into julienne
- 1/2 cup carrots, cut into julienne
- 1 tbsp olive oil
- 1 tbsp lemon juice
- 2 pats butter, melted
- Pepper
- Salt

Directions:
1. In a bowl, mix together butter, lemon juice, tarragon, and salt. Add vegetables and toss well. Set aside.
2. Take two parchments paper pieces to fold vegetables and fish.
3. Spray fish with cooking spray and season with pepper and salt.
4. Place a fish fillet on each parchment paper piece and top with vegetables.
5. Fold parchment paper around the fish and vegetables.
6. Place veggie fish packets into the air fryer basket and cook at 350 F for 15 minutes.
7. Serve and enjoy.

Nutritional Value (Amount per Serving):
- Calories 281
- Fat 8 g
- Carbohydrates 6 g
- Sugar 3 g
- Protein 41 g
- Cholesterol 100 mg

Air Fried Scallops

Preparation Time: 10 minutes; Cooking Time: 10 minutes; Serve: 2
Ingredients:
- 8 sea scallops
- 1 tbsp tomato paste
- 3/4 cup heavy whipping cream
- 12 oz frozen spinach, thawed and drained
- 1 tsp garlic, minced
- 1 tbsp fresh basil, chopped
- 1/2 tsp pepper
- 1/2 tsp salt

Directions:
1. Spray air fryer baking pan with cooking spray.
2. Add spinach in the pan.
3. Spray scallops with cooking spray and season with pepper and salt.
4. Place scallops on top of spinach.
5. In a small bowl, mix together garlic, basil, tomato paste, whipping cream, pepper, and salt and pour over scallops and spinach.
6. Place pan into the air fryer and cook at 350 F for 10 minutes.
7. Serve and enjoy.

Nutritional Value (Amount per Serving):
- Calories 311
- Fat 18.3 g
- Carbohydrates 12 g
- Sugar 1 g
- Protein 26 g
- Cholesterol 100 mg

Spicy Prawns

Preparation Time: 10 minutes; Cooking Time: 8 minutes; Serve: 2
Ingredients:
- 6 prawns
- 1/4 tsp pepper
- 1/2 tsp chili powder
- 1 tsp chili flakes
- 1/4 tsp salt

Directions:
1. Preheat the air fryer to 350 F.
2. In a bowl, mix together spices add prawns.
3. Spray air fryer basket with cooking spray.
4. Transfer prawns into the air fryer basket and cook for 8 minutes.
5. Serve and enjoy.

Nutritional Value (Amount per Serving):
- Calories 80
- Fat 1.2 g
- Carbohydrates 1 g
- Sugar 0.1 g

- Protein 15.2 g
- Cholesterol 140 mg

Simple Salmon Fillets

Preparation Time: 10 minutes; Cooking Time: 7 minutes; Serve: 2

Ingredients:
- 2 salmon fillets
- 2 tsp olive oil
- 2 tsp paprika
- Pepper
- Salt

Directions:
1. Rub salmon fillet with oil, paprika, pepper, and salt.
2. Place salmon fillets in the air fryer basket and cook at 390 F for 7 minutes.
3. Serve and enjoy.

Nutritional Value (Amount per Serving):
- Calories 280
- Fat 15 g
- Carbohydrates 1.2 g
- Sugar 0.2 g
- Protein 35 g
- Cholesterol 75 mg

Air Fried King Prawns

Preparation Time: 10 minutes; Cooking Time: 6 minutes; Serve: 4

Ingredients:
- 12 king prawns
- 1 tbsp vinegar
- 1 tbsp ketchup
- 3 tbsp mayonnaise
- 1/2 tsp pepper
- 1 tsp chili powder
- 1 tsp red chili flakes
- 1/2 tsp sea salt

Directions:
1. Preheat the air fryer to 350 F.
2. Spray air fryer basket with cooking spray.
3. Add prawns, chili flakes, chili powder, pepper, and salt to the bowl and toss well.
4. Transfer shrimp to the air fryer basket and cook for 6 minutes.
5. In a small bowl, mix together mayonnaise, ketchup, and vinegar.
6. Serve with mayo mixture and enjoy.

Nutritional Value (Amount per Serving):
- Calories 130
- Fat 5 g
- Carbohydrates 5 g
- Sugar 1 g
- Protein 15 g
- Cholesterol 0 mg

Spicy Shrimp

Preparation Time: 10 minutes; Cooking Time: 6 minutes; Serve: 2

Ingredients:
- 1/2 lb shrimp, peeled and deveined
- 1/2 tsp old bay seasoning
- 1 tsp cayenne pepper
- 1 tbsp olive oil
- 1/4 tsp paprika
- 1/8 tsp salt

Directions:

1. Preheat the air fryer to 390 F.
2. Add all ingredients into the bowl and toss well.
3. Transfer shrimp into the air fryer basket and cook for 6 minutes.
4. Serve and enjoy.

Nutritional Value (Amount per Serving):

- Calories 195
- Fat 9 g
- Carbohydrates 2 g
- Sugar 0.1 g
- Protein 26 g
- Cholesterol 0 mg

Lemon Butter Salmon

Preparation Time: 10 minutes; Cooking Time: 11 minutes; Serve: 2

Ingredients:

- 2 salmon fillets
- 1/2 tsp olive oil
- 2 tsp garlic, minced
- 2 tbsp butter
- 2 tbsp fresh lemon juice
- 1/4 cup white wine
- Pepper
- Salt

Directions:

1. Preheat the air fryer to 350 F.
2. Spray air fryer basket with cooking spray.
3. Season salmon with pepper and salt and place into the air fryer basket and cook for 6 minutes.
4. Meanwhile, in a saucepan, add remaining ingredients and heat over low heat for 4-5 minutes.
5. Place cooked salmon on serving dish then pour prepared sauce over salmon.
6. Serve and enjoy.

Nutritional Value (Amount per Serving):

- Calories 379
- Fat 23 g
- Carbohydrates 2 g
- Sugar 0.5 g
- Protein 35 g
- Cholesterol 0 mg

Cheese Crust Salmon

Preparation Time: 10 minutes; Cooking Time: 10 minutes; Serve: 5

Ingredients:

- 5 salmon fillets
- 1 tsp Italian seasoning
- 2 garlic cloves, minced
- 1 cup parmesan cheese, shredded
- 1 tsp paprika
- 1 tbsp olive oil
- 1/4 cup fresh parsley, chopped
- Pepper
- Salt

Directions:

1. Preheat the air fryer to 425 F.
2. Add salmon, seasoning, and olive oil to the bowl and mix well.

3. Place salmon fillet into the air fryer basket.
4. In another bowl, mix together cheese, garlic, and parsley.
5. Sprinkle cheese mixture on top of salmon and cook for 10 minutes.
6. Serve and enjoy.

Nutritional Value (Amount per Serving):
- Calories 333
- Fat 18 g
- Carbohydrates 2 g
- Sugar 0.4 g
- Protein 40 g
- Cholesterol 0 mg

Lemon Crab Patties

Preparation Time: 10 minutes; Cooking Time: 10 minutes; Serve: 4
Ingredients:
- 1 egg
- 12 oz crabmeat
- 2 green onion, chopped
- 1/4 cup mayonnaise
- 1 cup almond flour
- 1 tsp old bay seasoning
- 1 tsp red pepper flakes
- 1 tbsp fresh lemon juice

Directions:
1. Preheat the air fryer to 400 F.
2. Spray air fryer basket with cooking spray.
3. Add 1/2 almond flour into the mixing bowl.
4. Add remaining ingredients and mix until well combined.
5. Make patties from mixture and coat with remaining almond flour and place into the air fryer basket.
6. Cook patties for 5 minutes then turn to another side and cook for 5 minutes more.
7. Serve and enjoy.

Nutritional Value (Amount per Serving):
- Calories 184
- Fat 11 g
- Carbohydrates 5 g
- Sugar 1 g
- Protein 12 g
- Cholesterol 0 mg

Air Fried Catfish

Preparation Time: 10 minutes; Cooking Time: 20 minutes; Serve: 4
Ingredients:
- 4 catfish fillets
- 1 tbsp olive oil
- 1/4 cup fish seasoning
- 1 tbsp fresh parsley, chopped

Directions:
1. Preheat the air fryer to 400 F.
2. Spray air fryer basket with cooking spray.
3. Seasoned fish with seasoning and place into the air fryer basket.
4. Drizzle fish fillets with oil and cook for 10 minutes.
5. Turn fish to another side and cook for 10 minutes more.
6. Garnish with parsley and serve.

Nutritional Value (Amount per Serving):
- Calories 245
- Fat 15 g
- Carbohydrates 0.1 g
- Sugar 0 g
- Protein 24 g
- Cholesterol 0 mg

Easy Bacon Shrimp

Preparation Time: 10 minutes; Cooking Time: 7 minutes; Serve: 4

Ingredients:
- 16 shrimp, deveined
- 1/4 tsp pepper
- 16 bacon slices

Directions:
1. Preheat the air fryer to 390 F.
2. Spray air fryer basket with cooking spray.
3. Wrap shrimp with bacon slice and place into the air fryer basket and cook for 5 minutes.
4. Turn shrimp to another side and cook for 2 minutes more. Season shrimp with pepper.
5. Serve and enjoy.

Nutritional Value (Amount per Serving):
- Calories 515
- Fat 33 g
- Carbohydrates 2 g
- Sugar 0 g
- Protein 45 g
- Cholesterol 0 mg

Almond Coconut Shrimp

Preparation Time: 10 minutes; Cooking Time: 5 minutes; Serve: 4

Ingredients:
- 16 oz shrimp, peeled
- 1/2 cup almond flour
- 2 egg whites
- 1/4 tsp cayenne pepper
- 1/2 cup unsweetened shredded coconut
- 1/2 tsp salt

Directions:
1. Preheat the air fryer to 400 F.
2. Spray air fryer basket with cooking spray.
3. Whisk egg whites in a shallow dish.
4. In a bowl, mix together the shredded coconut, almond flour, and cayenne pepper.
5. Dip shrimp into the egg mixture then coat with coconut mixture.
6. Place coated shrimp into the air fryer basket and cook for 5 minutes.
7. Serve and enjoy.

Nutritional Value (Amount per Serving):
- Calories 200
- Fat 7 g
- Carbohydrates 4 g
- Sugar 1 g
- Protein 28 g
- Cholesterol 0 mg

Basil Parmesan Shrimp

Preparation Time: 10 minutes; Cooking Time: 10 minutes; Serve: 6

Ingredients:

- 2 lbs shrimp, peeled and deveined
- 1 tsp basil
- 1/2 tsp oregano
- 1 tsp pepper
- 2/3 cup parmesan cheese, grated
- 2 garlic cloves, minced
- 2 tbsp olive oil
- 1 tsp onion powder

Directions:

1. Add all ingredients into the bowl and toss well.
2. Spray air fryer basket with cooking spray.
3. Transfer shrimp into the air fryer basket and cook at 350 F for 10 minutes.
4. Serve and enjoy.

Nutritional Value (Amount per Serving):

- Calories 290
- Fat 10 g
- Carbohydrates 3 g
- Sugar 0.3 g
- Protein 40 g
- Cholesterol 0 mg

Cajun Cheese Shrimp

Preparation Time: 10 minutes; Cooking Time: 5 minutes; Serve: 4

Ingredients:

- 1 lb shrimp
- 1/2 cup almond flour
- 1 tsp olive oil
- 1 tbsp Cajun seasoning
- 2 tbsp parmesan cheese
- 2 garlic cloves, minced

Directions:

1. Add all ingredients into the bowl and toss well.
2. Spray air fryer basket with cooking spray.
3. Transfer shrimp mixture into the air fryer basket and cook at 390 F for 5 minutes. Shake halfway through.
4. Serve and enjoy.

Nutritional Value (Amount per Serving):

- Calories 175
- Fat 5 g
- Carbohydrates 3 g
- Sugar 0.2 g
- Protein 27 g
- Cholesterol 0 mg

Creamy Shrimp

Preparation Time: 10 minutes; Cooking Time: 8 minutes; Serve: 4

Ingredients:

- 1 lb shrimp, peeled
- 1 tbsp garlic, minced
- 1 tbsp tomato ketchup
- 3 tbsp mayonnaise
- 1/2 tsp paprika
- 1 tsp sriracha
- 1/2 tsp salt

Directions:

1. In a bowl, mix together mayonnaise, paprika, sriracha, garlic, ketchup, and salt. Add shrimp and stir well.
2. Add shrimp mixture into the air fryer baking dish and place in the air fryer.
3. Cook at 325 F for 8 minutes. Stir halfway through.
4. Serve and enjoy.

Nutritional Value (Amount per Serving):

- Calories 185
- Fat 5 g
- Carbohydrates 6 g
- Sugar 1 g
- Protein 25 g
- Cholesterol 0 mg

Cheesy Crab Dip

Preparation Time: 10 minutes; Cooking Time: 7 minutes; Serve: 4

Ingredients:

- 1 cup crabmeat, cooked
- 2 tbsp fresh parsley, chopped
- 2 tbsp fresh lemon juice
- 2 cups Jalapeno jack cheese, grated
- 2 tbsp hot sauce
- 1/2 cup green onions, sliced
- 1/4 cup mayonnaise
- 1 tsp pepper
- 1/2 tsp salt

Directions:

1. Add all ingredients except parsley and lemon juice in air fryer baking dish and stir well.
2. Place dish in the air fryer basket and cook at 400 F for 7 minutes.
3. Add parsley and lemon juice. Mix well.
4. Serve and enjoy.

Nutritional Value (Amount per Serving):

- Calories 305
- Fat 22 g
- Carbohydrates 5 g
- Sugar 1 g
- Protein 20 g
- Cholesterol 0 mg

Chili Garlic Shrimp

Preparation Time: 10 minutes; Cooking Time: 7 minutes; Serve: 4

Ingredients:

- 1 lb shrimp, peeled and deveined
- 1 tbsp olive oil
- 1 lemon, sliced
- 1 red chili pepper, sliced
- 1/2 tsp garlic powder
- Pepper
- Salt

Directions:

1. Preheat the air fryer to 400 F.
2. Spray air fryer basket with cooking spray.
3. Add all ingredients into the bowl and toss well.
4. Add shrimp into the air fryer basket and cook for 5 minutes. Shake basket twice.
5. Serve and enjoy.

Nutritional Value (Amount per Serving):
- Calories 170
- Fat 5 g
- Carbohydrates 3 g
- Sugar 0.5 g
- Protein 25 g
- Cholesterol 0 mg

Simple Salmon Patties

Preparation Time: 10 minutes; Cooking Time: 10 minutes; Serve: 2
Ingredients:
- 14 oz salmon
- 1/2 onion, diced
- 1 egg, lightly beaten
- 1 tsp dill
- 1/2 cup almond flour

Directions:
1. Spray air fryer basket with cooking spray.
2. Add all ingredients into the bowl and mix until well combined.
3. Spray air fryer basket with cooking spray.
4. Make patties from salmon mixture and place into the air fryer basket.
5. Cook at 370 F for 5 minutes.
6. Turn patties to another side and cook for 5 minutes more.
7. Serve and enjoy.

Nutritional Value (Amount per Serving):
- Calories 350
- Fat 15 g
- Carbohydrates 3 g
- Sugar 1 g
- Protein 44 g
- Cholesterol 0 mg

Thai Shrimp

Preparation Time: 10 minutes; Cooking Time: 10 minutes; Serve: 4
Ingredients:
- 1 lb shrimp, peeled and deveined
- 1 tsp sesame seeds, toasted
- 2 garlic cloves, minced
- 2 tbsp soy sauce
- 2 tbsp Thai chili sauce
- 1 tbsp arrowroot powder
- 1 tbsp green onion, sliced
- 1/8 tsp ginger, minced

Directions:
1. Spray air fryer basket with cooking spray.
2. Toss shrimp with arrowroot powder and place into the air fryer basket.
3. Cook shrimp at 350 F for 5 minutes. Shake basket well and cook for 5 minutes more.
4. Meanwhile, in a bowl, mix together soy sauce, ginger, garlic, and chili sauce.
5. Add shrimp to the bowl and toss well.
6. Garnish with green onions and sesame seeds.
7. Serve and enjoy.

Nutritional Value (Amount per Serving):
- Calories 155
- Fat 2 g
- Carbohydrates 6 g
- Sugar 2 g

- Protein 25 g
- Cholesterol 0 mg

Chapter 7: Meatless Meals Recipes

Crispy Pickles

Preparation Time: 10 minutes; Cooking Time: 6 minutes; Serve: 4

Ingredients:

- 16 dill pickles, sliced
- 1 egg, lightly beaten
- 1/2 cup almond flour
- 3 tbsp parmesan cheese, grated
- 1/2 cup pork rind, crushed

Directions:

1. Take three bowls. Mix together pork rinds and cheese in the first bowl.
2. In a second bowl, add the egg.
3. In the last bowl add the almond flour.
4. Coat each pickle slice with almond flour then dip in egg and finally coat with pork and cheese mixture.
5. Spray air fryer basket with cooking spray.
6. Place coated pickles in the air fryer basket.
7. Cook pickles for 6 minutes at 370 F.
8. Serve and enjoy.

Nutritional Value (Amount per Serving):

- Calories 245
- Fat 17 g
- Carbohydrates 4 g
- Sugar 2 g
- Protein 17 g
- Cholesterol 41 mg

Asian Broccoli

Preparation Time: 10 minutes; Cooking Time: 20 minutes; Serve: 4

Ingredients:

- 1 lb broccoli, cut into florets
- 1 tsp rice vinegar
- 2 tsp sriracha
- 2 tbsp soy sauce
- 1 tbsp garlic, minced
- 5 drops liquid stevia
- 1 1/2 tbsp sesame oil
- Salt

Directions:

1. In a bowl, toss together broccoli, garlic, oil, and salt.
2. Spread broccoli in air fryer basket and cook for 15-20 minutes at 400 F.
3. Meanwhile, in a microwave-safe bowl mix together soy sauce, vinegar, liquid stevia, and sriracha and microwave for 10 seconds.
4. Transfer broccoli to a bowl and toss well with soy mixture to coat.
5. Serve and enjoy.

Nutritional Value (Amount per Serving):

- Calories 94
- Fat 5.5 g
- Carbohydrates 9.3 g
- Sugar 2.1 g
- Protein 3.8 g
- Cholesterol 0 mg

Roasted Brussels sprouts

Preparation Time: 10 minutes; Cooking Time: 8 minutes; Serve: 4

Ingredients:

- 1 lb Brussels sprouts, cleaned and trimmed
- 1 tsp garlic powder
- 1 tsp dried parsley
- 2 tsp olive oil
- 1/2 tsp dried thyme
- 1/4 tsp salt

Directions:

1. Add all ingredients into the large bowl and toss well.
2. Pour Brussels sprout mixture into the air fryer basket.
3. Cook Brussels sprouts at 390 F for 8 minutes.
4. Serve and enjoy.

Nutritional Value (Amount per Serving):

- Calories 72
- Fat 2.7 g
- Carbohydrates 10.9 g
- Sugar 2.6 g
- Protein 4 g
- Cholesterol 0 mg

Quick Creamy Spinach

Preparation Time: 10 minutes; Cooking Time: 15 minutes; Serve: 2

Ingredients:

- 10 oz frozen spinach, thawed
- 1/4 cup parmesan cheese, shredded
- 1/2 tsp ground nutmeg
- 1 tsp pepper
- 4 oz cream cheese, diced
- 2 tsp garlic, minced
- 1 small onion, chopped
- 1 tsp salt

Directions:

1. Spray 6-inch pan with cooking spray and set aside.
2. In a bowl, mix together spinach, cream cheese, garlic, onion, nutmeg, pepper, and salt.
3. Pour spinach mixture into the prepared pan.
4. Place dish in air fryer basket and air fry at 350 F for 10 minutes.
5. Open air fryer basket and sprinkle parmesan cheese on top of spinach mixture and air fry at 400 F for 5 minutes more.
6. Serve and enjoy.

Nutritional Value (Amount per Serving):

- Calories 265
- Fat 21.4 g
- Carbohydrates 11.9 g
- Sugar 2.4 g
- Protein 10.2 g
- Cholesterol 65 mg

Perfect Crispy Tofu

Preparation Time: 10 minutes; Cooking Time: 20 minutes; Serve: 4

Ingredients:

- 1 block firm tofu, pressed and cut into 1-inch cubes
- 1 tbsp arrowroot flour
- 2 tsp sesame oil
- 1 tsp vinegar
- 2 tbsp soy sauce

Directions:
1. In a bowl, toss tofu with oil, vinegar, and soy sauce and let sit for 15 minutes.
2. Toss marinated tofu with arrowroot flour.
3. Spray air fryer basket with cooking spray.
4. Add tofu in air fryer basket and cook for 20 minutes at 370 F. Shake basket halfway through.
5. Serve and enjoy.

Nutritional Value (Amount per Serving):
- Calories 42
- Fat 0.5 g
- Carbohydrates 1.3 g
- Sugar 0.3g
- Protein 12.4 g
- Cholesterol 0 mg

Mushroom Bean Casserole

Preparation Time: 10 minutes; Cooking Time: 12 minutes; Serve: 6
Ingredients:
- 2 cups mushrooms, sliced
- 1 tsp onion powder
- 1/2 tsp ground sage
- 1/2 tbsp garlic powder
- 1 fresh lemon juice
- 1 1/2 lbs green beans, trimmed
- 1/4 tsp pepper
- 1/2 tsp salt

Directions:
1. In a large mixing bowl, toss together green beans, onion powder, sage, garlic powder, lemon juice, mushrooms, pepper, and salt.
2. Spray air fryer basket with cooking spray.
3. Transfer green bean mixture into the air fryer basket.
4. Cook for 10-12 minutes at 400 F. Shake after every 3 minutes.
5. Serve and enjoy.

Nutritional Value (Amount per Serving):
- Calories 45
- Fat 0.2 g
- Carbohydrates 9.8 g
- Sugar 2.3g
- Protein 3 g
- Cholesterol 0 mg

Crisp & Tender Brussels sprouts

Preparation Time: 10 minutes; Cooking Time: 10 minutes; Serve: 2
Ingredients:
- 2 cups Brussels sprouts, sliced
- 1 tbsp balsamic vinegar
- 1 tbsp olive oil
- 1/4 tsp sea salt

Directions:
1. Add all ingredients into the large bowl and toss well.
2. Spray air fryer basket with cooking spray.

3. Transfer Brussels sprouts mixture into the air fryer basket.
4. Cook Brussels sprouts at 400 F for 10 minutes. Shake basket halfway through.
5. Serve and enjoy.

Nutritional Value (Amount per Serving):
- Calories 100
- Fat 7.3 g
- Carbohydrates 8.1 g
- Sugar 1.9 g
- Protein 3 g
- Cholesterol 0 mg

Asian Green Beans

Preparation Time: 5 minutes; Cooking Time: 10 minutes; Serve: 2
Ingredients:
- 8 oz green beans, trimmed and cut in half
- 1 tsp sesame oil
- 1 tbsp tamari

Directions:
1. Add all ingredients into the large mixing bowl and toss well.
2. Spray air fryer basket with cooking spray.
3. Transfer green beans in air fryer basket and cook at 400 F for 10 minutes. Toss halfway through.
4. Serve and enjoy.

Nutritional Value (Amount per Serving):
- Calories 58
- Fat 2 g
- Carbohydrates 8 g
- Sugar 3 g
- Protein 3 g
- Cholesterol 0 mg

Roasted Squash

Preparation Time: 10 minutes; Cooking Time: 35 minutes; Serve: 6
Ingredients:
- 4 cups butternut squash, diced
- 1/4 cup dried cranberries
- 3 garlic cloves, minced
- 1 tbsp soy sauce
- 1 tbsp balsamic vinegar
- 1 tbsp olive oil
- 8 oz mushrooms, quartered
- 1 cup green onions, sliced

Directions:
1. In a large mixing bowl, mix together squash, mushrooms, and green onion and set aside.
2. In a small bowl, whisk together oil, garlic, vinegar, and soy sauce.
3. Pour oil mixture over squash and toss to coat.
4. Spray air fryer basket with cooking spray.
5. Add squash mixture into the air fryer basket and cook for 30-35 minutes at 400 F. Shake after every 5 minutes.
6. Toss with cranberries and serve hot.

Nutritional Value (Amount per Serving):
- Calories 82
- Fat 2.6 g
- Carbohydrates 14.5 g
- Sugar 3.3 g

- Protein 2.7 g
- Cholesterol 0 mg

Roasted Eggplant

Preparation Time: 10 minutes; Cooking Time: 12 minutes; Serve: 2

Ingredients:
- 1 eggplant, washed and cubed
- 1/2 tsp garlic powder
- 1/4 tsp marjoram
- 1/4 tsp oregano
- 1 tbsp olive oil

Directions:
1. Spray air fryer basket with cooking spray.
2. Add all ingredients into the mixing bowl and toss well.
3. Transfer eggplant mixture into the air fryer basket and cook at 390 F for 6 minutes.
4. Toss well and cook for 6 minutes more.
5. Serve and enjoy.

Nutritional Value (Amount per Serving):
- Calories 120
- Fat 7.5 g
- Carbohydrates 14.2 g
- Sugar 7.1 g
- Protein 2.4 g
- Cholesterol 0 mg

Curried Eggplant Slices

Preparation Time: 10 minutes; Cooking Time: 10 minutes; Serve: 2

Ingredients:
- 1 large eggplant, cut into 1/2-inch thick slices
- 1 garlic clove, minced
- 1 tbsp olive oil
- 1/2 tsp curry powder
- 1/8 tsp turmeric
- Salt

Directions:
1. Preheat the air fryer to 300 F.
2. Add all ingredients into the large mixing bowl and toss to coat.
3. Transfer eggplant slices into the air fryer basket.
4. Cook eggplant slices for 10 minutes or until lightly brown. Shake basket halfway through.
5. Serve and enjoy.

Nutritional Value (Amount per Serving):
- Calories 122
- Fat 7.5 g
- Carbohydrates 14.4 g
- Sugar 6.9 g
- Protein 2.4 g
- Cholesterol 0 mg

Healthy Green Beans

Preparation Time: 5 minutes; Cooking Time: 6 minutes; Serve: 4

Ingredients:
- 1 lb green beans, trimmed
- Pepper
- Salt

Directions:

1. Spray air fryer basket with cooking spray.
2. Preheat the air fryer to 400 F.
3. Add green beans in air fryer basket and season with pepper and salt.
4. Cook green beans for 6 minutes. Turn halfway through.
5. Serve and enjoy.

Nutritional Value (Amount per Serving):

- Calories 35
- Fat 0.1 g
- Carbohydrates 8.1 g
- Sugar 1.6 g
- Protein 2.1 g
- Cholesterol 0 mg

Healthy Air Fryer Mushrooms

Preparation Time: 10 minutes; Cooking Time: 12 minutes; Serve: 2

Ingredients:

- 8 oz mushrooms, sliced
- 1 tbsp parsley, chopped
- 1 tsp soy sauce
- 1/2 tsp garlic powder
- 1 tbsp olive oil
- Pepper
- Salt

Directions:

1. Add all ingredients into the mixing bowl and toss well.
2. Transfer mushrooms in air fryer basket and cook at 380 F for 10-12 minutes. Shake basket halfway through.
3. Serve and enjoy.

Nutritional Value (Amount per Serving):

- Calories 89
- Fat 7.4 g
- Carbohydrates 4.6 g
- Sugar 2.2 g
- Protein 3.9 g
- Cholesterol 0 mg

Tasty Okra

Preparation Time: 10 minutes; Cooking Time: 12 minutes; Serve: 2

Ingredients:

- 1/2 lb okra, ends trimmed and sliced
- 1 tsp olive oil
- 1/2 tsp mango powder
- 1/2 tsp chili powder
- 1/2 tsp ground coriander
- 1/2 tsp ground cumin
- 1/8 tsp pepper
- 1/4 tsp salt

Directions:

1. Preheat the air fryer to 350 F.
2. Add all ingredients into the large bowl and toss well.
3. Spray air fryer basket with cooking spray.
4. Transfer okra mixture into the air fryer basket and cook for 10 minutes. Shake basket halfway through.
5. Toss okra well and cook for 2 minutes more.

6. Serve and enjoy.

Nutritional Value (Amount per Serving):
- Calories 70
- Fat 2.8 g
- Carbohydrates 9.1 g
- Sugar 1.7 g
- Protein 2.4 g
- Cholesterol 0 mg

Cabbage Wedges

Preparation Time: 10 minutes; Cooking Time: 14 minutes; Serve: 6
Ingredients:
- 1 small cabbage head, cut into wedges
- 3 tbsp olive oil
- 1/4 tsp red chili flakes
- 1/2 tsp fennel seeds
- 1 tsp garlic powder
- 1 tsp onion powder
- Pepper
- Salt

Directions:
1. Spray air fryer basket with cooking spray.
2. In a small bowl, mix together garlic powder, red chili flakes, fennel seeds, onion powder, pepper, and salt.
3. Coat cabbage wedges with oil and rub with garlic powder mixture.
4. Place cabbage wedges into the air fryer basket and cook at 400 F for 8 minutes.
5. Turn cabbage wedges to another side and cook for 6 minutes more.
6. Serve and enjoy.

Nutritional Value (Amount per Serving):
- Calories 101
- Fat 7.2 g
- Carbohydrates 9.5 g
- Sugar 5.1 g
- Protein 2.1 g
- Cholesterol 0 mg

Roasted Broccoli

Preparation Time: 10 minutes; Cooking Time: 7 minutes; Serve: 4
Ingredients:
- 4 cups broccoli florets
- 1/4 cup water
- 1 tbsp olive oil
- 1/4 tsp pepper
- 1/8 tsp kosher salt

Directions:
1. Add broccoli, oil, pepper, and salt in a bowl and toss well.
2. Add 1/4 cup of water into the bottom of air fryer (under the basket).
3. Transfer broccoli into the air fryer basket and cook for 7 minutes at 400 F.
4. Serve and enjoy.

Nutritional Value (Amount per Serving):
- Calories 61
- Fat 3.8 g
- Carbohydrates 6.1 g
- Sugar 1.6 g
- Protein 2.6 g
- Cholesterol 0 mg

Air Fried Onion & Bell Peppers

Preparation Time: 10 minutes; Cooking Time: 25 minutes; Serve: 3
Ingredients:

- 6 bell pepper, sliced
- 1 tbsp Italian seasoning
- 1 tbsp olive oil
- 1 onion, sliced

Directions:

1. Add all ingredients into the large mixing bowl and toss well.
2. Preheat the air fryer to 320 F.
3. Transfer bell pepper and onion mixture into the air fryer basket and cook for 15 minutes.
4. Toss well and cook for 10 minutes more.
5. Serve and enjoy.

Nutritional Value (Amount per Serving):

- Calories 129
- Fat 6.1g
- Carbohydrates 14 g
- Sugar 10 g
- Protein 3 g
- Cholesterol 3 mg

Roasted Peppers

Preparation Time: 5 minutes; Cooking Time: 8 minutes; Serve: 3
Ingredients:

- 3 1/2 cups bell peppers, cut into chunks
- Pepper
- Salt

Directions:

1. Spray air fryer basket with cooking spray.
2. Add bell peppers into the air fryer basket and cook at 360 F for 8 minutes.
3. Season peppers with pepper and salt.
4. Serve and enjoy.

Nutritional Value (Amount per Serving):

- Calories 33
- Fat 0 g
- Carbohydrates 7 g
- Sugar 4 g
- Protein 1 g
- Cholesterol 0 mg

Roasted Cauliflower & Broccoli

Preparation Time: 10 minutes; Cooking Time: 15 minutes; Serve: 6
Ingredients:

- 3 cups cauliflower florets
- 3 cups broccoli florets
- 1/4 tsp paprika
- 1/2 tsp garlic powder
- 2 tbsp olive oil
- 1/8 tsp pepper
- 1/4 tsp sea salt

Directions:

1. Preheat the air fryer to 400 F.
2. Add broccoli in microwave-safe bowl and microwave for 3 minutes. Drain well.

3. Add broccoli in a large mixing bowl. Add remaining ingredients and toss well.
4. Transfer broccoli and cauliflower mixture into the air fryer basket and cook for 12 minutes.
5. Toss halfway through.
6. Serve and enjoy.

Nutritional Value (Amount per Serving):
- Calories 69
- Fat 4.9 g
- Carbohydrates 5.9 g
- Sugar 2 g
- Protein 2.3 g
- Cholesterol 0 mg

Parmesan Broccoli

Preparation Time: 10 minutes; Cooking Time: 5 minutes; Serve: 2

Ingredients:
- 3 cups broccoli florets
- 1/4 cup parmesan cheese, grated
- 2 tbsp olive oil
- 2 garlic cloves, minced

Directions:
1. Preheat the air fryer to 360 F.
2. Add all ingredients into the large bowl and toss well.
3. Transfer broccoli mixture into the air fryer basket and cook for 4-5 minutes.
4. Serve and enjoy.

Nutritional Value (Amount per Serving):
- Calories 182
- Fat 15.2 g
- Carbohydrates 10.2 g
- Sugar 2.4 g
- Protein 5.1 g
- Cholesterol 3 mg

Simple Air Fried Asparagus

Preparation Time: 5 minutes; Cooking Time: 7 minutes; Serve: 2

Ingredients:
- 1 lb asparagus
- 1/4 tsp olive oil
- Pepper
- Salt

Directions:
1. Brush asparagus with olive oil and season with pepper and salt.
2. Place asparagus into the air fryer basket and cook at 400 F for 7 minutes.
3. Shake halfway through.
4. Serve and enjoy.

Nutritional Value (Amount per Serving):
- Calories 51
- Fat 0.9 g
- Carbohydrates 8.8 g
- Sugar 4.3 g
- Protein 5 g
- Cholesterol 0 mg

Gluten-Free Beans

Preparation Time: 5 minutes; Cooking Time: 10 minutes; Serve: 2

Ingredients:

- 8 oz green beans, cut ends and cut beans in half
- 1 tsp sesame oil
- 1 tbsp tamari

Directions:

1. Add all ingredients into the zip-lock bag and shake well.
2. Place green beans into the air fryer basket and cook at 400 F for 10 minutes. Turn halfway through.
3. Serve and enjoy.

Nutritional Value (Amount per Serving):

- Calories 55
- Fat 2 g
- Carbohydrates 8 g
- Sugar 3 g
- Protein 3 g
- Cholesterol 0 mg

Air Fryer Mushrooms

Preparation Time: 5 minutes; Cooking Time: 8 minutes; Serve: 1
Ingredients:

- 12 button mushrooms, cleaned
- 1 tsp olive oil
- 1/4 tsp garlic salt
- Pepper
- Salt

Directions:

1. Add all ingredients into the bowl and toss well.
2. Spray air fryer basket with cooking spray.
3. Transfer mushrooms into the air fryer basket and cook at 380 F for 8 minutes. Toss halfway through.
4. Serve and enjoy.

Nutritional Value (Amount per Serving):

- Calories 62
- Fat 5 g
- Carbohydrates 3 g
- Sugar 2 g
- Protein 3 g
- Cholesterol 0 mg

Parmesan Asparagus

Preparation Time: 10 minutes; Cooking Time: 5 minutes; Serve: 4
Ingredients:

- 1 lb asparagus, cut the ends
- 1/2 cup parmesan cheese, grated
- 1 tbsp fresh lemon juice
- 1 tsp garlic powder
- 1 tbsp olive oil
- 1/4 tsp pepper
- 1/2 tsp sea salt

Directions:

1. Preheat the air fryer to 390 F.
2. In a large bowl, add asparagus.
3. In a small bowl, whisk together olive oil, garlic powder, pepper, and salt.
4. Pour oil mixture over asparagus and toss well.

5. Spread asparagus into the air fryer basket and cook for 5 minutes.
6. Pour lemon juice over cooked asparagus and sprinkle with grated cheese.
7. Serve and enjoy.

Nutritional Value (Amount per Serving):
- Calories 105
- Fat 6 g
- Carbohydrates 5 g
- Sugar 2 g
- Protein 7 g
- Cholesterol 8 mg

Roasted Acorn Squash

Preparation Time: 10 minutes; Cooking Time: 25 minutes; Serve: 4
Ingredients:
- 1 large acorn squash, cut in half lengthwise
- 2 tbsp olive oil
- 1/4 cup parmesan cheese, grated
- 1/4 tsp pepper
- 8 fresh thyme sprigs

Directions:
1. Preheat the air fryer to 370 F.
2. Remove seed from squash and cut into 3/4-inch slices.
3. Add squash slices, olive oil, thyme, parmesan cheese, pepper, and salt in a bowl and toss to coat.
4. Add squash slices into the air fryer basket and cook for 25 minutes. Turn halfway through.
5. Serve and enjoy.

Nutritional Value (Amount per Serving):
- Calories 250
- Fat 16.1 g
- Carbohydrates 11 g
- Sugar 0 g
- Protein 13 g
- Cholesterol 30 mg

Cheesy Broccoli

Preparation Time: 10 minutes; Cooking Time: 13 minutes; Serve: 4
Ingredients:
- 1 lb broccoli, cut into florets
- 1/2 cup mozzarella cheese, shredded
- 1/2 cup heavy cream
- 2 garlic cloves, minced
- 1/4 cup parmesan cheese, grated
- 1/2 cup gruyere cheese, shredded
- 1 tbsp butter, melted

Directions:
1. Preheat the air fryer to 350 F.
2. Toss broccoli with melted butter and season with pepper and salt.
3. Add broccoli into the air fryer basket and cook for 5 minutes.
4. Transfer broccoli into the air fryer baking dish.
5. Add garlic into the broccoli. Pour heavy cream over broccoli then top with parmesan, gruyere, and mozzarella cheeses.
6. Place baking dish in the air fryer and cook for 8 minutes.

7. Serve and enjoy.

Nutritional Value (Amount per Serving):
- Calories 220
- Fat 16 g
- Carbohydrates 8.5 g
- Sugar 2 g
- Protein 12 g
- Cholesterol 50 mg

Cheesy Ranch Broccoli

Preparation Time: 10 minutes; Cooking Time: 24 minutes; Serve: 6

Ingredients:
- 4 cups broccoli florets
- 1/2 cup cheddar cheese, shredded
- 1/4 cup ranch dressing
- 1/4 cup heavy whipping cream
- Pepper
- Salt

Directions:
1. Add all ingredients into the large bowl and toss well to coat.
2. Spread broccoli mixture into the air fryer baking dish and place into the air fryer.
3. Cook at 350 F for 24 minutes.
4. Stir well and serve.

Nutritional Value (Amount per Serving):
- Calories 80
- Fat 5 g
- Carbohydrates 4.5 g
- Sugar 1.4 g
- Protein 4 g
- Cholesterol 17 mg

Cheesy Brussels sprouts

Preparation Time: 10 minutes; Cooking Time: 8 minutes; Serve: 6

Ingredients:
- 2 lbs Brussels sprouts, cleaned and halved
- 1 cup heavy cream
- 4 oz cream cheese
- 1 cup Asiago cheese, shredded
- 2 tbsp water
- 2 tbsp butter

Directions:
1. Preheat the air fryer to 325 F.
2. Melt butter in a pan over medium-high heat. Add Brussels sprouts and water. Stir well.
3. Cover and steam for 5 minutes.
4. Transfer Brussels sprouts into the air fryer baking dish. Set aside.
5. Add cream cheese into the same pan and melt over medium heat.
6. Add cheese and heavy cream and whisk until smooth.
7. Pour cheese mixture over Brussels sprouts.
8. Place dish into the air fryer and cook for 8 minutes.
9. Serve and enjoy.

Nutritional Value (Amount per Serving):
- Calories 314
- Fat 25 g
- Carbohydrates 14 g
- Sugar 3 g

- Protein 12 g
- Cholesterol 78 mg

Parmesan Squash

Preparation Time: 10 minutes; Cooking Time: 12 minutes; Serve: 6
Ingredients:
- 2 lbs butternut squash, peeled and cut into 1-inch cubes
- 2 tbsp thyme, chopped
- 2 garlic cloves, minced
- 2 tbsp olive oil
- 1/2 cup parmesan cheese, grated
- 1 1/2 cups mozzarella cheese, shredded
- Pepper
- Salt

Directions:
1. Preheat the air fryer to 400 F.
2. Toss squash with thyme, garlic, and olive oil in a large bowl. Season pepper and salt.
3. Transfer squash mixture into the air fryer baking dish.
4. Place dish in the air fryer and cook squash for 10 minutes or until tender.
5. Top with parmesan and mozzarella cheese and cook for 2 minutes more or until cheese is melted.
6. Serve and enjoy.

Nutritional Value (Amount per Serving):
- Calories 130
- Fat 10.1 g
- Carbohydrates 3 g
- Sugar 1.7 g
- Protein 8 g
- Cholesterol 17 mg

Veggie Stuffed Peppers

Preparation Time: 10 minutes; Cooking Time: 20 minutes; Serve: 6
Ingredients:
- 4 bell peppers, halved and seeded
- 1/2 cup parmesan cheese, grated
- 1 1/2 cups mozzarella cheese, shredded
- 6 oz cream cheese, softened
- 10 oz frozen spinach, thawed and chopped
- 14 oz can artichoke hearts, drained and chopped
- 3 garlic cloves, minced
- 1/4 cup mayonnaise
- 1/4 cup sour cream
- 1 tbsp olive oil
- Pepper
- Salt

Directions:
1. Preheat the air fryer 370 F.
2. Spray air fryer basket with cooking spray.
3. Drizzle oil over bell peppers and season with pepper and salt.
4. In a large bowl, mix together artichoke, garlic, mayonnaise, sour cream, parmesan cheese, 1/2 cup mozzarella cheese, cream cheese, spinach, pepper, and salt.
5. Stuff artichoke mixture into the bell pepper halves and top with remaining mozzarella cheese.

6. Place stuff bell peppers into the air fryer basket and cook for 20 minutes. (Cook in batches)
7. Serve and enjoy.

Nutritional Value (Amount per Serving):
- Calories 220
- Fat 14 g
- Carbohydrates 14 g
- Sugar 4 g
- Protein 11 g
- Cholesterol 30 mg

Tasty Parmesan Cauliflower

Preparation Time: 10 minutes; Cooking Time: 47 minutes; Serve: 2

Ingredients:
- 1 cauliflower head, trim outer leaves
- 1 tsp garlic powder
- 1 lemon juice
- 4 tbsp butter, melted
- 3 tbsp Dijon mustard
- 1/4 cup parmesan cheese, grated
- 2 tbsp olive oil
- 1/2 tsp pepper
- 1/2 tsp salt

Directions:
1. Preheat the air fryer to 400 F.
2. In a small bowl, mix together butter, oil, lemon juice, mustard, garlic powder, pepper, and salt.
3. Brush cauliflower with butter mixture and place into the air fryer.
4. Cook cauliflower for 40-45 minutes or until tender.
5. Sprinkle with parmesan cheese and cook for 2-5 minutes more or until cheese melted.
6. Serve and enjoy.

Nutritional Value (Amount per Serving):
- Calories 655
- Fat 55 g
- Carbohydrates 5.1 g
- Sugar 1.5 g
- Protein 25 g
- Cholesterol 121 mg

Baked Cauliflower

Preparation Time: 10 minutes; Cooking Time: 35 minutes; Serve: 2

Ingredients:
- 1/2 cauliflower head, cut into florets
- 2 tbsp olive oil
- For seasoning:
- 1/2 tsp ground cumin
- 1/2 tsp black pepper
- 1/2 tsp white pepper
- 1 tsp onion powder
- 1 tbsp ground cayenne pepper
- 1/4 tsp dried oregano
- 1/4 tsp dried basil
- 1/4 tsp dried thyme
- 1/2 tsp garlic powder
- 2 tbsp ground paprika
- 2 tsp salt

Directions:
1. Preheat the air fryer to 370 F.
2. In a large bowl, mix together all seasoning ingredients. Add oil and stir well.

3. Add cauliflower to the bowl seasoning mixture and stir to coat.
4. Transfer cauliflower florets into the air fryer basket and cook for 30-35 minutes. Shake basket 3-4 times while cooking.
5. Serve and enjoy.

Nutritional Value (Amount per Serving):
- Calories 175
- Fat 15.6 g
- Carbohydrates 12 g
- Sugar 3.2 g
- Protein 3 g
- Cholesterol 0 mg

Cauliflower Rice

Preparation Time: 10 minutes; Cooking Time: 12 minutes; Serve: 3
Ingredients:
- 1 cauliflower head, cut into florets
- 2 tbsp olive oil
- 2 garlic cloves, chopped
- 1 tomato, chopped
- 1 onion, chopped
- 2 tbsp tomato paste
- 1 tsp white pepper
- 1 tsp pepper
- 1 tbsp dried thyme
- 2 chilies, chopped
- 1/2 tsp salt

Directions:
1. Preheat the air fryer to 370 F.
2. Add cauliflower florets into the food processor and process until it looks like rice.
3. Stir in tomato paste, tomatoes, and spices and mix well.
4. Add cauliflower mixture into the air fryer baking pan and drizzle with olive oil.
5. Place pan in the air fryer and cook for 12 minutes.
6. Serve and enjoy.

Nutritional Value (Amount per Serving):
- Calories 135
- Fat 9.7 g
- Carbohydrates 13 g
- Sugar 4 g
- Protein 3.2 g
- Cholesterol 0 mg

Squash Noodles

Preparation Time: 10 minutes; Cooking Time: 17 minutes; Serve: 2
Ingredients:
- 1 medium butternut squash, peel and spiralized
- 3 tbsp cream
- 1/4 cup parmesan cheese
- 1 tsp thyme, chopped
- 1 tbsp sage, chopped
- 1 tsp garlic powder
- 2 tbsp cream cheese

Directions:
1. Preheat the air fryer to 370 F.
2. In a bowl, mix together cream cheese, parmesan, thyme, sage, cream, and garlic powder.
3. Add noodles into the air fryer baking pan.
4. Place pan in the air fryer and cook for 15 minutes.

5. Spread cream cheese mixture over noodles and cook for 2-3 minutes more.
6. Serve and enjoy.

Nutritional Value (Amount per Serving):
- Calories 235
- Fat 15.8 g
- Carbohydrates 7 g
- Sugar 2.9 g
- Protein 17 g
- Cholesterol 40 mg

Roasted Carrots

Preparation Time: 10 minutes; Cooking Time: 25 minutes; Serve: 6
Ingredients:
- 16 small carrots
- 1 tbsp fresh parsley, chopped
- 1 tbsp dried basil
- 6 garlic cloves, minced
- 4 tbsp olive oil
- 1 1/2 tsp salt

Directions:
1. Preheat the air fryer to 350 F.
2. In a bowl, mix together oil, carrots, basil, garlic, and salt.
3. Transfer carrots into the air fryer basket and cook for 20-25 minutes. Shake basket 2-3 times while cooking.
4. Garnish with parsley and serve.

Nutritional Value (Amount per Serving):
- Calories 140
- Fat 9.4 g
- Carbohydrates 14 g
- Sugar 5 g
- Protein 1.3 g
- Cholesterol 0 mg

Cheese Eggplant Bites

Preparation Time: 10 minutes; Cooking Time: 12 minutes; Serve: 5
Ingredients:
- 1 egg
- 1 eggplant, sliced
- 1/4 cup parmesan cheese, grated
- 1/2 tbsp dried thyme
- 1/4 cup almond flour
- 1/2 cup cheese, grated
- 1/2 tbsp dried rosemary
- Pepper
- Salt

Directions:
1. Spray air fryer basket with cooking spray.
2. Place sliced eggplants into the air fryer basket season with pepper and salt.
3. Cook eggplant at 390 F for 6 minutes.
4. In a small bowl, mix together almond flour, dried rosemary, dried thyme, and grated cheese.
5. Remove from eggplant slices from air fryer and brush with beaten egg. Sprinkle with almond flour mixture and cook until cheese is melted, about 4-6 minutes more.
6. Serve and enjoy.

Nutritional Value (Amount per Serving):

- Calories 144
- Fat 9 g
- Carbohydrates 7.2 g

- Sugar 2 g
- Protein 8.5 g
- Cholesterol 50 mg

Broccoli Casserole

Preparation Time: 10 minutes; Cooking Time: 30 minutes; Serve: 8
Ingredients:
- 2 lbs broccoli florets
- 2 cups cheddar cheese, shredded
- 1/4 cup vegetable stock
- 1/2 cup heavy cream
- 2 garlic cloves, minced

- 4 oz cream cheese
- 1 cup mozzarella cheese
- 3 tbsp olive oil
- Pepper
- Salt

Directions:
1. Preheat the air fryer to 370 F.
2. Layer broccoli florets in an air fryer baking dish. Drizzle with olive oil and season with pepper and salt.
3. Cook broccoli in the air fryer for 15 minutes.
4. Meanwhile, combine together heavy cream, stock, garlic, cream cheese, mozzarella cheese, and 1 cup cheddar cheese in a medium saucepan over medium-low heat. Stir frequently.
5. Once broccoli is cooked then pour heavy cream mixture on top of broccoli and stir everything well.
6. Sprinkle remaining cheddar cheese on top and cook for 12 minutes more.
7. Serve and enjoy.

Nutritional Value (Amount per Serving):
- Calories 285
- Fat 23.4 g
- Carbohydrates 9 g

- Sugar 2.2 g
- Protein 12.5 g
- Cholesterol 55 mg

Creamy Spinach

Preparation Time: 10 minutes; Cooking Time: 16 minutes; Serve: 6
Ingredients:
- 1 lb fresh spinach
- 6 oz gouda cheese, shredded
- 8 oz cream cheese
- 1 tsp garlic powder

- 1 tbsp onion, minced
- Pepper
- Salt

Directions:
1. Preheat the air fryer to 370 F.
2. Spray air fryer baking dish with cooking spray and set aside.
3. Spray a large pan with cooking spray and heat over medium heat.
4. Add spinach to the pan and cook until wilted.
5. Add cream cheese, garlic powder, and onion and stir until cheese is melted.
6. Remove pan from heat and add Gouda cheese and season with pepper and salt.

7. Transfer spinach mixture to the prepared baking dish and place into the air fryer.
8. Cook for 16 minutes.
9. Serve and enjoy.

Nutritional Value (Amount per Serving):
- Calories 255
- Fat 21.3 g
- Carbohydrates 5 g
- Sugar 1.2 g
- Protein 12 g
- Cholesterol 74 mg

Roasted Cauliflower

Preparation Time: 10 minutes; Cooking Time: 12 minutes; Serve: 4
Ingredients:
- 1 large cauliflower head, cut into florets
- 1 lemon zest
- 3 tbsp olive oil
- 2 tsp lemon juice
- 1/2 tsp Italian seasoning
- 1/2 tsp garlic powder
- 1/4 tsp pepper
- 1/4 tsp salt

Directions:
1. Preheat the air fryer to 400 F.
2. In a bowl, combine together olive oil, lemon juice, Italian seasoning, garlic powder, lemon zest, pepper, and salt.
3. Add cauliflower florets to the bowl and toss well.
4. Add cauliflower florets into the air fryer basket and cook for 12 minutes. Shake basket halfway through.
5. Serve and enjoy.

Nutritional Value (Amount per Serving):
- Calories 145
- Fat 10.9 g
- Carbohydrates 11 g
- Sugar 5.2 g
- Protein 4.3 g
- Cholesterol 0 mg

Brussels sprouts with Garlic

Preparation Time: 10 minutes; Cooking Time: 30 minutes; Serve: 8
Ingredients:
- 2 lbs Brussels sprouts, trimmed and quartered
- 2 tbsp coconut oil, melted
- 5 garlic cloves, sliced
- 1/8 tsp pepper
- 1 tsp salt

Directions:
1. Preheat the air fryer to 370 F.
2. In a bowl, mix together Brussels sprouts, coconut oil, and garlic.
3. Transfer Brussels sprouts into the air fryer basket and cooks for 30 minutes. Shake basket halfway through.
4. Season with pepper and salt.
5. Serve and enjoy.

Nutritional Value (Amount per Serving):

- Calories 80
- Fat 3.8 g
- Carbohydrates 11 g
- Sugar 32.5 g
- Protein 4 g
- Cholesterol 0 mg

Beans with Mushrooms

Preparation Time: 10 minutes; Cooking Time: 20 minutes; Serve: 4

Ingredients:

- 2 cups green beans, clean and cut into pieces
- 1/4 cup olive oil
- 2 cups mushrooms, sliced
- 2 tsp garlic, minced
- 1 tsp pepper
- 1 tsp sea salt

Directions:

1. Preheat the air fryer to 370 F.
2. In a bowl, combine together olive oil, pepper, garlic, and salt.
3. Pour olive oil mixture over green beans and mushrooms and stir to coat.
4. Spread green beans and mushroom mixture into the air fryer basket and cook for 20 minutes.
5. Serve and enjoy.

Nutritional Value (Amount per Serving):

- Calories 135
- Fat 12.8 g
- Carbohydrates 6 g
- Sugar 1.4 g
- Protein 2.3 g
- Cholesterol 0 mg

Broccoli Cheese Stuff Pepper

Preparation Time: 10 minutes; Cooking Time: 20 minutes; Serve: 4

Ingredients:

- 4 eggs
- 2 medium bell peppers, cut in half and deseeded
- 1 tsp dried sage
- 2.5 oz cheddar cheese, grated
- 7 oz almond milk
- 1/4 cup baby broccoli florets
- 1/4 cup cherry tomatoes
- Pepper
- Salt

Directions:

1. Preheat the air fryer to 370 F.
2. In a bowl, whisk together eggs, milk, broccoli, cherry tomatoes, sage, pepper, and salt.
3. Spray air fryer basket with cooking spray.
4. Place bell pepper halves into the air fryer basket.
5. Pour egg mixture into the bell pepper halves.
6. Sprinkle cheese on top of bell pepper and cook for 20 minutes.
7. Serve and enjoy.

Nutritional Value (Amount per Serving):

- Calories 284
- Fat 25.2 g

- Carbohydrates 5.5 g
- Sugar 3.3 g
- Protein 12 g
- Cholesterol 167 mg

Broccoli with Almonds

Preparation Time: 10 minutes; Cooking Time: 16 minutes; Serve: 4
Ingredients:
- 1 1/2 lbs broccoli, cut into florets
- 3 tbsp olive oil
- 1 tbsp lemon juice
- 1/4 cup cheese, grated
- 3 tbsp slivered almonds, toasted
- 2 garlic cloves, sliced
- 1/4 tsp pepper
- 1/4 tsp salt

Directions:
1. Preheat the air fryer to 400 F.
2. Spray air fryer basket with cooking spray.
3. Add broccoli, pepper, salt, garlic, and oil in a large bowl and toss well.
4. Spread broccoli into the air fryer basket and cook for 16 minutes. Shake basket halfway through.
5. Add lemon juice, grated cheese, and almonds over broccoli and toss well.
6. Serve and enjoy.

Nutritional Value (Amount per Serving):
- Calories 205
- Fat 15 g
- Carbohydrates 13 g
- Sugar 3 g
- Protein 7 g
- Cholesterol 7 mg

Garlic Thyme Mushrooms

Preparation Time: 10 minutes; Cooking Time: 23 minutes; Serve: 2
Ingredients:
- 10 oz mushrooms, quartered
- 1 tsp thyme, chopped
- 2 tbsp olive oil
- 2 garlic cloves, sliced
- 1/4 tsp pepper
- 1/4 tsp salt

Directions:
1. Preheat the air fryer to 370 F.
2. Spray air fryer basket with cooking spray.
3. In a bowl, combine together mushrooms, pepper, salt, thyme, and oil.
4. Spread mushrooms into the air fryer basket and cook for 20 minutes. Shake basket halfway through.
5. Add garlic and stir well and cook for 2-3 minutes.
6. Serve and enjoy.

Nutritional Value (Amount per Serving):
- Calories 155
- Fat 14.5 g
- Carbohydrates 6 g
- Sugar 2.5 g
- Protein 5 g
- Cholesterol 0 mg

Ratatouille

Preparation Time: 10 minutes; Cooking Time: 25 minutes; Serve: 4
Ingredients:

- 1 tomato, cubed
- 1 zucchini, cubed
- 1/2 small eggplant, cubed
- 1 garlic clove, crushed
- 2 oregano sprigs, chopped
- 1 cayenne pepper, cubed
- 1/2 onion, cubed
- 1 bell pepper, cubed
- 1 tbsp vinegar
- 1 tbsp white wine
- 1 tbsp olive oil
- Pepper
- Salt

Directions:
1. Add all ingredients into the large mixing bowl and toss well.
2. Transfer vegetable mixture into the air fryer baking dish and place in the air fryer.
3. Cook at 400 F for 25 minutes. Stir after every 5 minutes.
4. Serve and enjoy.

Nutritional Value (Amount per Serving):
- Calories 79
- Fat 4 g
- Carbohydrates 10.3 g
- Sugar 5.2 g
- Protein 1.9 g
- Cholesterol 0 mg

Roasted Mushrooms

Preparation Time: 10 minutes; Cooking Time: 15 minutes; Serve: 4
Ingredients:

- 2 lbs mushrooms, clean and quarters
- 2 tbsp vermouth
- 2 tsp herb de Provence
- 1/2 tsp garlic powder
- 1 tbsp butter, melted

Directions:
1. Add mushrooms in a bowl with remaining ingredients and toss well.
2. Transfer mushrooms into the air fryer basket and cook at 320 F for 15 minutes. Toss halfway through.
3. Serve and enjoy.

Nutritional Value (Amount per Serving):
- Calories 253
- Fat 11.5 g
- Carbohydrates 8.5 g
- Sugar 4 g
- Protein 26.2 g
- Cholesterol 8 mg

Moroccan Spice Carrots

Preparation Time: 10 minutes; Cooking Time: 13 minutes; Serve: 4
Ingredients:

- 1 lb carrots, peeled and sliced
- 2 tbsp olive oil
- 1/2 tsp salt
- For the spice mix:

- 1/8 tsp cayenne pepper
- 1/8 tsp ground ginger
- 1/8 tsp ground allspice
- 1/8 tsp ground cinnamon
- 1/8 tsp paprika
- 1/4 tsp chili powder
- 1/4 tsp ground coriander
- 1/2 tsp ground cumin

Directions:
1. In a small bowl, mix together all spice ingredients.
2. Add carrots, oil, pepper, spice mix, and salt into the large bowl and toss well.
3. Transfer carrots into the air fryer basket and cook at 350 F for 8 minutes.
4. Toss well and cook for 5 minutes more.
5. Serve and enjoy.

Nutritional Value (Amount per Serving):
- Calories 109
- Fat 7.1 g
- Carbohydrates 11.6 g
- Sugar 5.6 g
- Protein 1 g
- Cholesterol 0 mg

Zucchini Fries

Preparation Time: 10 minutes; Cooking Time: 15 minutes; Serve: 2
Ingredients:
- 2 medium zucchini, cut into French fries shape
- 2 tbsp arrowroot powder
- 1 tbsp water
- 1/2 tbsp olive oil
- Salt

Directions
1. Preheat the air fryer to 390 F.
2. Add all ingredients into the bowl and mix well.
3. Place coated zucchini fries in air fryer basket and air fry for 15 minutes.
4. Serve and enjoy.

Nutritional Value (Amount per Serving):
- Calories 90
- Fat 4 g
- Carbohydrates 13 g
- Sugar 3.4 g
- Protein 2.4 g
- Cholesterol 0 mg

Simple Taro Fries

Preparation Time: 10 minutes; Cooking Time: 20 minutes; Serve: 2
Ingredients:
- 8 small taro, peel and cut into fries shape
- 1 tbsp olive oil
- 1/2 tsp salt

Directions:
1. Add taro slice in a bowl and toss well with olive oil and salt.
2. Transfer taro slices into the air fryer basket.
3. Cook at 360 F for 20 minutes. Toss halfway through.
4. Serve and enjoy.

Nutritional Value (Amount per Serving):

- Calories 115
- Fat 7 g
- Carbohydrates 12 g

- Sugar 0.2 g
- Protein 0.8 g
- Cholesterol 0 mg

Beetroot Chips

Preparation Time: 10 minutes; Cooking Time: 15 minutes; Serve: 4

Ingredients:
- 2 medium beetroot, wash, peeled, and sliced thinly
- 1 tsp olive oil

- 1 sprig rosemary, chopped
- Salt

Directions:
1. Sprinkle rosemary and salt on the beetroot slices.
2. Preheat the air fryer to 300 F.
3. Add beetroot slices into the air fryer basket. Drizzle beetroot slices with olive oil.
4. Cook for 15 minutes. Shake basket after every 5 minutes while cooking.
5. Serve and enjoy.

Nutritional Value (Amount per Serving):
- Calories 31
- Fat 1 g
- Carbohydrates 5 g

- Sugar 4 g
- Protein 0.5 g
- Cholesterol 0 mg

Delicious Ratatouille

Preparation Time: 10 minutes; Cooking Time: 15 minutes; Serve: 6

Ingredients:
- 1 eggplant, diced
- 3 garlic cloves, chopped
- 1 onion, diced
- 3 tomatoes, diced
- 2 bell peppers, diced

- 1 tbsp vinegar
- 1 1/2 tbsp olive oil
- 2 tbsp herb de Provence
- Pepper
- Salt

Directions:
1. Preheat the air fryer to 400 F.
2. Add all ingredients into the bowl and toss well and transfer into the air fryer baking dish.
3. Place dish into the air fryer and cook for 15 minutes. Stir halfway through.
4. Serve and enjoy.

Nutritional Value (Amount per Serving):
- Calories 60
- Fat 3 g
- Carbohydrates 7 g

- Sugar 4 g
- Protein 1 g
- Cholesterol 40 mg

Spicy Buffalo Cauliflower

Preparation Time: 10 minutes; Cooking Time: 15 minutes; Serve: 4

Ingredients:

- 8 oz cauliflower florets
- 1 tsp cayenne pepper
- 1 tsp chili powder
- 1 tsp olive oil
- 1 tsp garlic, minced
- 1 tomato, diced
- 6 tbsp almond flour
- 1 tsp black pepper
- 1/2 tsp salt

Directions:
1. Preheat the air fryer to 350 F.
2. Spray air fryer basket with cooking spray.
3. Add tomato, garlic, black pepper, olive oil, cayenne pepper, and chili powder into the blender and blend until smooth.
4. Add cauliflower florets into the bowl. Season with pepper and salt.
5. Pour blended mixture over cauliflower florets and toss well to coat.
6. Coat cauliflower florets with almond flour and place into the air fryer basket and cook for 15 minutes. Shake basket 2-3 times.
7. Serve and enjoy.

Nutritional Value (Amount per Serving):
- Calories 92
- Fat 6 g
- Carbohydrates 7 g
- Sugar 2 g
- Protein 3 g
- Cholesterol 0 mg

Basil Tomatoes

Preparation Time: 10 minutes; Cooking Time: 25 minutes; Serve: 4

Ingredients:
- 4 large tomatoes, halved
- 1 garlic clove, minced
- 1 tbsp vinegar
- 1 tbsp olive oil
- 2 tbsp parmesan cheese, grated
- 1/2 tsp fresh parsley, chopped
- 1 tsp fresh basil, minced
- Pepper
- Salt

Directions:
1. Preheat the air fryer to 320 F.
2. In a bowl, mix together oil, basil, garlic, vinegar, pepper, and salt.
3. Add tomatoes and toss to coat.
4. Place tomato halves into the air fryer basket and cook for 20 minutes.
5. Sprinkle tomatoes with cheese and cook for 5 minutes more.
6. Serve and enjoy.

Nutritional Value (Amount per Serving):
- Calories 85
- Fat 5 g
- Carbohydrates 7 g
- Sugar 4 g
- Protein 3 g
- Cholesterol 0 mg

Spiced Green Beans

Preparation Time: 10 minutes; Cooking Time: 10 minutes; Serve: 2

Ingredients:

- 2 cups green beans
- 1/8 tsp cayenne pepper
- 1/8 tsp ground allspice
- 1/4 tsp ground cinnamon
- 1/2 tsp dried oregano
- 2 tbsp olive oil
- 1/4 tsp ground coriander
- 1/4 tsp ground cumin
- 1/2 tsp salt

Directions:

1. Add all ingredients into the large bowl and toss well.
2. Spray air fryer basket with cooking spray.
3. Add bowl mixture into the air fryer basket.
4. Cook at 370 F for 10 minutes. Shake basket halfway through
5. Serve and enjoy.

Nutritional Value (Amount per Serving):

- Calories 155
- Fat 14 g
- Carbohydrates 8 g
- Sugar 1 g
- Protein 2 g
- Cholesterol 0 mg

Ricotta Mushrooms

Preparation Time: 10 minutes; Cooking Time: 12 minutes; Serve: 4

Ingredients:

- 4 large Portobello mushrooms caps
- 1 tbsp olive oil
- 1/4 cup parmesan cheese, grated
- 1/4 tsp rosemary, chopped
- 1 cup spinach, chopped
- 1/4 cup ricotta cheese

Directions:

1. Coat mushrooms with olive oil.
2. Transfer mushrooms into the air fryer basket and cook at 350 F for 2 minutes.
3. In a bowl, mix together remaining ingredients.
4. Stuff bowl mixture into the mushrooms and place into the air fryer basket and cook for 10 minutes more.
5. Serve and enjoy.

Nutritional Value (Amount per Serving):

- Calories 69
- Fat 5.1 g
- Carbohydrates 2.2 g
- Sugar 0.1 g
- Protein 3.5 g
- Cholesterol 6 mg

Squash Fritters

Preparation Time: 10 minutes; Cooking Time: 7 minutes; Serve: 4

Ingredients:

- 1 yellow summer squash, grated
- 1 egg, lightly beaten
- 3 oz cream cheese
- 2 tbsp olive oil
- 1/2 tsp dried oregano
- 1/4 cup almond flour
- 1/3 cup carrot, grated
- Pepper

- Salt

Directions:

1. Spray air fryer basket with cooking spray.
2. Add all ingredients into the mixing bowl and mix until well combined.
3. Make patties from bowl mixture and place into the air fryer basket and cook at 400 F for 7 minutes.
4. Serve and enjoy.

Nutritional Value (Amount per Serving):

- Calories 190
- Fat 18.6 g
- Carbohydrates 2.9 g
- Sugar 0.8 g
- Protein 4.4 g
- Cholesterol 64 mg

Shallots Almonds Green Beans

Preparation Time: 10 minutes; Cooking Time: 15 minutes; Serve: 6

Ingredients:

- 1/4 cup almonds, toasted
- 1 1/2 lbs green beans, trimmed and steamed
- 2 tbsp olive oil
- 1/2 lb shallots, chopped
- Pepper
- Salt

Directions:

1. Add all ingredients into the large bowl and toss well.
2. Transfer green bean mixture into the air fryer basket and cook at 400 F for 15 minutes.
3. Serve and enjoy.

Nutritional Value (Amount per Serving):

- Calories 125
- Fat 7 g
- Carbohydrates 14 g
- Sugar 2 g
- Protein 4 g
- Cholesterol 0 mg

Tasty Herb Tomatoes

Preparation Time: 10 minutes; Cooking Time: 15 minutes; Serve: 4

Ingredients:

- 2 large tomatoes, halved
- 1 tbsp olive oil
- 1/2 tsp thyme, chopped
- 2 garlic cloves, minced
- Pepper
- Salt

Directions:

1. Add all ingredients into the bowl and toss well.
2. Transfer tomatoes into the air fryer basket and cook at 390 F for 15 minutes.
3. Serve and enjoy.

Nutritional Value (Amount per Serving):

- Calories 49
- Fat 3.7 g
- Carbohydrates 4.1 g
- Sugar 2.4 g
- Protein 0.9 g
- Cholesterol 0 mg

Parmesan Dill Mushrooms

Preparation Time: 10 minutes; Cooking Time: 8 minutes; Serve: 4

Ingredients:

- 10 mushrooms
- 1 tbsp olive oil
- 2 tbsp mozzarella cheese, grated
- 1 tbsp Italian seasoning
- 2 tbsp cheddar cheese, grated
- 1 tbsp dill, chopped
- Pepper
- Salt

Directions:

1. In a bowl, mix together mushrooms, oil, dill, Italian seasoning, pepper, and salt.
2. Add mushrooms into the air fryer basket and sprinkle cheddar and mozzarella cheese on top.
3. Cook at 350 F for 8 minutes.
4. Serve and enjoy.

Nutritional Value (Amount per Serving):

- Calories 107
- Fat 8.4 g
- Carbohydrates 2.9 g
- Sugar 1.1 g
- Protein 6.5 g
- Cholesterol 14 mg

Curried Sweet Potato Fries

Preparation Time: 10 minutes; Cooking Time: 20 minutes; Serve: 3

Ingredients:

- 2 sweet potatoes, peeled and cut into fries shape
- 1/4 tsp ground coriander
- 1/2 tsp curry powder
- 2 tbsp olive oil
- Pepper
- Salt

Directions:

1. Add all ingredients into the mixing bowl and toss to coat.
2. Transfer sweet potato fries into the air fryer basket and cook at 370 F for 20 minutes. Toss halfway through.
3. Serve and enjoy.

Nutritional Value (Amount per Serving):

- Calories 118
- Fat 9 g
- Carbohydrates 9 g
- Sugar 2 g
- Protein 1 g
- Cholesterol 0 mg

Chapter 8: Desserts Recipes

Easy Lava Cake

Preparation Time: 10 minutes; Cooking Time: 9 minutes; Serve: 2

Ingredients:

- 1 egg
- 1/2 tsp baking powder
- 1 tbsp coconut oil, melted
- 1 tbsp flax meal
- 2 tbsp erythritol
- 2 tbsp water
- 2 tbsp unsweetened cocoa powder
- Pinch of salt

Directions:

1. Whisk all ingredients into the bowl and transfer in two ramekins.
2. Preheat the air fryer to 350 F.
3. Place ramekins in air fryer basket and bake for 8-9 minutes.
4. Carefully remove ramekins from air fryer and let it cool for 10 minutes.
5. Serve and enjoy.

Nutritional Value (Amount per Serving):

- Calories 119
- Fat 11 g
- Carbohydrates 4 g
- Sugar 0.3 g
- Protein 5 g
- Cholesterol 82 mg

Tasty Cheese Bites

Preparation Time: 10 minutes; Cooking Time: 2 minutes; Serve: 16

Ingredients:

- 8 oz cream cheese, softened
- 2 tbsp erythritol
- 1/2 cup almond flour
- 1/2 tsp vanilla
- 4 tbsp heavy cream
- 1/2 cup erythritol

Directions:

1. Add cream cheese, vanilla, 1/2 cup erythritol, and 2 tbsp heavy cream in a stand mixer and mix until smooth.
2. Scoop cream cheese mixture onto the parchment lined plate and place in the refrigerator for 1 hour.
3. In a small bowl, mix together almond flour and 2 tbsp erythritol.
4. Dip cheesecake bites in remaining heavy cream and coat with almond flour mixture.
5. Place prepared cheesecake bites in air fryer basket and air fry for 2 minutes at 350 F.
6. Make sure cheesecake bites are frozen before air fry otherwise they will melt.
7. Drizzle with chocolate syrup and serve.

Nutritional Value (Amount per Serving):

- Calories 80
- Fat 7 g
- Carbohydrates 2 g
- Sugar 1 g
- Protein 2 g
- Cholesterol 16 mg

Apple Chips with Dip

Preparation Time: 10 minutes; Cooking Time: 12 minutes; Serve: 4

Ingredients:

- 1 apple, thinly slice using a mandolin slicer
- 1 tbsp almond butter
- 1/4 cup plain yogurt
- 2 tsp olive oil
- 1 tsp ground cinnamon
- 4 drops liquid stevia

Directions:

1. Add apple slices, oil, and cinnamon in a large bowl and toss well.
2. Spray air fryer basket with cooking spray.
3. Place apple slices in air fryer basket and cook at 375 F for 12 minutes. Turn after every 4 minutes.
4. Meanwhile, in a small bowl, mix together almond butter, yogurt, and sweetener.
5. Serve apple chips with dip and enjoy.

Nutritional Value (Amount per Serving):

- Calories 86
- Fat 4.9 g
- Carbohydrates 10 g
- Sugar 7.1 g
- Protein 1.9 g
- Cholesterol 1 mg

Delicious Spiced Apples

Preparation Time: 10 minutes; Cooking Time: 10 minutes; Serve: 6

Ingredients:

- 4 small apples, sliced
- 1 tsp apple pie spice
- 1/2 cup erythritol
- 2 tbsp coconut oil, melted

Directions:

1. Add apple slices in a mixing bowl and sprinkle sweetener, apple pie spice, and coconut oil over apple and toss to coat.
2. Transfer apple slices in air fryer dish. Place dish in air fryer basket and cook at 350 F for 10 minutes.
3. Serve and enjoy.

Nutritional Value (Amount per Serving):

- Calories 73
- Fat 4.6 g
- Carbohydrates 8.2 g
- Sugar 5.4 g
- Protein 0 g
- Cholesterol 0 mg

Easy Cheesecake

Preparation Time: 10 minutes; Cooking Time: 10 minutes; Serve: 6

Ingredients:

- 2 eggs
- 16 oz cream cheese, softened
- 2 tbsp sour cream
- 1/2 tsp fresh lemon juice
- 1 tsp vanilla
- 3/4 cup erythritol

Directions:

1. Preheat the air fryer to 350 F.
2. Add eggs, lemon juice, vanilla, and sweetener in a large bowl and beat using a hand mixer until smooth.
3. Add cream cheese and sour cream and beat until fluffy.
4. Pour batter into the 2 four-inch spring-form pan and place in air fryer basket and cook for 8-10minutes at 350 F.
5. Remove from air fryer and let it cool completely.
6. Place in refrigerator for overnight.
7. Serve and enjoy.

Nutritional Value (Amount per Serving):

- Calories 296
- Fat 28 g
- Carbohydrates 2.4 g
- Sugar 0.4 g
- Protein 7.7 g
- Cholesterol 139 mg

Coconut Pie

Preparation Time: 10 minutes; Cooking Time: 12 minutes; Serve: 6
Ingredients:

- 2 eggs
- 1/2 cup coconut flour
- 1/2 cup erythritol
- 1 cup shredded coconut
- 1 1/2 tsp vanilla
- 1/4 cup butter
- 1 1/2 cups coconut milk

Directions:

1. Add all ingredients into the large bowl and mix until well combined.
2. Spray a 6-inch baking dish with cooking spray.
3. Pour batter into the prepared dish and place in the air fryer basket.
4. Cook at 350 F for 10-12 minutes.
5. Slice and serve.

Nutritional Value (Amount per Serving):

- Calories 282
- Fat 28.9 g
- Carbohydrates 6.3 g
- Sugar 3.2 g
- Protein 4 g
- Cholesterol 75 mg

Strawberry Muffins

Preparation Time: 10 minutes; Cooking Time: 15 minutes; Serve: 12
Ingredients:

- 3 eggs
- 1 tsp ground cinnamon
- 2 tsp baking powder
- 2 1/2 cups almond flour
- 2/3 cup fresh strawberries, diced
- 1/3 cup heavy cream
- 1 tsp vanilla
- 1/2 cup Swerve
- 5 tbsp butter

Directions:

1. Preheat the air fryer 325 F.
2. Add butter and sweetener in a bowl and beat using a hand mixer until smooth.
3. Add eggs, cream, and vanilla and beat until frothy.
4. In another bowl, sift together almond flour, cinnamon, baking powder, and salt.
5. Add almond flour mixture to wet ingredients and mix until well combined.
6. Add strawberries and fold well.
7. Pour batter into the silicone muffin molds and place into the air fryer basket in batches.
8. Cook muffins for 15 minutes.
9. Serve and enjoy.

Nutritional Value (Amount per Serving):
- Calories 205
- Fat 18 g
- Carbohydrates 6 g
- Sugar 1.5 g
- Protein 6 g
- Cholesterol 58 mg

Pecan Muffins

Preparation Time: 10 minutes; Cooking Time: 15 minutes; Serve: 12
Ingredients:
- 4 eggs
- 1 tsp vanilla
- 1/4 cup almond milk
- 2 tbsp butter, melted
- 1/2 cup swerve
- 1 tsp psyllium husk
- 1 tbsp baking powder
- 1/2 cup pecans, chopped
- 1/2 tsp ground cinnamon
- 2 tsp allspice
- 1 1/2 cups almond flour

Directions:
1. Preheat the air fryer to 370 F.
2. Beat eggs, almond milk, vanilla, sweetener, and butter in a bowl using a hand mixer until smooth.
3. Add remaining ingredients and mix until well combined.
4. Pour batter into the silicone muffin molds and place into the air fryer basket in batches.
5. Cook muffins for 15 minutes.
6. Serve and enjoy.

Nutritional Value (Amount per Serving):
- Calories 204
- Fat 18 g
- Carbohydrates 6 g
- Sugar 1.2 g
- Protein 5 g
- Cholesterol 60 mg

Chocolate Brownie

Preparation Time: 10 minutes; Cooking Time: 16 minutes; Serve: 4
Ingredients:
- 1 cup bananas, overripe
- 1 scoop protein powder
- 2 tbsp unsweetened cocoa powder
- 1/2 cup almond butter, melted

Directions:

1. Preheat the air fryer to 325 F.
2. Spray air fryer baking pan with cooking spray.
3. Add all ingredients into the blender and blend until smooth.
4. Pour batter into the prepared pan and place in the air fryer basket.
5. Cook brownie for 16 minutes.
6. Serve and enjoy.

Nutritional Value (Amount per Serving):
- Calories 80
- Fat 2.1 g
- Carbohydrates 11.4 g
- Protein 7 g
- Sugars 5 g
- Cholesterol 15 mg

Blueberry Muffins

Preparation Time: 10 minutes; Cooking Time: 20 minutes; Serve: 12
Ingredients:
- 3 large eggs
- 1/3 cup coconut oil, melted
- 1 1/2 tsp gluten-free baking powder
- 1/2 cup erythritol
- 2 1/2 cups almond flour
- 3/4 cup blueberries
- 1/2 tsp vanilla
- 1/3 cup unsweetened almond milk

Directions:
1. Preheat the air fryer to 325 F.
2. In a large bowl, stir together almond flour, baking powder, erythritol.
3. Mix in the coconut oil, vanilla, eggs, and almond milk. Add blueberries and fold well.
4. Pour batter into the silicone muffin molds and place into the air fryer basket in batches.
5. Cook muffins for 20 minutes.
6. Serve and enjoy.

Nutritional Value (Amount per Serving):
- Calories 215
- Fat 19 g
- Carbohydrates 5 g
- Sugar 2 g
- Protein 7 g
- Cholesterol 45 mg

Pumpkin Muffins

Preparation Time: 10 minutes; Cooking Time: 20 minutes; Serve: 10
Ingredients:
- 4 large eggs
- 1/2 cup pumpkin puree
- 1 tbsp pumpkin pie spice
- 1 tbsp baking powder, gluten-free
- 2/3 cup erythritol
- 1 tsp vanilla
- 1/3 cup coconut oil, melted
- 1/2 cup almond flour
- 1/2 cup coconut flour
- 1/2 tsp sea salt

Directions:
1. Preheat the air fryer to 325 F.
2. In a large bowl, stir together coconut flour, pumpkin pie spice, baking powder, erythritol, almond flour, and sea salt.

3. Stir in eggs, vanilla, coconut oil, and pumpkin puree until well combined.
4. Pour batter into the silicone muffin molds and place into the air fryer basket in batches.
5. Cook muffins for 20 minutes.
6. Serve and enjoy.

Nutritional Value (Amount per Serving):
- Calories 150
- Fat 13 g
- Carbohydrates 7 g
- Sugar 2 g
- Protein 5 g
- Cholesterol 75 mg

Cappuccino Muffins

Preparation Time: 10 minutes; Cooking Time: 20 minutes; Serve: 12
Ingredients:
- 4 eggs
- 2 cups almond flour
- 1/2 tsp vanilla
- 1 tsp espresso powder
- 1/2 cup sour cream
- 1 tsp cinnamon
- 2 tsp baking powder
- 1/4 cup coconut flour
- 1/2 cup Swerve
- 1/4 tsp salt

Directions:
1. Preheat the air fryer to 325 F.
2. Add sour cream, vanilla, espresso powder, and eggs in a blender and blend until smooth.
3. Add almond flour, cinnamon, baking powder, coconut flour, sweetener, and salt. Blend again until smooth.
4. Pour batter into the silicone muffin molds and place into the air fryer basket. (Cook in batches)
5. Cook muffins for 20 minutes.
6. Serve and enjoy.

Nutritional Value (Amount per Serving):
- Calories 150
- Fat 13 g
- Carbohydrates 5.3 g
- Sugar 0.8 g
- Protein 6 g
- Cholesterol 59 mg

Moist Cinnamon Muffins

Preparation Time: 10 minutes; Cooking Time: 12 minutes; Serve: 20
Ingredients:
- 1 tbsp cinnamon
- 1 tsp baking powder
- 2 scoops vanilla protein powder
- 1/2 cup almond flour
- 1/2 cup coconut oil
- 1/2 cup pumpkin puree
- 1/2 cup almond butter

Directions:
1. Preheat the air fryer to 325 F.
2. In a large bowl, combine together all dry ingredients and mix well.
3. Add wet ingredients into the dry ingredients and mix until well combined.

4. Pour batter into the silicone muffin molds and place into the air fryer basket. (Cook in batches)
5. Cook muffins for 12 minutes.
6. Serve and enjoy.

Nutritional Value (Amount per Serving):

- Calories 80
- Fat 7.1 g
- Carbohydrates 1 g
- Sugar 0.4 g
- Protein 3 g
- Cholesterol 0 mg

Cream Cheese Muffins

Preparation Time: 10 minutes; Cooking Time: 16 minutes; Serve: 10
Ingredients:

- 2 eggs
- 1/2 cup erythritol
- 8 oz cream cheese
- 1 tsp ground cinnamon
- 1/2 tsp vanilla

Directions:
1. Preheat the air fryer to 325 F.
2. In a bowl, mix together cream cheese, vanilla, erythritol, and eggs until soft.
3. Pour batter into the silicone muffin molds and sprinkle cinnamon on top.
4. Place muffin molds into the air fryer basket and cook for 16 minutes.
5. Serve and enjoy.

Nutritional Value (Amount per Serving):

- Calories 90
- Fat 8.8 g
- Carbohydrates 13 g
- Sugar 12.2 g
- Protein 2.8 g
- Cholesterol 58 mg

Cinnamon Apple Chips

Preparation Time: 10 minutes; Cooking Time: 8 minutes; Serve: 6
Ingredients:

- 3 Granny Smith apples, wash, core and thinly slice
- 1 tsp ground cinnamon
- Pinch of salt

Directions:
1. Rub apple slices with cinnamon and salt and place into the air fryer basket.
2. Cook at 390 F for 8 minutes. Turn halfway through.
3. Serve and enjoy.

Nutritional Value (Amount per Serving):

- Calories 41
- Fat 0 g
- Carbohydrates 11 g
- Sugar 8 g
- Protein 0 g
- Cholesterol 0 mg

Choco Mug Cake

Preparation Time: 5 minutes; Cooking Time: 20 minutes; Serve: 1

Ingredients:
- 1 egg, lightly beaten
- 1 tbsp heavy cream
- ¼ tsp baking powder
- 2 tbsp unsweetened cocoa powder
- 2 tbsp Erythritol
- ½ tsp vanilla
- 1 tbsp peanut butter
- 1 tsp salt

Directions:
1. Preheat the air fryer to 400 F.
2. In a bowl, mix together all ingredients until well combined.
3. Spray mug with cooking spray.
4. Pour batter in mug and place in the air fryer and cook for 20 minutes.
5. Serve and enjoy.

Nutritional Value (Amount per Serving):
- Calories 241
- Fat 19 g
- Carbohydrates 10 g
- Sugar 2 g
- Protein 12 g
- Cholesterol 184 mg

Almond Bars

Preparation Time: 10 minutes; Cooking Time: 35 minutes; Serve: 12
Ingredients:
- 2 eggs, lightly beaten
- 1 cup erythritol
- ½ tsp vanilla
- ¼ cup water
- ½ cup butter, softened
- ¾ cup cherries, pitted
- 1 ½ cup almond flour
- 1 tbsp xanthan gum
- ½ tsp salt

Directions:
1. In a bowl, mix together almond flour, erythritol, eggs, vanilla, butter, and salt until dough is formed.
2. Press dough in air fryer baking dish.
3. Place in the air fryer and cook at 375 F for 10 minutes.
4. Meanwhile, mix together cherries, xanthan gum, and water.
5. Pour cherry mixture over cooked dough and cook for 25 minutes more.
6. Slice and serve.

Nutritional Value (Amount per Serving):
- Calories 168
- Fat 15 g
- Carbohydrates 5 g
- Sugar 1.8 g
- Protein 4 g
- Cholesterol 48 mg

Coconut Berry Pudding

Preparation Time: 10 minutes; Cooking Time: 15 minutes; Serve: 6
Ingredients:
- 2 cups coconut cream
- 1 lime zest, grated
- 3 tbsp erythritol
- ¼ cup blueberries

- 1/3 cup blackberries

Directions:
1. Add all ingredients into the blender and blend until well combined.
2. Spray 6 ramekins with cooking spray.
3. Pour blended mixture into the ramekins and place in the air fryer.
4. Cook at 340 F for 15 minutes.
5. Serve and enjoy.

Nutritional Value (Amount per Serving):
- Calories 190
- Fat 19 g
- Carbohydrates 6 g
- Sugar 3.7 g
- Protein 2 g
- Cholesterol 0 mg

Strawberry Cheese Cake

Preparation Time: 10 minutes; Cooking Time: 35 minutes; Serve: 6
Ingredients:
- 1 cup almond flour
- 3 tbsp coconut oil, melted
- ½ tsp vanilla
- 1 egg, lightly beaten
- 1 tbsp fresh lime juice
- ¼ cup erythritol
- 1 cup cream cheese, softened
- 1 lb strawberries, chopped
- 2 tsp baking powder

Directions:
1. Add all ingredients into the large bowl and mix until well combined.
2. Spray air fryer cake pan with cooking spray.
3. Pour batter into the prepared pan and place into the air fryer and cook at 350 F for 35 minutes.
4. Allow to cool completely.
5. Slice and serve.

Nutritional Value (Amount per Serving):
- Calories 195
- Fat 17.3 g
- Carbohydrates 3.2 g
- Sugar 1 g
- Protein 7.2 g
- Cholesterol 52 mg

Coffee Cookies

Preparation Time: 10 minutes; Cooking Time: 15 minutes; Serve: 12
Ingredients:
- 1 cup almond flour
- 2 eggs, lightly beaten
- 2 tsp baking powder
- ½ tbsp cinnamon
- ¼ cup erythritol
- ¼ cup brewed espresso
- ½ cup ghee, melted

Directions:
1. Add all ingredients into the bowl and mix until well combined.
2. Place cookie sheet into the air fryer basket.

3. Make small cookies from mixture and place into the air fryer basket on cookie sheet.
4. Cook at 350 F for 15 minutes.
5. Serve and enjoy.

Nutritional Value (Amount per Serving):
- Calories 141
- Fat 14 g
- Carbohydrates 2.8 g
- Sugar 0.4 g
- Protein 3 g
- Cholesterol 49 mg

Ricotta Cheese Cake

Preparation Time: 10 minutes; Cooking Time: 30 minutes; Serve: 8

Ingredients:
- 3 eggs, lightly beaten
- 1 tsp baking powder
- ½ cup ghee, melted
- 1 cup almond flour
- 1/3 cup erythritol
- 1 cup ricotta cheese, soft

Directions:
1. Add all ingredients into the bowl and mix until well combined.
2. Pour batter into the greased air fryer baking dish and place into the air fryer.
3. Cook at 350 F for 30 minutes.
4. Slice and serve.

Nutritional Value (Amount per Serving):
- Calories 259
- Fat 23 g
- Carbohydrates 5 g
- Sugar 0.5 g
- Protein 8 g
- Cholesterol 104 mg

Cinnamon Pineapple Slices

Preparation Time: 5 minutes; Cooking Time: 20 minutes; Serve: 4

Ingredients:
- 4 pineapple slices
- 1 tsp cinnamon
- 2 tbsp erythritol

Directions:
1. Add pineapple slices, sweetener, and cinnamon into the zip-lock bag. Shake well and place into the refrigerator for 30 minutes.
2. Preheat the air fryer to 350 F.
3. Place pineapples slices into the air fryer basket and cook for 2o minutes. Turn halfway through.
4. Serve and enjoy.

Nutritional Value (Amount per Serving):
- Calories 46
- Fat 0 g
- Carbohydrates 10 g
- Sugar 10 g
- Protein 0 g
- Cholesterol 0 mg

Delicious Vanilla Custard

Preparation Time: 10 minutes; Cooking Time: 20 minutes; Serve: 2
Ingredients:

- 5 eggs
- 2 tbsp swerve
- 1 tsp vanilla
- ½ cup unsweetened almond milk
- ½ cup cream cheese

Directions:
1. Add eggs in a bowl and beat using a hand mixer.
2. Add cream cheese, sweetener, vanilla, and almond milk and beat for 2 minutes more.
3. Spray two ramekins with cooking spray.
4. Pour batter into the prepared ramekins.
5. Preheat the air fryer to 350 F.
6. Place ramekins into the air fryer and cook for 20 minutes.
7. Serve and enjoy.

Nutritional Value (Amount per Serving):

- Calories 381
- Fat 32 g
- Carbohydrates 5 g
- Sugar 1.2 g
- Protein 18 g
- Cholesterol 473 mg

Quick Blueberry Muffins

Preparation Time: 5 minutes; Cooking Time: 14 minutes; Serve: 2
Ingredients:

- 1 egg
- 1 tsp baking powder
- 3 tbsp butter, melted
- ¾ cup blueberries
- 2/3 cup almond flour
- 2 tbsp erythritol
- 1/3 cup unsweetened almond milk

Directions:
1. Spray silicone muffins molds with cooking spray and set aside.
2. Add all ingredients into the bowl and mix until well combined.
3. Pour batter into the prepared molds and place into the air fryer basket.
4. Cook at 320 F for 14 minutes.
5. Serve and enjoy.

Nutritional Value (Amount per Serving):

- Calories 283
- Fat 24 g
- Carbohydrates 13 g
- Sugar 6 g
- Protein 5 g
- Cholesterol 128 mg

Berry Cobbler

Preparation Time: 10 minutes; Cooking Time: 10 minutes; Serve: 6
Ingredients:

- 1 egg, lightly beaten
- 1 tbsp butter, melted

- 2 tsp swerve
- ½ tsp vanilla
- 1 cup almond flour
- ½ cup raspberries, sliced
- ½ cup strawberries, sliced

Directions:

1. Preheat the air fryer to 360 F.
2. Add sliced strawberries and raspberries into the air fryer baking dish.
3. Sprinkle sweetener over berries.
4. Mix together almond flour, vanilla, and butter in the bowl.
5. Add egg in almond flour mixture and stir well to combine.
6. Spread almond flour mixture over sliced berries. Cover dish with foil and place into the air fryer and cook for 10 minutes.
7. Serve and enjoy.

Nutritional Value (Amount per Serving):

- Calories 66
- Fat 5 g
- Carbohydrates 3 g
- Sugar 1 g
- Protein 2 g
- Cholesterol 32 mg

Cashew Pie

Preparation Time: 10 minutes; Cooking Time: 18 minutes; Serve: 8
Ingredients:

- 1 egg
- 2 oz cashews, crushed
- ½ tsp baking soda
- 1/3 cup heavy cream
- 1 oz dark chocolate, melted
- 1 tbsp butter
- 1 tsp vinegar
- 1 cup coconut flour

Directions:

1. Add egg in a bowl and beat using a hand mixer. Add coconut flour and stir well.
2. Add butter, vinegar, baking soda, heavy cream, and melted chocolate and stir well.
3. Add cashews and mix well.
4. Preheat the air fryer to 350 F.
5. Add prepared dough in air fryer baking dish and flatten it into a pie shape.
6. Cook for 18 minutes.
7. Slice and serve.

Nutritional Value (Amount per Serving):

- Calories 105
- Fat 8 g
- Carbohydrates 5 g
- Sugar 2.4 g
- Protein 2.4 g
- Cholesterol 32 mg

Almond Pumpkin Cookies

Preparation Time: 10 minutes; Cooking Time: 8 minutes; Serve: 8
Ingredients:

- ¼ cup almond flour
- ½ cup pumpkin puree
- 3 tbsp swerve
- ½ tsp baking soda

- 1 tbsp coconut flakes
- ½ tsp cinnamon
- Pinch of salt

Directions:
1. Preheat the air fryer to 360 F.
2. Add all ingredients into the bowl and mix until well combined.
3. Spray air fryer basket with cooking spray.
4. Make cookies from bowl mixture and place into the air fryer and cook for 8 minutes.
5. Serve and enjoy.

Nutritional Value (Amount per Serving):
- Calories 30
- Fat 2 g
- Carbohydrates 3 g
- Sugar 0.7 g
- Protein 1 g
- Cholesterol 0 mg

Vanilla Butter Pie

Preparation Time: 10 minutes; Cooking Time: 20 minutes; Serve: 8
Ingredients:
- 1 egg
- 2 tbsp erythritol
- ½ cup butter, melted
- 1 tsp vanilla
- 1 cup almond flour
- 1 tsp baking soda
- 1 tbsp vinegar

Directions:
1. Mix together almond flour and baking soda in a bowl.
2. In a separate bowl, whisk the egg with sweetener and vanilla.
3. Pour whisk egg, vinegar, and butter in almond flour and mix until dough is formed.
4. Preheat the air fryer to 340 F.
5. Roll dough using the rolling pin in air fryer baking dish size.
6. Place rolled dough in air fryer baking dish. Place in the air fryer and cook for 20 minutes.
7. Slice and serve.

Nutritional Value (Amount per Serving):
- Calories 132
- Fat 13.8 g
- Carbohydrates 0.9 g
- Sugar 0.3 g
- Protein 1.6 g
- Cholesterol 51 mg

Choco Chips Cookies

Preparation Time: 10 minutes; Cooking Time: 15 minutes; Serve: 4
Ingredients:
- 1 egg
- 3 tbsp butter
- 1 tsp vanilla
- ¼ tsp baking powder
- 2 tbsp macadamia nuts, crushed
- 1 cup almond flour
- 2 tbsp unsweetened chocolate chips
- Pinch of salt

Directions:
1. In a bowl, beat egg using a hand mixer.

2. Add almond flour, butter, vanilla, baking powder, and salt and stir well.
3. Add Chocó chips and macadamia nuts and mix until dough is formed.
4. Preheat the air fryer to 360 F.
5. Make cookies from dough and place into the air fryer and cook for 15 minutes.
6. Serve and enjoy.

Nutritional Value (Amount per Serving):
- Calories 215
- Fat 20 g
- Carbohydrates 4.5 g
- Sugar 0.7 g
- Protein 4 g
- Cholesterol 64 mg

Almond Coconut Cheese Muffins

Preparation Time: 10 minutes; Cooking Time: 10 minutes; Serve: 8

Ingredients:
- 1 egg
- 1 tsp baking soda
- 1 cup almond flour
- 2 tbsp coconut flakes
- 2 tsp erythritol
- 1 tsp vinegar
- 1 cup cream cheese
- Pinch of salt

Directions:
1. Beat cream cheese and egg in a bowl until well combined.
2. Add almond flour, vinegar, baking soda, coconut flakes, sweetener, and salt and beat until well combined.
3. Preheat the air fryer to 360 F.
4. Pour batter into silicone muffin molds and place into the air fryer.
5. Cook for 10 minutes.
6. Serve and enjoy.

Nutritional Value (Amount per Serving):
- Calories 134
- Fat 12 g
- Carbohydrates 1 g
- Sugar 0.5 g
- Protein 3.7 g
- Cholesterol 52 mg

Chocolate Soufflé

Preparation Time: 10 minutes; Cooking Time: 12 minutes; Serve: 6

Ingredients:
- 3 eggs, separated
- 1 tsp vanilla
- ¼ cup swerve
- 5 tbsp butter, melted
- 2 tbsp heavy cream
- 2 tbsp almond flour
- 2 oz dark chocolate, melted

Directions:
1. Mix together melted chocolate and butter.
2. In a bowl, whisk egg yolk with sweetener until combined.
3. Add almond flour, heavy cream, and vanilla and whisk well.
4. In a separate bowl, whisk egg white s until soft peaks form.

5. Add the egg white to the chocolate mixture slowly and fold well.
6. Pour chocolate mixture into the ramekins and place into the air fryer.
7. Cook at 330 F for 12 minutes.
8. Serve and enjoy.

Nutritional Value (Amount per Serving):
- Calories 240
- Fat 21 g
- Carbohydrates 8 g
- Sugar 5 g
- Protein 5 g
- Cholesterol 116 mg

Fluffy Butter Cake

Preparation Time: 10 minutes; Cooking Time: 35 minutes; Serve: 8
Ingredients:
- 6 egg yolks
- 3 cups almond flour
- 2 tsp vanilla
- 1 egg, lightly beaten
- ¼ cup erythritol
- 1 cup butter
- Pinch of salt

Directions:
1. Preheat the air fryer to 350 F.
2. In a bowl, beat butter and sweetener until fluffy.
3. Add vanilla, egg yolks and beat until well combined.
4. Add remaining ingredients and beat until combined.
5. Pour batter into air fryer cake pan and place into the air fryer and cook for 35 minutes.
6. Slice and serve.

Nutritional Value (Amount per Serving):
- Calories 315
- Fat 32 g
- Carbohydrates 2 g
- Sugar 0.5 g
- Protein 5 g
- Cholesterol 239 mg

Peanut Butter Cookies

Preparation Time: 5 minutes; Cooking Time: 12 minutes; Serve: 15
Ingredients:
- 1 egg
- ¼ cup erythritol
- 1 cup peanut butter

Directions:
1. Preheat the air fryer to 325 F.
2. Add all ingredients into the bowl and mix until well combined.
3. Make cookies from mixture and place into the air fryer and cook for 12 minutes.
4. Serve and enjoy.

Nutritional Value (Amount per Serving):
- Calories 105
- Fat 8 g
- Carbohydrates 3 g
- Sugar 1 g
- Protein 4 g
- Cholesterol 11 mg

Fudgy Brownies

Preparation Time: 10 minutes; Cooking Time: 16 minutes; Serve: 6
Ingredients:
- 3 eggs
- ½ tsp baking powder
- ¾ cup erythritol
- 2 oz dark chocolate
- ¾ cup butter softened
- ½ cup almond flour
- ¼ cup of cocoa powder

Directions:
1. Preheat the air fryer to 325 F.
2. Spray air fryer baking dish with cooking spray and set aside.
3. In a bowl, mix together chocolate and butter and microwave for 30 seconds or until melted. Stir well.
4. Mix together almond flour, baking powder, cocoa powder, and sweetener.
5. In a large bowl beat eggs using a hand mixer. Add chocolate-butter mixture and beat until combined.
6. Slowly add dry ingredients and mix until well combined.
7. Pour batter into the prepared dish and place into the air fryer.
8. Cook for 16 minutes.
9. Slice and serve.

Nutritional Value (Amount per Serving):
- Calories 307
- Fat 29 g
- Carbohydrates 8 g
- Sugar 5 g
- Protein 5 g
- Cholesterol 145 mg

Coconut Cheese Cookies

Preparation Time: 10 minutes; Cooking Time: 12 minutes; Serve: 30
Ingredients:
- 8 oz cream cheese
- 1 tsp vanilla
- 1 tbsp baking powder
- ¾ cup coconut flakes
- 1 cup swerve
- ¾ cup butter, softened
- 1 ¼ cup coconut flour
- Pinch of salt

Directions:
1. Preheat the air fryer to 325 F.
2. Beat cream cheese, butter, and sweetener in a bowl using a hand mixer until fluffy.
3. Add vanilla and stir well.
4. Add coconut flour, baking powder, and salt and mix until well combined.
5. Add coconut flakes and mix to combine.
6. Make cookies from mixture and place on a plate.
7. Place cookies in batches in the air fryer and cook for 12 minutes.
8. Serve and enjoy.

Nutritional Value (Amount per Serving):

- Calories 78
- Fat 8 g
- Carbohydrates 1.2 g
- Sugar 0.2 g
- Protein 0.8 g
- Cholesterol 21 mg

Cheesecake

Preparation Time: 10 minutes; Cooking Time: 28 minutes; Serve: 6
Ingredients:
- For crust:
- 2 tbsp butter, melted
- ¼ tsp cinnamon
- 1 tbsp swerve
- ½ cup almond flour
- Pinch of salt
- For Cheesecake:
- 1 egg
- ½ tsp vanilla
- ½ cup swerve
- 8 oz cream cheese

Directions:
1. Preheat the air fryer to 280 F.
2. Spray air fryer baking dish with cooking spray.
3. Add all crust ingredients into the bowl and mix until combined. Transfer crust mixture into the prepared baking dish and press down into the bottom of the dish.
4. Place dish in the air fryer and cook for 12 minutes.
5. In a large bowl, beat cream cheese using a hand mixer until smooth.
6. Add egg, vanilla, and salt and stir to combine.
7. Pour cream cheese mixture over cooked crust and cook for 16 minutes.
8. Allow to cool completely.
9. Slice and serve.

Nutritional Value (Amount per Serving):
- Calories 191
- Fat 18 g
- Carbohydrates 2 g
- Sugar 0.3 g
- Protein 4.3 g
- Cholesterol 79 mg

Ricotta Lemon Cake

Preparation Time: 10 minutes; Cooking Time: 40 minutes; Serve: 8
Ingredients:
- 1 lb ricotta
- 4 eggs
- 1 lemon juice
- 1 lemon zest
- ¼ cup erythritol

Directions:
1. Preheat the air fryer to 325 F.
2. Spray air fryer baking dish with cooking spray.
3. In a bowl, beat ricotta cheese until smooth.
4. Whisk in the eggs one by one.
5. Whisk in lemon juice and zest.
6. Pour batter into the prepared baking dish and place into the air fryer.

7. Cook for 40 minutes.
8. Allow to cool completely then slice and serve.

Nutritional Value (Amount per Serving):
- Calories 110
- Fat 6.7 g
- Carbohydrates 3.1 g
- Sugar 0.4 g
- Protein 9.2 g
- Cholesterol 99 mg

Brownie Bites

Preparation Time: 10 minutes; Cooking Time: 12 minutes;Serve: 16

Ingredients:
- ¾ cup almond flour
- ½ tsp vanilla
- 2 eggs
- ½ cup unsweetened cocoa powder
- ¾ cup swerve
- 4 tbsp butter, melted
- Pinch of salt

Directions:
1. Preheat the air fryer to 325 F.
2. In a bowl, whisk together butter, vanilla, eggs, cocoa powder, sweetener, and salt.
3. Add almond flour and stir to combine.
4. Pour batter into the mini silicone molds and place into the air fryer.
5. Cook for 12 minutes or until done.
6. Serve and enjoy.

Nutritional Value (Amount per Serving):
- Calories 48
- Fat 4.5 g
- Carbohydrates 1.9 g
- Sugar 0.2 g
- Protein 1.5 g
- Cholesterol 28 mg

Coconut Sunflower Cookies

Preparation Time: 10 minutes; Cooking Time: 10 minutes; Serve: 8

Ingredients:
- 5 oz sunflower seed butter
- 6 tbsp coconut flour
- 1 tsp vanilla
- ¼ tsp olive oil
- 2 tbsp swerve
- Pinch of salt

Directions:
1. Add all ingredients into the bowl and mix until dough is formed.
2. Preheat the air fryer to 360 F.
3. Make cookies from mixture and place into the air fryer and cook for 10 minutes.
4. Serve and enjoy.

Nutritional Value (Amount per Serving):
- Calories 152
- Fat 10 g
- Carbohydrates 11 g
- Sugar 0.8 g
- Protein 5 g
- Cholesterol 0 mg

Sponge Cake

Preparation Time: 10 minutes; Cooking Time: 40 minutes; Serve: 12
Ingredients:
- 4 eggs
- ½ cup swerve
- 2 cups almond flour
- 1 tsp vanilla
- 1 cup margarine

Directions:
1. Preheat the air fryer to 350 F.
2. Spray air fryer cake pan with cooking spray and set aside.
3. In a large bowl, beat margarine and sweetener using a hand mixer until light and fluffy.
4. Add egg one by one and beat well.
5. Add vanilla and almond flour and mix until well combined.
6. Pour batter into the prepared pan and place into the air fryer.
7. Cook for 40 minutes.
8. Slice and serve.

Nutritional Value (Amount per Serving):
- Calories 184
- Fat 18 g
- Carbohydrates 1.4 g
- Sugar 0.3 g
- Protein 3 g
- Cholesterol 55 mg

Almond Coconut Lemon Cake

Preparation Time: 10 minutes; Cooking Time: 48 minutes; Serve: 10
Ingredients:
- 4 eggs
- 2 tbsp lemon zest
- 1/2 cup butter softened
- 2 tsp baking powder
- 1/4 cup coconut flour
- 2 cups almond flour
- 1/2 cup fresh lemon juice
- 1/4 cup swerve
- 1 tbsp vanilla

Directions:
1. Preheat the air fryer to 280 F.
2. Spray air fryer baking dish with cooking spray and set aside.
3. In a large bowl, beat all ingredients using a hand mixer until a smooth.
4. Pour batter into the prepared dish and place into the air fryer and cook for 48 minutes.
5. Slice and serve.

Nutritional Value (Amount per Serving):
- Calories 245
- Fat 22 g
- Carbohydrates 5 g
- Sugar 2 g
- Protein 7 g
- Cholesterol 24 mg

Vanilla Butter Cheese Cake

Preparation Time: 10 minutes; Cooking Time: 32 minutes; Serve: 9

Ingredients:
- 5 eggs
- 1 cup erythritol
- 4 oz cream cheese, softened
- 1 tsp vanilla
- 1 tsp baking powder
- 6.5 oz almond flour
- 1/2 cup butter, softened

Directions:
1. Preheat the air fryer to 325 F.
2. Spray air fryer cake pan with cooking spray and set aside.
3. Add all ingredients into the large bowl and beat until fluffy.
4. Pour batter into the prepared pan and place into the air fryer and cook for 32 minutes.
5. Slice and serve.

Nutritional Value (Amount per Serving):
- Calories 290
- Fat 27 g
- Carbohydrates 5 g
- Sugar 1 g
- Protein 8 g
- Cholesterol 36 mg

Cinnamon Pecan Muffins

Preparation Time: 10 minutes; Cooking Time: 15 minutes; Serve: 12
Ingredients:
- 4 eggs
- 1 1/2 cups almond flour
- 1 tsp vanilla
- 1/4 cup unsweetened almond milk
- 2 tbsp butter, melted
- 1/2 cup erythritol
- 1 tsp psyllium husk
- 1/2 cup pecans, chopped
- 1/2 tsp ground cinnamon
- 2 tsp allspice
- 1 tbsp baking powder

Directions:
1. Preheat the air fryer to 400 F.
2. Beat eggs, milk, vanilla, sweetener, and butter in a bowl using a hand mixer until smooth.
3. Add remaining ingredients and stir until combined.
4. Pour batter into silicone muffin molds and place in the air fryer. In batches.
5. Cook for 15 minutes.
6. Serve and enjoy.

Nutritional Value (Amount per Serving):
- Calories 95
- Fat 8 g
- Carbohydrates 3 g
- Sugar 0.5 g
- Protein 3 g
- Cholesterol 28 mg

Poppyseed Muffins

Preparation Time: 10 minutes; Cooking Time: 14 minutes; Serve: 12
Ingredients:
- 3 eggs
- 4 true lemon packets
- 2 tbsp poppy seeds
- 1/4 cup coconut oil

- 1/4 cup ricotta cheese
- 1 tsp baking powder
- 1 cup almond flour
- 1 tsp lemon extract
- 1/4 cup heavy whipping cream
- 1/3 cup swerve

Directions:

1. Add all ingredients into the large bowl and beat using a hand mixer until fluffy.
2. Pour batter into the silicone muffin molds and place in the air fryer. In batches.
3. Cook at 320 F for 14 minutes.
4. Serve and enjoy.

Nutritional Value (Amount per Serving):

- Calories 90
- Fat 8 g
- Carbohydrates 3 g
- Sugar 2 g
- Protein 3 g
- Cholesterol 35 mg

Easy Mug Brownie

Preparation Time: 5 minutes; Cooking Time: 10 minutes; Serve: 1
Ingredients:

- 1 scoop chocolate protein powder
- 1 tbsp cocoa powder
- 1/2 tsp baking powder
- 1/4 cup unsweetened almond milk

Directions:

1. Add baking powder, protein powder, and cocoa powder in a mug and mix well.
2. Add milk in a mug and stir well.
3. Place the mug in the air fryer and cook at 390 F for 10 minutes.
4. Serve and enjoy.

Nutritional Value (Amount per Serving):

- Calories 80
- Fat 2 g
- Carbohydrates 6 g
- Sugar 1 g
- Protein 10 g
- Cholesterol 25 mg

Yummy Brownies

Preparation Time: 10 minutes; Cooking Time: 10 minutes; Serve: 4
Ingredients:

- 2 tbsp cocoa powder
- 1/4 tsp baking powder
- 1/2 tsp baking soda
- 2 tbsp unsweetened applesauce
- 1 tsp liquid stevia
- 1 tbsp coconut oil, melted
- 3 tbsp almond flour
- 1/2 tsp vanilla
- 1 tbsp unsweetened almond milk
- 1/2 cup almond butter
- 1/4 tsp sea salt

Directions:

1. Preheat the air fryer to 350 F.
2. Grease air fryer baking dish with cooking spray and set aside.
3. In a small bowl, mix together almond flour, baking soda, cocoa powder, baking powder, and salt. Set aside.

4. In a small bowl, add coconut oil and almond butter and microwave until melted.
5. Add sweetener, vanilla, almond milk, and applesauce in the coconut oil mixture and stir well.
6. Add dry ingredients to the wet ingredients and stir to combine.
7. Pour batter into prepared dish and place into the air fryer and cook for 10 minutes.
8. Slice and serve.

Nutritional Value (Amount per Serving):
- Calories 175
- Fat 15 g
- Carbohydrates 7 g
- Sugar 2 g
- Protein 5 g
- Cholesterol 24 mg

Almond Cinnamon Mug Cake

Preparation Time: 5 minutes; Cooking Time: 10 minutes; Serve: 1
Ingredients:
- 1 scoop vanilla protein powder
- 1/2 tsp cinnamon
- 1 tsp granulated sweetener
- 1 tbsp almond flour
- 1/2 tsp baking powder
- 1/4 tsp vanilla
- 1/4 cup unsweetened almond milk

Directions:
1. Add protein powder, cinnamon, almond flour, sweetener, and baking powder into the mug and mix well.
2. Add vanilla and almond milk and stir well.
3. Place mug in the air fryer and cook at 390 F for 10 minutes
4. Serve and enjoy.

Nutritional Value (Amount per Serving):
- Calories 181
- Fat 6 g
- Carbohydrates 8 g
- Sugar 2 g
- Protein 23 g
- Cholesterol 31 mg

Egg Custard

Preparation Time: 10 minutes; Cooking Time: 32 minutes; Serve: 6
Ingredients:
- 2 egg yolks
- 3 eggs
- 1/2 cup erythritol
- 2 cups heavy whipping cream
- 1/2 tsp vanilla
- 1 tsp nutmeg

Directions:
1. Preheat the air fryer to 325 F.
2. Add all ingredients into the large bowl and beat until well combined.
3. Pour custard mixture into the greased baking dish and place into the air fryer.
4. Cook for 32 minutes.
5. Let it cool completely then place in the refrigerator for 1-2 hours.
6. Serve and enjoy.

Nutritional Value (Amount per Serving):
- Calories 190
- Fat 19 g
- Carbohydrates 2 g
- Sugar 0.5 g
- Protein 5 g
- Cholesterol 26 mg

Chocolate Custard

Preparation Time: 10 minutes; Cooking Time: 32 minutes; Serve: 4
Ingredients:
- 2 eggs
- 1 tsp vanilla
- 1 cup heavy whipping cream
- 1 cup unsweetened almond milk
- 2 tbsp unsweetened cocoa powder
- 1/4 cup Swerve
- Pinch of salt

Directions:
1. Preheat the air fryer to 305 F.
2. Add all ingredients into the blender and blend until well combined.
3. Pour mixture into the ramekins and place into the air fryer.
4. Cook for 32 minutes.
5. Serve and enjoy.

Nutritional Value (Amount per Serving):
- Calories 156
- Fat 15 g
- Carbohydrates 3 g
- Sugar 0.5 g
- Protein 4 g
- Cholesterol 35 mg

Chocolate Coconut Cake

Preparation Time: 10 minutes; Cooking Time: 20 minutes; Serve: 9
Ingredients:
- 6 eggs
- 2 tsp baking powder
- 3 oz unsweetened cocoa powder
- 5 oz erythritol
- 3.5 oz coconut flour
- 1 tsp vanilla
- 3 oz butter, melted
- 11 oz heavy cream

Directions:
1. Preheat the air fryer to 325 F.
2. In a bowl, mix together coconut flour, butter, 5 oz heavy cream, eggs, baking powder half cocoa powder, and 3 oz sweetener until well combined.
3. Pour batter into the greased cake pan and place into the air fryer and cook for 20 minutes.
4. Allow to cool completely.
5. In a large bowl, beat remaining heavy cream, cocoa powder, and sweetener until smooth.
6. Spread the cream on top of cake and place in the refrigerator for 30 minutes.
7. Slice and serve.

Nutritional Value (Amount per Serving):
- Calories 280
- Fat 25 g

- Carbohydrates 10 g
- Sugar 1 g
- Protein 7 g
- Cholesterol 15 mg

Choco Fudge Cake

Preparation Time: 10 minutes; Cooking Time: 24 minutes; Serve: 12
Ingredients:
- 6 eggs
- 1 1/2 cup swerve
- 10 oz unsweetened chocolate, melted
- 1/2 cup almond flour
- 10 oz butter, melted
- Pinch of salt

Directions
1. Preheat the air fryer to 325 F.
2. Spray air fryer cake pan with cooking spray and set aside.
3. In a large bowl, beat eggs until foamy. Add sweetener and stir well.
4. Add melted butter, chocolate, almond flour, and salt and stir to combine.
5. Pour batter into the prepared pan and place into the air fryer and cook for 24 minutes.
6. Slice and serve.

Nutritional Value (Amount per Serving):
- Calories 359
- Fat 38 g
- Carbohydrates 7 g
- Sugar 0.5 g
- Protein 7 g
- Cholesterol 15 mg

Cranberry Almond Cake

Preparation Time: 10 minutes; Cooking Time: 16 minutes; Serve: 6
Ingredients:
- 4 eggs
- 1 tsp orange zest
- 2 tsp mixed spice
- 2 tsp cinnamon
- 1/4 cup swerve
- 1 cup butter, softened
- 2/3 cup dried cranberries
- 1 1/2 cups almond flour
- 1 tsp vanilla

Directions:
1. Preheat the air fryer to 325 F.
2. In a bowl, add sweetener and melted butter and beat until fluffy.
3. Add cinnamon, vanilla, and mixed spice and stir well.
4. Add eggs stir until well combined.
5. Add almond flour, orange zest, and cranberries and stir to combine.
6. Pour batter in a greased air fryer cake pan and place into the air fryer.
7. Cook cake for 16 minutes.
8. Slice and serve.

Nutritional Value (Amount per Serving):
- Calories 485
- Fat 48 g
- Carbohydrates 8 g
- Sugar 2 g
- Protein 11 g
- Cholesterol 35 mg

Pumpkin Custard

Preparation Time: 10 minutes; Cooking Time: 32 minutes; Serve: 6
Ingredients:

- 4 egg yolks
- 1/2 tsp cinnamon
- 15 drops liquid stevia
- 15 oz pumpkin puree
- 3/4 cup coconut cream
- 1/8 tsp cloves
- 1/8 tsp ginger

Directions:

1. Preheat the air fryer to 325 F.
2. In a large bowl, combine together pumpkin puree, cinnamon, swerve, cloves, and ginger.
3. Add egg yolks and beat until combined.
4. Add coconut cream and stir well.
5. Pour mixture into the six ramekins and place into the air fryer.
6. Cook for 32 minutes.
7. Let it cool completely then place in the refrigerator.
8. Serve chilled and enjoy.

Nutritional Value (Amount per Serving):

- Calories 131
- Fat 11 g
- Carbohydrates 3 g
- Sugar 2 g
- Protein 4 g
- Cholesterol 12 mg

Cheese Butter Cookies

Preparation Time: 10 minutes; Cooking Time: 12 minutes; Serve: 8
Ingredients:

- 2 eggs
- 5 tbsp butter, melted
- 1/3 cup sour cream
- 1/3 cup mozzarella cheese, shredded
- 1 1/4 cup almond flour
- 1/2 tsp baking powder
- 1/2 tsp salt

Directions:

1. Preheat the air fryer to 370 F.
2. Add all ingredients into a large bowl and mix using a hand mixer.
3. Spoon batter into the mini silicone muffin molds and place into the air fryer and cook for 12 minutes.
4. Serve and enjoy.

Nutritional Value (Amount per Serving):

- Calories 205
- Fat 20 g
- Carbohydrates 4 g
- Sugar 1 g
- Protein 6 g
- Cholesterol 25 mg

Vanilla Coconut Cheese Cookies

Preparation Time: 10 minutes; Cooking Time: 12 minutes; Serve: 15

Ingredients:
- 1 egg
- 1/2 tsp baking powder
- 1 tsp vanilla
- 1/2 cup swerve
- 1/2 cup butter, softened
- 3 tbsp cream cheese, softened
- 1/2 cup coconut flour
- Pinch of salt

Directions:
1. In a bowl, beat together butter, sweetener, and cream cheese.
2. Add egg and vanilla and beat until smooth and creamy.
3. Add coconut flour, salt, and baking powder and beat until combined. Cover and place in the fridge for 1 hour.
4. Preheat the air fryer to 325 F.
5. Make cookies from dough and place into the air fryer and cook for 12 minutes.
6. Serve and enjoy.

Nutritional Value (Amount per Serving):
- Calories 65
- Fat 7 g
- Carbohydrates 1 g
- Sugar 0.5 g
- Protein 1 g
- Cholesterol 34 mg

Pumpkin Cookies

Preparation Time: 10 minutes; Cooking Time: 20 minutes; Serve: 27
Ingredients:
- 1 egg
- 2 cups almond flour
- 1/2 tsp baking powder
- 1 tsp vanilla
- 1/2 cup butter
- 15 drops liquid stevia
- 1/2 tsp pumpkin pie spice
- 1/2 cup pumpkin puree

Directions:
1. Preheat the air fryer to 280 F.
2. In a large bowl, add all ingredients and mix until well combined.
3. Make cookies from mixture and place into the air fryer and cook for 20 minutes.
4. Serve and enjoy.

Nutritional Value (Amount per Serving):
- Calories 80
- Fat 7 g
- Carbohydrates 2 g
- Sugar 1 g
- Protein 3 g
- Cholesterol 25 mg

Chia Chocolate Cookies

Preparation Time: 5 minutes; Cooking Time: 8 minutes; Serve: 20
Ingredients:
- 2 1/2 tbsp ground chia
- 2 tbsp chocolate protein powder
- 1 cup sunflower seed butter
- 1 cup almond flour

Directions:
1. Preheat the air fryer to 325 F.

2. In a large bowl, add all ingredients and mix until combined.
3. Make cookies from bowl mixture and place into the air fryer and cook for 8 minutes.
4. Serve and enjoy.

Nutritional Value (Amount per Serving):
- Calories 110
- Fat 9 g
- Carbohydrates 5 g
- Sugar 0.5 g
- Protein 4 g
- Cholesterol 35 mg

Cinnamon Ginger Cookies

Preparation Time: 10 minutes; Cooking Time: 12 minutes; Serve: 8
Ingredients:
- 1 egg
- 1/2 tsp vanilla
- 1/8 tsp ground cloves
- 1 tsp baking powder
- 3/4 cup erythritol
- 2/4 cup butter, melted
- 1 1/2 cups almond flour
- 1/4 tsp ground nutmeg
- 1/4 tsp ground cinnamon
- 1/2 tsp ground ginger
- Pinch of salt

Directions:
1. In a large bowl, mix together all dry ingredients.
2. In a separate bowl, mix together all wet ingredients.
3. Add dry ingredients to the wet ingredients and mix until dough is formed. Cover and place in the fridge for 30 minutes.
4. Preheat the air fryer to 325 F.
5. Make cookies from dough and place into the air fryer and cook for 12 minutes.
6. Serve and enjoy.

Nutritional Value (Amount per Serving):
- Calories 230
- Fat 22 g
- Carbohydrates 4 g
- Sugar 1 g
- Protein 5 g
- Cholesterol 24 mg

Crustless Pie

Preparation Time: 10 minutes; Cooking Time: 24 minutes; Serve: 4
Ingredients:
- 3 eggs
- 1/2 cup pumpkin puree
- 1/2 tsp cinnamon
- 1 tsp vanilla
- 1/4 cup erythritol
- 1/2 cup cream
- 1/2 cup unsweetened almond milk

Directions:
1. Preheat the air fryer to 325 F.
2. Spray air fryer baking dish with cooking spray and set aside.
3. In a large bowl, add all ingredients and beat until smooth.

4. Pour pie mixture into the prepared dish and place into the air fryer and cook for 24 minutes.
5. Let it cool completely and place into the refrigerator for 1-2 hours.
6. Slice and serve.

Nutritional Value (Amount per Serving):

- Calories 85
- Fat 5 g
- Carbohydrates 4 g
- Sugar 1 g
- Protein 5 g
- Cholesterol 35 mg

Tasty Peanut Butter Bars

Preparation Time: 10 minutes; Cooking Time: 24 minutes; Serve: 9
Ingredients:

- 2 eggs
- 1 tbsp coconut flour
- 1/2 cup butter, softened
- 1/2 cup peanut butter
- 1/4 cup almond flour
- 1/2 cup swerve

Directions:
1. Spray air fryer baking pan with cooking spray and set aside.
2. In a bowl, beat together butter, eggs, and peanut butter until well combined.
3. Add dry ingredients and mix until a smooth batter is formed.
4. Spread batter evenly in prepared pan and place into the air fryer and cook at 325 F for 24 minutes.
5. Slice and serve.

Nutritional Value (Amount per Serving):

- Calories 215
- Fat 20 g
- Carbohydrates 4 g
- Sugar 2 g
- Protein 6 g
- Cholesterol 26 mg

Chapter 9: 21-Day Meal Plan

Day 1

Breakfast-Radish Hash Browns

Lunch-Chicken Popcorn

Dinner-Perfect Salmon Fillets

Day 2

Breakfast-Spicy Cauliflower Rice

Lunch-Delicious Whole Chicken

Dinner-Nutritious Salmon

Day 3

Breakfast-Broccoli Stuffed Peppers

Lunch-Quick & Easy Steak

Dinner-Shrimp Scampi

Day 4

Breakfast-Zucchini Muffins

Lunch-Perfect Cheeseburger

Dinner-Lemon Chili Salmon

Day 5

Breakfast-Jalapeno Breakfast Muffins

Lunch-Steak Bites with Mushrooms

Dinner-Pesto Salmon

Day 6

Breakfast-Zucchini Noodles

Lunch-Simple & Tasty Pork Chops

Dinner-Veggie Pork Tenderloin

Day 7

Breakfast-Mushroom Frittata

Lunch-Delicious Crab Cakes

Dinner-Lemon Herb Lamb Chops

Day 8

Breakfast-Vegetable Egg Cups

Lunch-Tuna Patties

Dinner-Crispy & Juicy Whole Chicken

Day 9

Breakfast-Spinach Frittata

Lunch-Crispy Fish Sticks

Dinner-Juicy Turkey Breast Tenderloin

Day 10

Breakfast-Omelette Frittata

Lunch-Flavorful Parmesan Shrimp

Dinner-Flavorful Cornish Hen

Day 11

Breakfast-Cheese Soufflés

Lunch-Quick & Easy Meatballs

Dinner-Chicken Vegetable Fry

Day 12

Breakfast-Simple Egg Soufflé

Lunch-Lemon Pepper Chicken Wings

Dinner-Cilantro Lime Chicken

Day 13

Breakfast-Vegetable Egg Soufflé

Lunch-BBQ Chicken Wings

Dinner-Delicious Chicken Casserole

Day 14

Breakfast-Asparagus Frittata

Lunch-Flavorful Fried Chicken

Dinner-Chicken with Mushrooms

Day 15

Breakfast-Egg Muffins

Lunch-Yummy Chicken Nuggets

Dinner-Parmesan Walnut Salmon

Day 16

Breakfast-Bacon Egg Muffins

Lunch-Crisp Pork Chops

Dinner-Pesto Salmon

Day 17

Breakfast-Zucchini Cheese Quiche

Lunch-Parmesan Pork Chops

Dinner-Mustard Pork Tenderloin

Day 18

Breakfast-Breakfast Casserole

Lunch-Meatloaf Sliders

Dinner-McCornick Pork Chops

Day 19

Breakfast-Egg Cups

Lunch-Simple Air Fryer Salmon

Dinner-Sweet Mustard Pork Chops

Day 20

Breakfast-Spinach Muffins

Lunch-Delicious White Fish

Dinner-BBQ Ribs

Day 21

Breakfast-Broccoli Muffins

Lunch-Shrimp with Veggie

Dinner-Vietnamese Pork Chop

Conclusion

We have to see a healthy diet popularly known as a ketogenic diet. It will change the eating habits of many people and gives them a healthy lifestyle. In this book, we have to see different types of 450 healthy and delicious recipes. Here we have made different and fabulous ketogenic recipes into the air fryer. In this book, we also see the benefits of the ketogenic diet and air frying foods.